TREATING
SEXUAL SHAME

TREATING SEXUAL SHAME

A NEW MAP FOR OVERCOMING DYSFUNCTION, ABUSE, AND ADDICTION

Anne Stirling Hastings, Ph.D.

JASON ARONSON INC.
Northvale, New Jersey
London

The author gratefully acknowledges the permission of Randy Fitzgerald and Cindy Rushin-Gallagher to reproduce two case histories in detail, and the *Seattle Gay News* for permission to quote from an article by Ken Lovering.

This book was set in 11 pt. New Baskerville by Alabama Book Composition of Deatsville, Alabama and printed and bound by Book-mart Press, Inc. of North Bergen, New Jersey.

Library of Congress Cataloging-in-Publication Data

Hastings, Anne Stirling, 1943–
      Treating sexual shame : a new map for overcoming dysfunction,
   abuse, and addiction / Anne Stirling Hastings.
         p.   cm.
      Includes bibliographical references and index.
      ISBN 0-7657-0103-0 (alk. paper)
      1. Sex therapy.   2. Sex.   3. Sex (Psychology)   I. Title.
   RC557.H29   1997
   616.85'8306—DC21   97-15765

Printed in the United States of America on acid-free paper. Jason Aronson Inc. offers books and cassettes. For information and catalog write to Jason Aronson Inc., 230 Livingston Street, Northvale, New Jersey 07647-1731. Or visit our website: http://www.aronson.com

Contents

PART III: A NEW LOOK

PART IV: ADDRESSING SEXUALITY IN THERAPY

Preface

Early in my psychology practice I didn't understand sexual issues brought by my clients—or my own, even after years of psychoanalysis. I read books on sex therapy, and I treated couples along with a male co-therapist. But even after a year of working with clients with sexual dysfunction, I was unprepared for a client who came to me with depression or marital problems and then mentioned going to an adult bookstore to masturbate, or for one who asked, with trepidation, if masturbation was okay. All I could say, after reading Masters and Johnson, was that this behavior wasn't bad. When women told me they felt awful when their husbands wanted them to wear sexy lingerie to enhance their arousal, or how they used fantasy to become aroused, I could do no more than nod and say that this is common and recommended by sex therapists. Even with training, I generally felt incompetent to assess, understand, and help clients with sexual issues.

After I was divorced in 1983, I began my own informal study with an N of 1—myself. I abandoned the idea of monogamy and all other social rules about sexuality. Through a series of sexual relationships—some concurrent, some with married men—I followed my intuition, gathering information. I worked through much of my own history of sexual abuse—abuse by adults when I was a child, and abuse by the culture's attitudes about sex.

Finally, when I met my current husband, I was able to fully experience the transition from a loving friendship, to the introduction of sex, followed by an intense desire to be together, and, after a few weeks, to the loss of sexual interest in anyone else. Because this relationship was mostly free of childhood influences, and free from a cultural belief that monogamy was natural or right, I was able to observe the nature of monogamous, sexual bonding emerging from the inside out, monogamous bonding very different from one based on fear of loss. This bonding enhanced the relationship, expanded it, and made it stronger. We felt no sacrifice, no constriction, no compromise. Now ten years later, monogamy continues to support our love.

I saw that I was charting a new map to understanding sexuality. As I worked with clients, additional observational data supported my own experience. Finally, after I began speaking and writing about sex, I received the support of other therapists who had not been able to articulate their own similar learning as they worked with incest survivors who were no longer able to engage in culturally prescribed sexual practices.

Once I began specializing in sexuality, I worked with many clients who had been to other therapists with whom they hadn't been able to describe their difficulties. I could see that I had been one of those therapists—the one to whom clients wouldn't reveal their deepest secrets, because they sensed I couldn't help, and worse than that perhaps I would bring on even more shame. After spending several years on my own sexual recovery, I began to bring a sense of understanding to my work that allowed clients to feel safe enough to talk. Even now, when I have probably heard every imaginable story, clients generally test the waters with a little information in early sessions, and then later drop their defenses and tell what they feel are the really shameful parts.

Sexuality is different from other issues because of the shame that is elicited by open, nondefended conversation about sexual behavior. Most therapists don't have the opportunity to address sex in the way we address most other subjects brought up by clients—free of our own shame. Education, training, and consultation groups typically do not address sexual issues, preventing therapists from preparing themselves to help with sexuality (Pope et al. 1993).

I provided myself with this education in part by attending workshops with people in sexual recovery, and by asking more questions of my clients while facing my own shame. Soon my clients were revealing far more than any had a few years before. Now I hear the stories of my new clients who were unable to talk about sex with past therapists. I have empathy for both my clients and their former therapists.

More recent education has come from five years in a peer consultation group with three women from three different backgrounds specializing in sexuality. Instead of creating conflict, our differences broaden each of us as we hear about new concepts and different interventions. We have in common the understanding that sexuality cannot be isolated from the rest of a person's emotional healing, and that sexual healing is a complex, difficult, and long project. Louisa Turner, Ph.D., takes a self psychology and psychoanalytic approach to addressing sexual (and other) issues. Jill Seipel, ACSW, approaches sexuality and relationships from a family systems and object-relations theory orientation. Cindy Rushin-Gallagher, M.A., began as a traditional sex therapist, and has evolved her cognitive/behavioral training into the broader picture of sexual healing.

The fields of psychotherapy and counseling are impacted by our culture's attachment of shame to sex. I have written this book to help ameliorate this impact. I do this through numerous case examples, offered so the therapist and student of therapy can more readily perceive clients' expression of sexual issues. I encourage therapists to take a look at their own shame that might prevent offering a shame-free environment for the client to bring up sexual issues. To this end, I offer suggestions about how to reduce therapist shame that can be used in a training or consultation group. As I discovered myself, this can change the way we are with clients, giving them tacit permission to talk about this most difficult subject.

1

Beyond Dysfunction, Abuse, and Addiction

Three areas of professional practice address sexuality. These are sex therapy, the treatment of sexual abuse, and sexual addiction/compulsivity (see Chapters 4, 5, and 6). Each area has a body of research and methods of practice. But they do not sufficiently overlap. Nor do they deal with other sexual issues. We need an integrated, broader perspective.

A fourth area, the treatment of sex offenders, is highly specialized, and requires additional certification in most states to offer court-mandated treatment. This book doesn't address this issue because sex offenders generally don't seek therapy on their own. If a client admits to having performed a sex act with a child, therapists are required by all the states to report it to the legal authorities, at which point the court system takes over.

THE CULTURE INHIBITS THERAPISTS AND CLIENTS

The role of sexuality in the symptoms of our clients is far greater than dysfunction, abuse, and addiction, as I have described in *Body and Soul: Sexuality on the Brink of Change* (1996). We live in a highly sexual culture, as evidenced by the media, while at the same time, open, intimate, real conversation about sex elicits feelings of embarrassment and shame. Therapists live in this culture, and so for us to ask probing questions about sexuality requires that we overcome our own inclination not to. In addition, the sexuality of all of us has been culturally shamed, a feeling that will be elicited by discussion with clients until we face our own shame and begin to address it.

After a decade of talking with clients who want to face their sexuality, I have come to see from their reports of sessions with other therapists how most therapists are not able to hear subtle indications that a client needs to address sexual shame. There are two main reasons for this. First is the therapist's shame. As members of this culture, therapists who have not addressed their own sexual shame will become uncomfortable when openly listening to sexual information. This might be particularly true if the therapist experiences sexual arousal or attraction. Second, clients are rarely able to say outright that sexual issues have to be addressed. It is more difficult to ask for help for sexual problems than for relationship problems or problems with one's children.

Clients with sexual issues need to know that the therapist won't shame them before most can reveal their issues.

THE THREE AREAS OF STUDY ARE NOT INTEGRATED

A person specializing in one area of treatment of sexual issues might not know about the other two areas. Traditional sex therapists focus on sexual behavior, even when childhood sexual abuse or sexual addiction becomes evident. Therapists treating sexual abuse might not see evidence of sexual addiction. Sexual addiction training does pay attention to the importance of sexual abuse, but less to healthy sexual functioning. The best specialists will understand all three areas (as well as the paths to sexual healing) and be able to move among them to address the client's needs. The nonspecializing therapist needs to at least understand all three areas in order to integrate sexuality into psychotherapy, and to know when to refer clients to a specialist.

Alecia was approaching 60 when she read a book on sex addiction. Her husband, Paul, hadn't wanted sex with her since they married in their early twenties. They had gone to several therapists, including the Masters and Johnson clinic, and while they were having more sex, his addiction to illicit affairs and "bad" women had not been addressed. Nor had the layers of sexual shame that resulted from a number of childhood influences. Among them were living in a culture that shames sex, observing his mother repeatedly lock his father out of the bedroom to avoid his violent demands for sex, and exposure to pornography and prostitutes with a "good old boy" attitude toward the fun of being bad.

Alecia raged over the time she had spent learning how to be more provocative with her husband, and how she had watched pornographic movies in order to help him become aroused so he could have sex with her. While sex therapists had not shamed Paul for his lack of interest, they had not been able to help him address the fact that arousal was limited to "shameful" acts. The first time he masturbated without using fantasy or pornography to distract himself from shame, he was deeply touched. It helped him continue the work that resulted in intimate, less shame-based sex with his wife.

Hearing about their long search brought me sadness, but I also felt great satisfaction in helping them become more sexually comfortable. They renewed their wedding vows on their fortieth anniversary, really marrying for the first time, as they were able at last to share loving sexuality.

MOVING BEYOND DYSFUNCTION, ABUSE, AND ADDICTION

Most clients with sexual issues do not place themselves into one of the three categories of help. Even people who directly ask for help see only a fraction of their issues. Many clients seek therapy because they know something is wrong but have difficulty naming it. Even people who have been sexually abused may not understand how the abuse causes sexual difficulties, and so they don't present them as issues.

In my practice I frequently see couples who cannot define what is wrong, and who have no understanding of how to change. One partner often brings (or sends) the other partner to be helped because he or she may be sexually addicted or sexually inhibited, which are maneuvers to avoid sexual shame. Neither understands why conflicts exist, or how to begin addressing them. Popular books and magazine articles give suggestions that are unworkable for most people. In addition, the culture prescribes correct sexual frequency, and fosters the myth that married couples will automatically want to have sex—then offers common sense interpretations when they don't.

> Jackie made an appointment to see me because her husband Richard, a professional in his early thirties, had lost interest in sex after the first six months of their relationship. He had sex occasionally in order to pacify Jackie, but she knew he didn't like to. They named the issue as Richard's lack of sexual desire—he seemed to be asexual. I began working alone with Richard, planning to bring Jackie in once he and I had more understanding. He could talk more easily without his wife present.
>
> Richard felt a great deal of shame about sex, so we went slowly, talking first about his relationship history, and later asking how sex evolved in each relationship. Over several sessions, he continued to appear almost asexual—until I asked him if he masturbated.
>
> Richard was terribly uncomfortable with my question, moving in his chair, trying to begin sentences, until finally he admitted that he did masturbate. While Richard was unusually reluctant in answering this question, almost all people are uncomfortable going beyond yes—unless they have come to see me for that purpose and have rehearsed what they want to say.

With shame pouring out, Richard told me how he looked at an attractive woman, often during his lunch hour at work, and then spent the afternoon imagining he had a relationship with her. He felt like he was in love. During the evening he masturbated to the images of making love to her. Having sex with an imaginary person was easier than with a real one. Masturbation became a solution to his aversion to having sex, allowing him to have a sex life.

Part of our work was now identified. We began exploring why sex was so difficult with his wife—or any woman. He had a pattern of not being able to make love after the first few months. I asked about the feelings it brought up, the revulsion and fear. We explored his history to learn how he had come to associate sex with displeasure. And we learned more about the nature of his masturbation.

I asked Richard if he would go without creating the fantasy, or masturbating, for one week and see how it went. He readily agreed, relieved by having a reason to stop.

At the beginning of the next session, Richard told me he had been unable to abstain more than two days. He could now reveal that it happened not two to three times a week, as he had said, but every day. His daily life included knowing in the morning that he would find a new "partner" by noon, spending the afternoon falling in love, looking forward to sex with the new lover, and the day would end with the fantasy of making love. The fact that he could not stop identified Richard as a sex addict.

If he were being seen by a therapist with no background in sexual addiction, a referral would be appropriate at this time. An experienced therapist who was studying sexual addiction, who could consult with an expert, and who could recommend a therapy group for sexual addicts when the time was right, would be able to continue working with Richard. A therapy group or twelve-step program is usually necessary for recovery from sexual addiction.

If a referral is to be made, it might need to be discussed for several more sessions. In Richard's case, his developing trust that I would not shame him was very important, and a referral would have been painful.

It is sometimes helpful for the referring therapist to continue seeing the client while the client begins seeing a specialist. Once the connection is made with the new therapist, then it could be decided if the client would continue to see both. While there are times when it is best to work with one therapist, when confronting sexual shame the experience of working with two therapists can help the early de-shaming of sexuality. This might be an intermediate step between individual therapy and the addition of group therapy, where several accepting people are available to listen.

I have on a number of occasions been the specialist, while the client continued to see the referring therapist, who continues to be the main therapist. It has usually served the client to come to me for painful exploration, and return to the referring therapist for support and integration. This process also educates the referring therapist about long-term issues that need to be addressed. Until shame about sexuality is manageable, the client can work with both therapists.

HELP FOR UNUSUAL AROUSAL PATTERNS

A client with a specific issue, such as a man who needs to wear women's lingerie in order to become sexually aroused, doesn't have a place to turn. Specialists in sexual abuse don't begin with the adult sexual symptom. A client has to know that he has been sexually abused in the past in order to seek help from such a specialist.

A sex therapist would help this client accept his arousal patterns and would assume they cannot be changed. The client would reduce his shame by talking about the symptom, and by meeting with other people who share the same sexual pattern. His mate might be included in sessions in order to integrate his use of lingerie into their sex life.

The sexual addiction field may be able to help if the behavior is also addictive. If it isn't, then none of the three areas of specialization can help him relinquish a mode of sexual arousal in order to have a loving, intimate sexual exchange with his mate. Such men need to know that a process of moving to healthy sexuality will better serve him.

> When Bob entered therapy he was worried about his use of women's lingerie to become aroused. He spoke in generalities for three sessions, uncomfortable with the shame that accompanied such conversation. But at our fourth meeting, he said he wanted to unburden himself and he told the whole history of how he had started masturbating into women's underpants from the time he reached puberty, beginning with his mother's, and then stealing them from neighbors' homes. As I could listen to his story, nod, take him seriously, and express sympathy for the fear and shame he had been tolerating, his shame decreased. Immediately he set up an appointment to bring his wife, Jennifer, to a session so he could further relieve his shame over hiding this information the entire twelve years of their marriage. He became happier as the shame decreased.

I explained to Bob and Jennifer the concept of cross-wiring—a term I use to reflect the association of anything that isn't sexual with sexual arousal or sexual bonding. Wearing women's underwear isn't sexual—it became sexual to Bob for reasons we had yet to determine. The term *cross-wiring* offers a nonshaming label, in contrast to perversion or paraphilia (see Chapter 8). The term made intuitive sense to Bob, as it does to many people who have a particular need in order to become aroused.

Bob and Jennifer questioned what they should do next. Bob's preference was to wear women's underwear when he and Jennifer had sex, but she felt torn. She wanted to relieve his feelings of shame, but she didn't like him to be already aroused by the underwear before they decided to have sex. The underwear felt like the "other woman" who aroused him before he had sex with her.

By exploring Jennifer's feelings, we discovered that Bob was not only sexually responsive to lingerie, he used the arousal addictively. He could see that it was one thing to have a sexual association to lingerie, but it was another to crave it, or require it in order to be aroused. If a person isn't addicted to sexual arousal, then the association with lingerie or anything else won't have the power to cause a person to be sexual. The stimulus can be ignored, and sex can be used in a loving way with a partner. For example, most people will become aroused when observing others being sexual, as in the movies or on television, but won't choose to be sexual as a result, or seek out situations where they can watch people. This distinction between sexually arousing stimuli and the addictive use of the arousal is addressed in Chapter 8.

We began examining Bob's addictive use of his sexuality, and at the same time we explored the reasons he responded to this particular stimulus. We are discovering his gender confusion, evidenced by his desire to look like a woman, concealing his genitals in women's underwear, and we are looking at his relationship with his mother, an aunt, and a neighbor, all of whom shamed him for being male.

Traditional sex therapists accept behaviors such as cross-dressing, but it is possible to look further. If Bob were encouraged to accept his use of lingerie, and Jennifer encouraged to join him in the use of it, this would only further his addiction. Jennifer needed to know that her reactions were healthy and her concerns respected in order to create room for intimate sexual interaction.

THE POSSIBILITY OF HEALTHY, INTIMATE SEX

Throughout this book I refer to the kind of sexual experience that is possible when a couple is capable of intimacy and love (see Hastings 1993, Schnarch 1991). Reaching this place is usually a long process that requires reducing sexual shame and removing relationship obstacles. Some writers say that when the relationship is going well, good sex will follow. I have not found this to be so. A well-functioning relationship is needed to obtain deeply intimate sex, but the influence of our culture must also be shed. This might be accomplished without the help of therapy, but for most couples help of some kind will be needed. It is no small task to relinquish our culture's stereotypes about lust, sexual "need," sexual roles, definitions of having sex, and definitions of being a man or woman. Much of what has become "normal" isn't optimal. The norms have come from shared attempts to override shame (see Chapter 3).

The sex therapy (and *DSM-IV*) definition of *desire* as the first phase in sexual activity comes from studying sexuality within the context of the culture, where a specific feeling of wanting sex is necessary for sexual activity to take place. Without desire, couples who cannot access a *natural* reason to interact sexually will not do so. A client who is unable to override sexual shame with desire is diagnosed as having inhibited sexual desire.

Couples who have achieved deep sexual intimacy don't experience the kind of desire represented by the slang term *horny*. Better terms might be *sexual opening*, or *sexually receptive* (for both men and women), or *sexually welcoming*. An individual can *feel sexual* all by herself or himself. We are sexual people, and sexual feelings might come and go as our energy flows. But our culture (and sex therapy) has attached to this solitary feeling the urge to act on it. In contrast, gentle sexual energy filling the body, or even full sexual arousal, can be enjoyed for itself—without sex with a partner—and with or without masturbation.

Couples who have found deep sexual intimacy will not begin with desire, as it is understood in our culture. Instead, they will feel intimate, and then sexual arousal may emerge. The couple will follow the energy, allowing it to rise and fall. They will become passionately intense with gentle stimulation, discovering if this activity ends with orgasm or a fully satisfying final drop in arousal. When in this state, arousal, decrease of arousal, and orgasms of both partners occur at the same time, directed by their bodies, not by their minds. (There is no formula for reaching this place. It cannot be defined as a goal of therapy. It is an outcome of sexual healing.)

Therapists can help by recognizing when a couple has reached new levels—even if the therapist has not reached them. A couple comes to a session delightedly recounting how they had sex, telling about how the arousal faded with no orgasm, and they were totally satisfied. They need a therapist who will nod and smile, and otherwise affirm that they have found a new level of obeying their bodies instead of superimposing the need for orgasms in order to think they have had good sex.

Therapists who see orgasm as a positive indicator might react with neutrality, or even suggest they would have orgasms next time. With a preconceived view that good sex includes orgasm, a therapist is going to communicate this criterion directly or indirectly. It will take the couple more time, and perhaps ending therapy to realize that what they had was *just right*. There was nothing missing. (Of course, when a person cannot have orgasms because of emotional inhibitors, then orgasm takes on a different meaning.)

PATHS TO SEXUAL HEALING

The three areas of help for sexual issues may merge in the future. A therapist specializing in sexuality will be able to evaluate and treat any sexual problem. One client might focus on sexual abuse from childhood, and follow this by turning to healthy sexuality in a relationship. Another might begin by addressing sexual addiction, move on to sexual abuse, and then discover the causes of a lack of interest in sex with the partner. An integrated view of sexual issues can facilitate greater possibilities for each client.

Part I

Sexual Shame

2

Shame—The Root of Problems with Sex

The past three decades have seen a dramatic reduction in negative views of sexual activity. Articles in women's magazines address it overtly, and the "sexual revolution" of the '60s and '70s brought sex into the open. Prime-time television includes frequent, sometimes helpful, references to sex. Talk shows have created a new model for acceptable conversation about strange and bizarre uses of sexuality, and have educated the public about the pervasiveness of sexual abuse of children. But in spite of the dramatic increase in the amount of time sex is discussed on television and in classrooms, and the fact that many people are now able to identify their own sexual problems and seek help, shame remains attached to the subject on a cultural level. Few people can have comfortable, non-erotic conversations about sexual activity, such as asking friends how they have sex as they might ask about cooking or recreation, or telling a parent about going to a movie on a date and then describing the sex that followed. Sitting on a Lake Washington dock with my laptop computer, I attracted the curiosity of an adolescent boy who asked if I wrote books. When I said yes, he eagerly asked for the titles. As I told him, his face lost interest, he backed away from me, and ran to his siblings. Minutes later I heard them laughing as they discharged their embarrassment over hearing that I wrote about sex. These children demonstrated how it is possible to talk about sex by using laughter and secrecy to reduce the experience of the shame that is attached to the subject.

Masturbation is almost universally experienced as shameful. The past three decades have had less impact on removing shame from masturbation than from sex with a partner. Men in my men's therapy group can refer easily to masturbation, even gesturing the stroking of the penis. But when the conversation becomes more explicit, the room quickly becomes humid and warm as they experience shameful feelings they describe as bad, dirty, unacceptable, and self abusive. Some also fear becoming aroused, which they view as unacceptable in this setting.

In addition to acculturated shame, shame is introduced to individual children and young people in countless ways. Some of these are sexual abuse, emotional abuse of sexuality, sexual secrecy, exposure to pornography in a sexualized manner, religious shaming, taking on the disowned sexual shame of a parent, being dressed to hide the body, and leading a promiscuous lifestyle. Even moderate parental discomfort with talking about sexual things, including first bras, first menstruation, sexual body parts, erections, and ejaculations conveys to the child that these things are shameful. While parenting is improving in these areas, few therapy clients will have received sexual education that is free from the shame of the parent.

Sexual shame inhibits sexual loving, and addressing this issue is a top priority for sexual healing. Shame underlies most sexual symptoms and is relevant to each of the three fields of sexual treatment.

If evidence of our sexuality had not been shamed, and we emerged from the wombs of women who loved their bodies, and lived in a culture where sexuality was not shamed, we would grow up to discover the real nature of sexuality in our own developmental time schedule. We would discover its purpose, and learn through trial and error without admonishments from others. But we aren't born into such an environment. Instead, shame is focused on sexuality more than any other human quality—worldwide.

The shaming that accompanies most expressions of sexuality becomes attached to it, so that when we are sexual, we evoke shame along with arousal (internalized shame). This puts into motion *distortions of sexual expression* in both universal and unique ways, which presents an enormously difficult task for therapists who want to help clients have healthier, happier lives. The task is similar to helping women live fully in the face of a culture that still discriminates against them.

The culture's attitudes change slowly. Clients who are able to substantially heal their sexual problems will feel like misfits if they no longer laugh at sexual jokes, and will trigger the shame and defensiveness of others. As we remove shame from any culturally shamed facet of ourselves (race, gender, socioeconomic status, sexual orientation, height, weight, appearance, level of success, age, etc.) we become different in ways that make us more approachable, and at the same time, make others uncomfortable. Sexual healing doesn't mean fitting in, adjusting, coping, or compromising. Clients can discover what is right for them, and learn how to set limits about how they will use sexual energy.

OUR CULTURE HOLDS NEGATIVE
VIEWS OF SEX

While sex is considered a wonderful, enjoyable aspect of being human, at the same time, a seemingly contradictory cultural belief that it is wrong and bad still underlies the more positive view. Viewing one aspect of our nature as bad contaminates the rest of our view of ourselves. The perception of sexual badness influences feelings about the body, attractiveness, value to others, and even the right to be alive. This perception falls on a continuum from people who are only mildly affected and have been able to develop a happy use of sexual energy, to those whose lives have been devastated by sexual addiction or sexual inhibition.

PUBERTY

Women in my workshops and groups have few good stories of first menstruation, first bras, and body development, but rather a host of painful experiences.

The association of shame with masturbation engenders even more shame at puberty. Once masturbation begins, it is no longer an abstract idea associated with concepts like *self-abuse* or *impure thoughts.* It becomes real. For those with a tendency to become addicted to sexual feelings, puberty is a natural time for addiction to begin or strengthen in an attempt to reduce the increased feelings of shame.

My men's therapy group learned from the dictionary that the word *masturbation* is based on "self-mutilation!" Even today most people keep their practices secret, and few talk openly with their partners about when and where and how they touch themselves.

The men in the therapy group didn't believe they had much shame about masturbation, until I brought in a large watercolor of several abstract penises in differing stages of erection, all ejaculating. Then, latent shameful feelings emerged. These penises were in bright colors, representing the recovery of the artist. In spite of the healthy nature of the picture (very different from erotic art or pornography) the men had reactions of embarrassment (a form of shame) and discomfort, even after extensive exposure to pornography. The painting broke through the shame barriers that allow men to talk about so-called shameful things without feeling shame. (See Chapter 3 for a discussion of how people make shame congruent with the experience of self.) By the end of two hours of conversation, the picture was no longer a stimulus for shame. (In a women's therapy group this picture created equally intense, but different, reactions.)

SEXUAL RELATIONSHIPS PRODUCE SHAME

Sexually bonded relationships are, by definition, sexual. If sex equates to shame, then being in a sexual relationship will bring up shame. Getting married announces to the world that sex is involved.

Sexual activity (as with masturbation) attaches more shame to sex. Even the girls who were "good" and didn't have sex were shaming their sexuality. This vital part of themselves was declared bad, and withheld from expression. Marriage, which is supposed to make sex acceptable, doesn't remove this shame.

Long-term relationships create the most difficult arena in which to be sexual. Avoiding shame while *in* a relationship is more difficult than in one-night stands and short-term affairs. It is more difficult to avoid shame with a loved one who is part of "normal" life than in a situation that is defined as shameful.

Frustration typically evolves because partners usually have different ways of avoiding the experience of shame. For example, a woman may feel violated by a man's desire for her to wear sexy clothes or view pornography with him. She will take on additional shame if she does so.

And then her negative reaction brings on *his* shame, reminding him that men are seen as "perverts," who only want to use women for sex. This attitude toward himself, supported by the culture, makes him feel like a bad person.

Men often feel violated by a woman's desire to be romanced to avoid her own feelings of shame. He feels pressured to act romantic, but she will know he doesn't really want to. His lack of interest in romance brings on her false belief that all he wants is sex, and that he doesn't really care about her (Hastings 1993). This can be the source of some of the conflict between women and men.

SEXUAL SHAME PRODUCES COUPLING DISTRESSES

Couples may not be aware that sexual shame increases as the relationship progresses because our culture does not provide language for it. The result is an unnamable distress. A man cannot say he is angry with his wife for triggering his sexual interest (and consequent shame), when he knows she is supposed to do just that. He may have to use lust or pornography to override his shame. A woman cannot expect her partner to stop initiating sex so her sexual shame isn't triggered. These and countless other conflicts resulting from sexual shame can result in fights as the couple tries to *find namable reasons for their anger.* Many couples don't get to sexually bond and re-bond comfortably. This may be from sexual abuse during childhood, but living in our culture is also a likely cause.

Some choose not to be in long-term relationships to avoid this shame.

HOMOSEXUAL SHAME

To be sexual with someone of the same gender is one of the most shamed forms of sex. As a result, gay men are culturally programmed to be sexually addictive to provide enough sexual stimulus to override this great amount of shame. Gay men and lesbian women have few ways to feel normal and have a sense of belonging to our culture when they are in homosexual relationships. To have loving sex with a partner brings up more cultural shaming, and makes it more difficult to avoid shame with lustful addiction (see Chapter 11).

"BEING A GOOD PERSON" AS A SOLUTION
TO SHAME

Our culture offers an antidote to badness—becoming a good person, an upstanding member of the community, a good Christian, a family person.

Most religions and other organizations offer a set of rules to follow, which can appeal to people who carry shame. Failure to obey the rules, however, results in more shame. Religions don't offer methods to remove shame. When clients are dogmatically religious, they may be trying to cope with sexual shame.

Jerry, who sexually abused his younger brother as a teen, belongs to a cult that controls his life. He is raising his children within the cult. He writes his brother sentimental letters that sound loving and committed to family even while he has isolated himself from his family of origin, except for brief romanticized contact. Jerry hasn't been able to release his shame. Instead, he follows the rules, and remains locked into a shame-based life.

A sexually addicted client had been a member of a Christian organization for years as he sought to belong to a group with strong values that dictated how to behave. His recovery from sexual addiction didn't begin until he left this group. Once able to admit to sexual addiction, he could accept help with reducing the shame. Only then was he able to look at the function of his sexual activities, and the damage from childhood abuses that led to it. As a gay man, he and his sexuality, as well as his addiction, weren't acceptable to the church.

Membership in a community that adheres to a hierarchic structure, with authorities to set and enforce rules, does not remove shame from one's view of one's self; it further reinforces it. Even when a person does good things, the perception of self is not changed by accolades. Many clients have described themselves as frauds, waiting to be found out. Facing shame, talking about it, revealing acts that have been harmful to others without being shamed for them, and taking responsibility for change, can release shame.

WHEN SEX IS BORING

Boring sex is a profound effect of shame. Sex becomes hard to start and "too much work." Alcohol, drugs, pornography, fantasy, and new relationships are used to override boredom.

Long-term relationships are likely to elicit lack of interest because it becomes increasingly difficult to use cross-wired stimulators in a normal situation. Women's magazines publish articles about how to spice up sex, reflecting the pervasiveness of boredom. None seriously addresses the reasons behind it.

Intimate sex is never boring even when using the same activities, the same positions, no sex toys, and gentle stimulation. Such sex would look boring in a sex video! Passion and intense arousal don't necessarily show on the outside. When they do, they may take the form of laughter or shouts that don't sound "sexual" according to our culture's presentation of passionate sex in movies, television, and pornography.

The next chapter demonstrates how shame is unconsciously dealt with in order to override boredom and the overt experience of shame.

3

Making Sexual Shame Congruent with Self

BEING A SEXUAL PERSON

As long as shame is attached to sexuality, then sexual activity or awareness of oneself as a sexual person will bring unpleasant feelings. It is natural for us to want to avoid shame, but refraining from sex and divorcing oneself from sexuality is no solution. We must be sexual people for our species to continue, as well as for each person to feel whole.

CONGRUENCY WITH SHAME

Each of us learns a variety of maneuvers to continue being sexual and at the same time not feel shame. These maneuvers do not remove shame from sex, but will allow a person to feel sexual without awareness of the shame. Only a small percentage of people give up sexual feelings as a means of avoiding shame.

"It's okay to be bad," is one belief that allows shame and sexuality to coexist. If we can figure out how to accept being "sexually bad," then it becomes possible to engage in sexual activities and not feel shame. Ruth Westheimer's "Dr. Ruth" book (1986) teaches readers how to accept their badness by using words such as *raunchy, naughty,* and *the dirty deed* to describe sexual activities. A "doctor" is saying you can do these bad things and enjoy them—even enjoy them more because you are being naughty. Sex therapists are quoted in women's magazines as giving this kind of encouragement.

It's okay to be bad is the only possible solution until shame is removed from sexuality, allowing a person to feel like a good person while fully enjoying sex. Approaching sex from the perspective that it is acceptable to be bad can be a first step toward seeing that one isn't bad for being sexual. Such an approach brings sex out in the open and allows previously inhibited people to drop their inhibition and explore sex. This is certainly what has happened in our culture. In the '60s and '70s people began building into subcultures the acceptance of sexual activity. This contributed to the beginning of the reporting of memories of sexual abuse in childhood, which has fostered the sexual healing of millions of people. Clients addressing sexual issues might have to go through a similar process to remove shame and discover healthy sexuality.

Ginger hated having sex with her husband, and when they divorced, she set out to have a variety of sexual experiences, including casual sex with men she had just met, and a short-term relationship that was almost entirely sexual in nature. While I didn't support these activities as healthy lifestyle choices, I could see that Ginger was challenging the side of her that believed all sex was evil. I took the stand of supporting her explorations by helping her examine the function they were serving, knowing she would move through this stage and on to a better use of sexuality. Because she discussed her activities with an accepting, nonshaming therapist, she was able to engage in shameful sex without internalizing additional shame. Consciousness of her choices allowed her to remove shame. Over a period of years she was able to discover sexuality that allowed her to bond monogamously with her second husband. They achieved an "inside out" sexuality, one that emerged from within each of them, different from her old "outside-in" sexuality based on rules and myths about how sex should be. She could look back at the earlier period with appreciation for what she learned.

CONGRUENCY MANEUVERS

Shame compartment is a term I use for the emotional experience of congruency with shame. When in the shame compartment, we identify as sexual/shameful people, and so we can be sexual. But if something comes along and elicits the shame, then it becomes difficult to be sexual. For example, if your mother knocks on the bedroom door, do you ask her to wait in the living room until you are through with sex? Unlikely. Instead, our culture tells you to stop and pretend that nothing was going on.

The following are examples of how people get into the shame compartment.

1. *Sexual addiction* makes sex so desirable it overrides shame and revulsion. Men who give up their addiction often find themselves repulsed by their partners' bodies—something they would have vehemently denied was possible because when in addiction they desperately wanted a partner's body. (This is not the only reason for sexual addiction, of course.)

2. *The boys-out-on-the-town mentality* allows men to gather together and feel that being bad is fun. (Girls'-night-out is becoming increasingly accepted, as women imitate male freedom.) Going together to strip clubs allows men to be sexual together, and affirms that if other men who are respected, even admired, are doing this, it must be acceptable. These men may be shamed for it by women, particularly their partners, but they get to join together to combat the shaming that they feel toward themselves—internalized shame. Men say that they deserve to have a night out with the guys.

This activity will not produce sexual healing. Such a man needs the help of a therapist who can accept him even with his shame-avoiding maneuver, and know that healing will bring about a healthier, shame-free use of sexuality. Then he will no longer need the boys' night out in order to feel sexual without shame. A man in a relationship needs a mate who understands and knows how to support his sexual recovery without shaming him. Sexual recovery is greatly enhanced when both partners are involved, and willing to understand each other's symptoms.

3. *Pornography and sexual fantasy* also prevent feeling shame by eliciting intense arousal. I ask people who attend my groups or workshops to try masturbating without pornography, without fantasy, and when they are not already

aroused. Many are able to do this, but a common response is no arousal. Some find themselves fantasizing when they hadn't intended to. Fantasy appears in order to cut off the shame emerging from touching one's genitals with the intention of arousal.

Paul was amazed by the idea that he could masturbate without pornography. At first he became only mildly aroused, but was eager to continue. But time after time, he would discover himself lapsing into sexual fantasy— internal pornography. We talked about not scolding himself for it. While he was pleased to find he was capable of remaining aware while being sexual, his shame and fear still emerged. After more than thirty years of shame-based sex, he was taking on this important task. Many of my clients try the exercise, but the lurking shame is so strong, they put it off until they have been in therapy for many months or years.

4. *Lusting for strangers who look "sexy"* overrides shame, eliciting arousal that can be used for a sexual "hit," or masturbation, or finding a partner to have sex with. Men will look at women together (women are increasingly looking at men together, too), a briefer version of the boys' night out, and reduce shame by approving each other's response. Our culture accepts this behavior as long as it isn't too intrusive. Women feel pressure to be looked at so they can feel sexually valuable. When they achieve it, most don't like being lusted after by men who aren't interesting to them, or who cross the line of appropriateness. The sexual addiction twelve-step groups call it "lustful looking," a form of sexual addiction. Many sex addicts find it the hardest form of addiction to stop. The stimulus is everywhere, and the hit is received

before it is possible to make a decision to avoid it, in contrast to purchasing pornography or sexual services, or seducing a partner.

5. *Romantic fantasies and activities* make sex into something more than what it is—the love of a lifetime, marriage made in heaven, soul mates, being swept away. The feeling can be fueled by gifts and other proof that the relationship is extraordinary. Romantic feeling will set shame aside, and sexual activity can appear to be the completion of a magnificent relationship. This maneuver is considered not only acceptable but desirable for women. But it cannot last, eliciting the corresponding negative feeling of tragedy.

Women (and some men) bring partners to therapy with the complaint that he isn't romantic enough, all he wants is sex. If the partner is a sex addict, the complaint could reflect his emotional absence, but romance isn't a healthy alternative. Romance and loving feelings are not the same thing.

6. *Idiosyncratic arousers* will temporarily eliminate shame. Examples include searching (for a prostitute, one-night stand, one's lover, an affair), being sought after, an intense sexual charge from specific sexual activities, and imagining particular fantasies to become aroused. The content of the activities is determined by a number of things, including childhood sexual abuse, adult abuse, our culture's definition of "sexy," and observing sexual activity during the formative years. But whatever the original cause, these arousers override shame and allow access to the shame compartment.

7. *Drugs and alcohol* are effective tools to get into the shame compartment by preventing shame and fear. However, shame returns "the morning after." A high proportion of recovering alcoholics and drug addicts find they are no longer interested in sex when they stop using alcohol and drugs because the method that worked best to remove

shame is no longer available. Other substance-addicted sex addicts discover that sexual addiction intensifies after they stop using substances.

8. *Transforming shame into arousal,* such as having sex in public where it is possible to get caught, shaming one or both partners, dominance and submission, and other sado-masochistic acts, can convert shame into arousal.

> Marc entered therapy because his wife was no longer willing to stay married after discovering he visited a dominating prostitute who humiliated him while he obeyed her and masturbated in the nude. Over time we discovered that he had felt like his mother's servant, loved only when she shamed him. He went to just one prostitute, developing a relationship with her that extended outside their sessions, and he gave her the role of a new mother. I coached him in how he could interact with her to challenge his belief that he was only safe and loved when submitting. For example, I asked what it would be like to rise up off the floor and tell her that she had to love him as he was, that she was wrong to demand these things of him. He laughed at the thought. It was novel to expect to be loved as his powerful self. Over a few months he did change his interactions with her, gathering evidence that she cared for him as a person during their meetings for coffee after sessions. He was able to reduce the association between humiliation and sexuality.
>
> Marc's sexual relationship with his wife improved dramatically during the months we worked together as he was increasingly able to feel aroused by loving sex. His wife continued to feel anger about his visits to a prostitute, and learned how to express it. This gave him

immediate information about how his choices were affecting her, as well as drawing him into an increasingly monogamous relationship.

A client watched a documentary about a Jew who hired another man to dress up as a Nazi and pretend to torture him, forcing him to do humiliating, degrading things. He had had experiences as a child during the Holocaust that were similar to what he acted out. At that time there was no pleasure. He learned how to take devastating experiences and make them seem pleasurable. This maneuver is useful for someone unwilling to have the feelings of devastation in order to heal from them. The man in the documentary was able to make the connection between his sexual interests and actual experiences. Most clients don't know what they are acting out.

9. *Feeling "horny"* is almost universally seen as the beginning of sexual activity (for the initiator, at least). I am using the slang expression because there is no clinical term for the powerful urge for sexual activity.

The horny person approaches the partner to see if he or she is horny, too. Sexual arousal obviates sexual shame, and allows sexual activity. Intense desire isn't natural to sexuality; instead, it is a species-preserving feeling that is strong enough to override sexual repression. When shame is removed from sexuality, sexual activity can come from a more gentle place, a nonsexual connection between partners evolving into sexual interest and activity. If sex is based on horniness, then when horniness drops during sexual activity shame can prevent further interest. Other methods might then be employed to keep arousal going, such as sexual fantasy. People who are responding to an intuitive interest in sex will be able to allow arousal to rise and fall as needed.

10. *Not wanting to have sex* or doing so infrequently allows some women to avoid shame. They can also set aside shame by having sex because they are "supposed to," or otherwise letting the partner make the decision.

11. *Feeling "swept off one's feet"* can override shame with romance and love. Some women become congruent with shame by becoming prostitutes, sexual dancers, or strippers, or by having sex with a series of men because there seems to be no reason not to.

SEX CAN DRIVE PARTNERS APART

There are many ways sexual shame creates difficulty for couples. One of the most obvious has been called the "goddess–whore" dichotomy, where a man is able to have sex with the "whore" but is unable to be sexual with his mate, the "goddess." The man feels sexual shame when he is not able to make shame congruent with self, which is more difficult in the "good" marital bed. Feelings of badness when being sexual prevent him from having intimate sex with a woman he loves. Instead, he needs a woman who will join him in the shame compartment to override his shame. He needs her to be lustful, "talk dirty," use drugs and alcohol, break a taboo, engage in sexual acts that trigger shame-based sexuality, or otherwise engage his sexual addiction. Prostitutes and strippers can offer this "bad" sex. He must have strong arousal in order to be sexual in spite of shame. Men with this dynamic can work on removing the shame, even though it is a painful process. As this process proceeds they can become increasingly available to their mates in an intimate way.

SHAMEFUL SEX AND LOVING BONDING ARE INCOMPATIBLE

Paul (discussed earlier) spent thirty years struggling with how to have loving, bonding, *and* shameful sex. He loved his wife and wanted to be married and have children. But immediately after the wedding, he found that he couldn't maintain sexual interest. (They had not had sex before, and he had never felt very sexual with Alecia.) Even with fantasy and pornography, he felt asexual.

A year or so into the marriage, Paul had his first affair. He was relieved to have erections and inter-course. He decided to continue affairs with married women who would not interrupt his marriage. Through three decades of affairs, he was never tempted to leave his wife.

In therapy, Paul was able to see that he had developed a strong connection between shame and sexuality. Prostitution was legal where he grew up, and "real men" were not monogamous. He had been filled with ideas about how good women don't like sex, and how men hurt them with their penises. He could not switch into the shame compartment in order to avoid feeling shame when with his wife, while doing so easily with "bad" women.

Alecia was deeply pained by the lack of sex with her husband. They adopted two children when it became obvious that she would not conceive. After a decade she had her own affair to prove she was attractive to a man who enjoyed being sexual with her. Now in their sixties, they are glad the sexual difficulties didn't drive them apart.

Alecia consulted several therapists who counseled her to make herself into the kind of woman Paul found sexually attractive. She did. She became glamorous, sexy, and interesting. She went back to school, and worked in a profession in which she knew many interesting people and did many activities. Paul supported her development, but his disinclination to be sexual with her didn't change. She could not solve the problem by becoming his sex object. To him she remained the "good" woman.

Late in their thirty-year marriage, they found a sex therapist who helped them discover how they could be more sexual. Paul was able to override his shame sufficiently to experiment with oral and manual stimulation. They were told to watch pornographic movies and become aroused together. Alecia was glad they were relating sexually, but still she felt something was wrong.

Finally introduced to the ideas of sexual addiction, cross-wiring, and sexual shame, both Paul and Alecia could see that there was more to their problems than whether she was sexually attractive to him. As we mapped out his past he could see that his feelings had nothing to do with loving his wife, and that he was not a bad person. Alecia finally saw that his reactions had nothing to do with her sexual desirability or his love for her.

Women's socialization allows them to abandon sexual expression more easily than does men's. If Paul had stopped having sex, his self-esteem might have dropped more than it did from affairs. He had learned that men who don't have sex aren't men. He was encouraged by uncles and cousins to have prostitutes and affairs, and they kept the secret for him.

Women, on the other hand, are culturally allowed to stop being sexual in order to avoid shame. Women are not provided with mechanisms to move easily into shame congruence, and instead are revered as pure and good. Until sex therapy became popularized, there was no sanctioning of shameful sex except for romantic affairs. This solution required focusing on the "relationship" rather than sexual activity.

Abandoning sexual activity or pleasure is a solution that allows women to reduce the experience of shame. As women become mothers, particularly if they don't feel like good mothers, the desire to avoid sexual shame can become even stronger. A client may be able to recognize issues of parenting, without knowing that issues of sexual shame and/or the desire to give up sexual activity lie underneath. For example, a couple who came to me about the husband's sexual addiction soon discovered that the wife was sexually bonded with their 4-year-old daughter. She was not being sexual with the child, but emotional incest had created a monogamous bond that excluded the husband. As we explored this, we identified the numerous complications that prevented the father and daughter from having a lovingly bonded relationship. The wife had diverted her sexual bonding energy onto the daughter, with consequences that reverberated throughout the family. The issues were seen as the husband's difficulty bonding with the child, his dislike for her, and his refusal to participate in her care. When the couple successfully addressed the wife's bond with the child, the other issues fell away.

The culture encourages women to focus on the coupling bond. Sexual energy feeds this bond even without sexual activity. In the past when young people were chaperoned on dates, they were still able to use sexual energy to bond by looking deeply into each other's eyes and expressing sexual energy in a touch of the hand or a kiss on the cheek. A woman needn't feel shameful about this form of sexual energy—it had cultural approval. But once she married, and was required to have sex, then she often had difficulties. She had to engage in this shamed activity to meet her husband's needs and to have children.

Women are now permitted to express sexuality with sex. However, much confusion has arisen over this change because now women are *culturally required* to integrate the shameful "whore" in the bedroom with the daytime idealized mother. These issues will continue to influence every person in the culture until shame is reduced at an individual and cultural level. The incest recovery movement, propelling people toward healthier sexuality, is making this increasingly possible.

CULTURAL COPING WITH SHAME DAMAGES MEN

The expressions "men are like that" and "boys will be boys" mean that men automatically lust after attractive women. Construction workers have the reputation for taking note of women who pass by. The culture says that women, particularly these men's partners, are to find this objectionable. A charming man is fascinating until he marries, then his wife objects to charm directed toward other women.

The tragedy here is that men have been trained to feel self-esteem, and express sexuality, in spite of shame, through using these maneuvers to get into the shame compartment. Until that is appreciated, feminist discourse about how men harm women cannot lead to change. Men are victims of their acculturated sexuality until they can enter sexual recovery.

As therapists, we must address the sexuality of men as if they were sexual abuse survivors, even if they weren't touched sexually. Male acculturation produces intense violation of a man's sexuality, of his body, and his overall self. Men have been traumatized by the culture's view of sexuality and masculinity.

As therapists we can work with men as if they are suffering the adult effects of sexual abuse by making room for memories of how sex was shamed, what first masturbation was like, how first sexual contact went, and education about the role of shame in creating their approach to sex. We can help men remove the obstacles to discovering a more satisfying use of sexuality, and lead the kind of life that allows self esteem to grow.

> Kenneth started therapy thinking that all interaction with women was sexual. He flirted with women in grocery stores by commenting on items in their baskets. He pursued prostitutes and sexualized all of his wife's friends. We worked on his sexual addiction immediately, and then, over time, we talked about how flirting with strangers wasn't a healthy use of his sexuality. Because Kenneth was a severe sexual addict, and had to stop all of his sexual behavior and begin again, he quickly realized how he had to give up everything but intimate sex.

The stories of men like Kenneth (told in *The Centerfold Syndrome* [Brooks 1995]) have made possible an appreciation for how little of acculturated male sexuality is healthy, and how the recovery of many sex addicts has created a broader understanding of healthy sexuality and how to achieve it.

> After more than three years of recovery, and divorce, Kenneth spent a summer pursuing women with a sexually addicted friend who was not in recovery. He came to group with stories about how he had met women. Each time his initial interest was lusting and getting sex, but then he got to know the woman and watched her change from a sex object into a person with feelings and a personality. His lust would drop, and he would find himself no longer even sexually attracted if the woman wasn't someone he was interested in dating. Eventually he met a woman he wanted to be with, and the sexual attraction remained. They lived together, and then married. Now six years after beginning recovery from a very strong addiction to sex, Kenneth is free of the compulsion, with only occasional confusion about how to relate with women without sexual energy. He is now addressing his compulsive use of money.

The change experienced by Kenneth and many other sex addicts did not come from shaming the behaviors, or from a decision to stop them. It came from years of examination of his sexual history, with the support of other recovering addicts. He gradually removed the shame attached to sex by our culture, and by sexual abuse in his childhood.

Part II

Dysfunction, Abuse, and Addiction

4

First Came Sex Therapy

Sex therapy is the oldest of the three areas of research and treatment. Becoming popular in the 1970s following research by Masters and Johnson (begun in the 1950s), sex therapy is only 25 years old. Masters and Johnson (1966, 1970), followed by Helen Singer Kaplan (1974), and then a host of sex therapists in the 1980s and 1990s, delineated a series of sexual dysfunctions and behavior modification techniques devised to help people obtain better sexual functioning (Hartman and Fithian 1994, Hawton 1985, Heiman and Lopiccolo 1988, Leiblum and Rosen 1988, 1989, Szasz 1990, and Tiefer 1995). These dysfunctions, listed in *DSM-IV*, are called inhibited sexual desire, sexual aversion, sexual arousal disorder, rapid ejaculation, retarded ejaculation, impotence, secondary impotence, and anorgasmia.

The implied philosophy of sex therapy is that more sex is desirable, and the therapist's job is to help people accomplish that. When a therapist suggests that a couple stop having sex, it is to change their interaction so they can eventually have more sex.

WHAT IS SEX THERAPY?

Sex therapy focuses on difficulties (or dysfunctions) in performing sexual activities. Masters and Johnson (1970) classified sexual problems of women into three categories— orgasmic dysfunction, vaginismus (spasms of the muscles around the entrance of the vagina inhibiting or preventing intercourse) and dyspareunia (pain during intercourse)— and problems of men into four categories—impotence, premature ejaculation, ejaculatory incompetence, and dyspareunia. Sexual dysfunction has been defined as the persistent impairment of the normal patterns of sexual interest or response (Hawton 1985).

Beginning with the work of Masters and Johnson (1970), behavioral techniques have been devised for specific dysfunctions. These original methods were further developed by later researchers, including Kaplan (1974).

Hawton (1985) offers an easy to read, straightforward approach to sex therapy, including information on sexual anatomy and sexual response, the nature of sexual problems, the causes, assessment, and homework assignments for couples and individuals who are embarking on behavioral programs. Hawton's book is useful for all therapists, not just sex therapists. Leiblum and Rosen (1989) offer a more comprehensive explanation of sex therapy.

THE INFLUENCE OF SEX THERAPY ON CULTURE

Sex therapy has had a positive effect on our culture by bringing sex out in the open, and making it more acceptable to seek treatment for sexual dysfunction. In addition, common sexual practices, such as oral sex, and the use of pornography and fantasy for arousal, have been addressed as acceptable. The therapist's taking a "sexual history," a common first step, offers clients an experience they have never had before: an accepting, nonshaming, matter-of-fact therapist asks questions to understand the particular issues of the client. What should be ordinary is a radically new experience. This step offers an opportunity to remove a great deal of shame just by talking. Such interviews must allow the client to pace the timing and to refuse to answer questions; otherwise the experience can be violating (see Chapter 15).

In a student discussion of sexuality led by a college junior, the students responded to a list of questions provided by the counseling center. (No professional participated, although I was an observer.) The participants were fascinated, asked each other questions, and listened carefully to the answers. Meetings of this kind are an outgrowth of the impact of sex therapy in bringing sex out in the open.

The University of Washington recently offered a presentation on dominance-submission, or sadomasochistic sexual activities, suggesting how these arousal stimuli might be incorporated into a couple's sex life. The effect of increasingly open discussion has reduced sexual shame for millions of people. But it has not eliminated it. Sex remains attached to shame because of the culture. Being a sexual person brings shame of varying degrees because virtually all cultures pass sexual shame on to each member. (A brief look at the practices of all major cultures demonstrates how women are treated as inferior, with little control over their sexuality. This fact alone supports the experience of sexual shame, which is then conveyed to succeeding generations.) Traditional sex therapy, taking a behavioral approach to symptom change, does not address our culture's damaging effects from the beginning of life. It does not go far enough to meet the needs of most clients and offer some hope for change of sexual functioning.

WHEN SEX THERAPY IS APPROPRIATE

When prospective clients call for an appointment, I ascertain if they are interested in the long-term sexual healing I offer. Some people are interested not in a deep healing process but in a behavioral approach to reducing symptoms. If a man wants to spend eight to twelve sessions learning how to delay orgasm, I refer him to a certified sex therapist. If his relationship is troubled, however, or he wants to change because his partner is nagging him, I invite him for a session to determine if his issue is really rapid orgasm, or if there are personality or relationship dynamics that manifest in sexual symptoms.

Some people are clear that they want a rapid, symptom-focused solution, but others don't understand the options and need help evaluating their problem. Many begin talking about orgasms or failed erections, but then launch into a look at their nonsexual lives or their history. Sex was merely an identifiable symptom that allowed them to seek help, while other issues were difficult to define.

Brian came to me because, at 28, he hadn't been able to sustain a relationship beyond three months. He attributed this to the fact that he couldn't maintain an erection once he started intercourse. I didn't question him about sex therapy because he already told me there were other issues.

In the first two sessions we talked about the loss of erections, identifying some of the related issues, including performance anxiety when he thinks he must have an erection, needing to feel like a man by having sex with every woman on the first date, and preference for masturbation because it's easier than trying to satisfy a woman. After this discussion, his shame dropped rapidly. In the third session he realized that he wanted to examine his whole way of life, having known something was wrong from the time he was a child. His stepfather had physically abused him from age 5, and he was emotionally abused by his alcoholic parents. The resulting levels of distrust made it impossible to bond trustingly with a woman. He became emotionally absent when experiencing physical contact with a partner—or anyone else.

We put sex on the back burner, knowing it would resurface. Months later he realized that his dependency on masturbation was strong, and began examining how he used it addictively. He wasn't able to talk about it until he developed sufficient trust in me. In addition, he wasn't prepared to give up the imitation feeling of love until he was able to have such feelings in real life.

When Brian fell in love several months after beginning therapy, he consistently obtained and maintained an erection, even though we had spent little time directly discussing the symptom. His increasing trust in women removed the need to avoid sex.

LISTENING FOR SEXUAL INFORMATION

I suggest paying close attention any time a client mentions sex. Given the massive connection of shame with sexuality, most people are going to toss out a crumb and not follow it up unless the therapist asks questions, genuinely making room for further information (but without a demand for more than the client is able to reveal).

Early in my practice, I saw Greg, who wanted support in divorcing his wife from whom he had been separated for years. While he dated other women, he couldn't seem to let go of the final thread. Being "married" allowed him to avoid bonding with a new partner, which frightened him. After several sessions, he mentioned that he had gone to an adult bookstore to masturbate to videos. He said nothing more, moving on to a different subject. At that time I didn't know the significance of this revelation, or that he needed me to ask about it. Questions like, "Do you go to the adult bookstore often?" or "I'd like to hear more about that part of your life; it sounds important," could have encouraged him to continue. It can be assumed that such a shame-loaded subject, discussed with no one else in his life, will need to be encouraged, probably more than once. Greg needed me to take this behavior seriously without shaming him or labeling it as wrong, and to know it was a symptom that would be helpful to change.

BENEFITS OF STUDYING SEX THERAPY

Therapists who want to help with sexual issues can learn basic information about causes of sexual symptoms and about behavioral techniques. Even therapists who focus on deep sexual healing will find use for short-term, primarily behavioral approaches.

A client was unable to have erections after he lost his job. His self-esteem dropped even further from not having sex and the resulting loss of closeness with his wife.

I told him in the first session that loss of sexual interest was a symptom of depression, and that a job loss was cause for a temporary depression that would pass as he moved on to new employment. I suggested that he talk with his wife about giving up trying to have sex for now, and instead, to meet both their needs for affection by cuddling.

He came back the next session to tell me it was working well. By telling her what I had said, she was able to let go of her own concern that something was wrong with the relationship. This decreased his urge to "perform."

In our third and last session, he was having erections again, now free from believing he had to. In addition, he had been offered an interesting new job, removing much of his distress. In this case, the circumscribed symptom resulting from specific causes in the very recent past didn't need deep sexual healing.

SEXUAL POTENTIAL INSTEAD OF SEXUAL FUNCTIONING

David Schnarch (1991), a radical sex therapist, addresses the profound limitations of sex therapy. He offers an alternative to the goal of more sex and consistent orgasms. He calls this alternative "the pursuit of sexual potential." He helps his clients relinquish the limited goals of more sex and better orgasms in order to discover a deeper kind of sex—one that doesn't focus on orgasms, in which orgasms occur spontaneously when the time is right, or don't occur, even when sex has been highly satisfying.

Therapists who limit themselves to traditional sex therapy training may not be able to see that there are more options, and they may have difficulty validating the experience of clients who have moved beyond our culture's limited views. Traditional sex therapy teachings don't include an understanding of couples who feel satisfied with sex without having orgasms.

Schnarch describes the experiences of his clients who have been able to obtain more than high sexual frequency, the ability to obtain and maintain arousal and have orgasms. Shame reduction from talking with an accepting therapist allows clients to explore their sexuality in new ways, often discovering an experience that doesn't match our culture's limited view. Schnarch's descriptions indicate that he was able to hear experiences that transcend the usual hot, frenzied sexual encounters that characterize Dr. Ruth's (Westheimer 1986) proclaimed good sex. Schnarch's ability to reflect the accomplishment of his clients' sexual evolution encouraged them to continue. Sex therapy training, however, doesn't go beyond success in sexual functioning to include Schnarch's "sexual potential."

Schnarch cites research that supports the need for a broader view of sexuality than the four phases of sexual activity—desire, arousal, orgasm, and resolution. *Physiological* levels of arousal correlate poorly with the *experience* of arousal. This lack of correlation is consistent with arousal based on electromagnetic energy (the English term for the Chinese experience of *Chi*, or the Hindu experience of *Chakras*). Since this energy is not measured in sex therapy research (it is only beginning to be measured in medical research), it is not scientifically understood how the ordinary experience of arousal with full physiological evidence (erection in men, tumescence and lubrication in women) can be multiplied many times by those who can allow body energy to supplement sexual sensation. The experience is a vibration that swells within each person, and moves back and forth between partners. One of Schnarch's clients describes this as "the quiet," or "seeing God," noting that time stops. There are no English words to express this experience.

Intense arousal is brought about by gentle and slow stimulation. Schnarch frequently advises his clients to slow down intercourse and other stimulation in order to become *more* aroused. Fast, hard stimulation inhibits energy-based arousal. Intense stimulation, a variety of positions, fantasy, pornography, and sex "toys" become necessary to create sufficient arousal to override sexual inhibition, or cover up shame, for those who are sexually addicted or otherwise needing to avoid intimacy during sex.

For those who are able to access strong exchange of energy, sex can never be boring. Having sex in the same position time after time with no outward variety (but total inward variety) can be fully satisfying. Such experience of sex is not shown in pornographic videos—it looks boring to those who are seeking external stimulation.

The field of sex therapy is evolving, and Schnarch is supporting this development. He has not, however, integrated the research and practice of sexual addiction recovery, or of sexual abuse recovery, into his understanding of sexuality.

"DR. RUTH'S" SEX THERAPY

There are numerous books on how to achieve better sex. Some can be downright damaging, while others are helpful but inadequate. The "Dr. Ruth" books are among the most harmful, as Ruth Westheimer advocates the use of alcohol to relax, and lying to partners to make them feel better. Her writing reflects the traditional sex therapy belief that orgasms are a good indicator of healthy sex. She believes in "taking care of each other's sexual needs," and uses expressions like "raunchy," and "the dirty deed," suggesting that sex is naughty. This attitude encourages sexual addiction, and offers no understanding of how removing shame can permit healthy sexuality.

Women's magazines publish articles about how to have sex that is better, hotter, lustier, and more frequent. These articles reflect traditional sex therapy practices and quote sex therapists. As a result, many clients think this is how their sex lives should be. Unfortunately, they are then unwilling to raise sexual issues in therapy because they aren't open to trying the methods they have read about. Because the articles quote sex therapists, readers are led to believe this is the only possibility. People who have been sexually abused in childhood (half of all women [Russell 1986]) will not be able to use those methods, or will have to leave emotionally (dissociate) in order to follow instructions.

Women with a history of many partners who then became emotionally unable to have sex will be particularly harmed by the suggestion to force arousal. These women (and men) may not bring up their sexual issues in therapy, or will search for indicators that the therapist will not respond like the "experts." If any suggestion of sexual issues emerges for women clients, it can be helpful to mention that the ideas of healthy sex presented in the media are distorted. This could open a door for further discussion, as the client can see that the therapist might be of more help than the quoted experts.

THERAPISTS' SEXUAL HEALING

Traditional sex therapists recommend that clients use fantasy and pornography to increase sexual arousal. This instruction reduces shame about using strong arousers, and more sexual activity is a likely result. But the acceptance of these maneuvers deprives people of intimate sex. People who have spent years healing their sexuality learn (from the inside out) that sexual fantasy or pornography takes them away from themselves, and thus away from their partner, and they choose not to do so. Therapists who accept and recommend these sexual stimuli will not be able to help a client find the true nature of their sexuality.

If therapists work on freeing their own sexuality from cultural influences they will better understand what clients can achieve.

5

Treatment of Sexual Abuse

When I was in school in the 1970s, the issues of sexual abuse of children and the recovery of adults who had been violated during childhood were not addressed. In 1982 I led a group of adult survivors and began an experiential education along with psychotherapists across the country. The time was right for people to come forward and tell about their history of abuse. Now the subject has become a primary focus of clinical research and practice.

Self-help books describe the healing process for those who were sexually violated. (Some of these are: Bass and Davis (1988), Courtois (1988), Davis (1991), Elliott (1993), Fraser (1987), Gil (1983), Hunter (1990), Lew (1990), Maltz and Holman (1987), and Stein (1973).) The popularity of this recovery is encouraging a worldwide look at the role of sexual violation of children, and the healing of millions is bringing about a movement toward radical changes in the use of sexuality. As I address audiences, and have conversations with therapists who work with incest survivors, I am seeing that therapists who treat sexual abuse victims are learning from their clients (and some from their own lives) about a healthier use of sexuality. The person who has been in sexual recovery no longer tolerates the culture's attitudes toward sex. When enough people experience a healthier use of sexuality, the culture will change.

Some clients seek therapy because they were abused sexually as children and want to remove the effects. Therapist training in sexual abuse has increased as clients have come forward with this issue. Research studies conclude that, conservatively, a third of women have been touched sexually as children (Russell 1983, 1984, 1986). When Russell asked about noncontact abuse, half of the sample had been sexually abused. About 17 percent of men reported sexual abuse as children, with an additional 9 to 14 percent reporting noncontact abuse (Lisak et al. 1996). We might assume that those seeking therapy reflect a higher proportion of survivors, increasing these percentages among our clients. Other countries, including massively populated India and China, have far higher rates.

The abuse of sexuality is built in to our culture. The overt physical form is at one end of a continuum of damage. On the other end is silence regarding, for example, a baby's genitals, the sexual feelings of 3-year-olds, the beginning of menstruation, and first orgasms of pubescent children. Silence conveys the shameful nature of sexuality. Somewhere in the middle of the continuum is shaming of evidence of sexuality in children and young adults, such as telling a child to stop touching herself, or discouraging explicit questions about sex.

Helping people recover from the effects of sexual abuse includes helping people *recover from the ways our culture has damaged all of us.* As therapists we have been affected by the culture, and must actively work on our own cultural denial. Then we can be available to our clients when they bring up damage from actions that are culturally accepted.

IDENTIFYING ABUSE

To recover from sexual abuse, therapy clients first need to know they were abused. The perceptive therapist can note signs, and ask questions that might elicit this information, but it is particularly difficult to uncover abuses that occurred in the early years, or that were prevented from registering in language and images through the process of dissociation. These clients have sexual issues resulting from early abuse that can be addressed even without obtaining concrete memories. For example, lusting for very large breasts can come from breast-feeding—when the mother was aroused and felt guilty, or used the arousal for her pleasure, or hated the child for causing it. Sexual energy is transmitted in the same way it is with a sexual partner, where each partner's arousal fuels the other's. If a mother is sexually boundaried (her sexual energy is not broadcast to anyone who is not appropriate for sexual relating) the child will be aware of the mother's sexual energy, but it will not be transmitted to the child. (Preoccupation with large breasts can also result from exposure to pornography in one's teen years. A symptom cannot be automatically connected to a cause.)

Repression and dissociation in response to sexual violation are thoroughly and beautifully covered in *Memories of
Sexual Betrayal: Truth, Fantasy, Repression, and Dissociation*
(Gartner 1997). Even though written by psychoanalysts (from
the perspective of interpersonal and relational psychoanalysis), the book is easily readable, and applies to psychotherapy
of all orientations. For example, the relational psychoanalytic approach has integrated trauma theory and research
into analytic practice. Jody Messler Davies' chapter shows
how we don't need to dwell on retrieving memory, which is
perhaps impossible when memory has been dissociated at
the time the events were taking place. Instead, we can see
how the story is told through the transference and countertransference, allowing us to witness the abuses for the client.
The client can be seen, and the abuses validated, even when
the specific act and the person who perpetrated it may not
be remembered.

Some clients can remember what happened, but will
deny that harm was caused. For example, some postpubes-
cent boys who are seduced by older girls or women don't
consider it abuse, but rather their good fortune. Other
examples are parents' shaming comments about body parts
and looks, violation of physical privacy, inability to tell
parents when sexual abuse has occurred, rough handling
when being bathed, unnecessary or sexualized enemas,
sexualized comments about developing body or body parts,
sexualized relating among parents and their friends, and
anything that doesn't respect the natural evolution of the
child's sexuality. Taking a look at these events usually
requires questions from the therapist and education about
the potential damage. A primary task of therapy is teaching
the client that what has occurred is, indeed, abuse.

Beth had difficulty believing her father had sexually abused her because she has no memory of intercourse. They went on trips, slept in the same bed, and took showers together to save water until she was 14. She wakes up frightened at night, convinced her husband is masturbating in bed, and freezes in fear of what he will do to her. While she knows this reflects the nights in her father's bed, she cannot let herself know that her sexuality was abused. Even though she herself is a therapist, and she knows that her own clients were abused when they had experiences like hers, she denies the significance of her own. She understood her denial when she confronted her parents several years ago. They angrily denied everything, and cut off all contact with her and her children. They also believe no sexual abuse occurred because no intercourse took place.

MEMORY

Gartner (1997) synthesizes new information about the process of memory that can help clinicians work with abuse that cannot be remembered or named. He discusses the biology of traumatic memory. Traumatic memory is encoded (into images, language, or other symbols) differently than conventional memory. He describes a study in which a beta blocker was administered to subjects who were then exposed to neutral and traumatic stories. The beta blocker significantly impaired memory of an emotionally arousing story, but not a neutral story, demonstrating the experimental induction of the process of dissociation. Gartner explains how this study suggests a separate biological system for encoding and recalling emotional trauma. The implication of the study is that children use dissociation to cope with traumatic sexual abuse, which results in a physiological inability to remember what happened even when the child is old enough to remember neutral events. If this is true, it can help therapists accept that a client was sexually abused without having to obtain proof, or focus on remembering in the conventional sense.

> A client did not remember being sexually abused by her father, even though she could piece together information that suggested this had happened. Early in our work she described feeling aroused as if being kissed, then touched, and finally she approached orgasm. She wasn't touching herself, and I was six feet away in my chair. She said with surprise, "I feel like I'm going to have an orgasm!" She didn't, probably only because she was in a therapist's office. When her arousal subsided, I repeated what she had said, and then asked what she felt had happened. She responded, "Well, it seems like someone was sexual with me. I couldn't do anything about it. I couldn't keep myself from feeling sexual. And coming. But I don't remember anything like that happening." As her witness, I said, "Someone was sexual with you when you didn't want him to be. Your body remembers." I didn't know if it was her father. I didn't have to know in order to affirm that something had happened that she needed me to see. This memory, and others like it, were the only evidence she had. In spite of this, she was able to free herself from the effects of childhood violation.

Gartner also describes a longitudinal study by Linda Meyer Williams (1994) in which she studied the recall of women whose childhood sexual abuse was documented by hospital records. Seventeen years later 38 percent of the women did not remember the abuse for which they had received medical attention. When girls younger than 7 were removed from the study to eliminate the possibility that age could have prevented memory, 28 percent still did not recall the abuse. Williams also discovered that abuse at very young ages was more likely to be forgotten than at later ages, and that abuse by a family member is more readily forgotten than abuse by a stranger.

This study relieves therapists of having to question how a person could not remember sexual abuse while having all the symptoms of childhood sexual violation. We can change our focus from learning if a person was or was not sexually abused to paying attention to other methods of storytelling, such as body memory and relationship dynamics in adulthood. Working with this evidence can be useful even if the truth of what happened cannot be verified.

NONCONTACT ABUSE

Sexual abuse is generally considered to include physical contact, but it has been discovered that noncontact abuse can be as devastating (Love 1990).

> Monica came to therapy because she stopped wanting sex with her boyfriend, a pattern that had occurred over the twenty years she had been in relationships. In the past she would find a new lover and then break up with the old one. She didn't want to do that again. In addition, she had had sex with anyone who wanted it during her high school years.

As we talked about sex in the present, and in her childhood, she assured me that she hadn't been sexually abused. I could believe she hadn't been touched sexually. But as we talked about her relationship with her parents, it became clear that her father was a sexual addict, and his sexual energy spilled onto her. She was the "cute" daughter, and her sister felt jealous of her relationship with their father, even though Monica didn't experience it as a good one. While the father found Monica sexually appealing (even before puberty, but more so after) he didn't like reacting to her sexually. Blaming her for his sexual arousal, he criticized any evidence of her attractiveness and developing sexuality. He poked at her breasts, making fun of them. He didn't want her to date, and tried to screen her boyfriends. When she was 16 he began spending all his time with his future wife, and was no longer around to control her.

Monica couldn't see this treatment as abusive. Even when I phrased it as abuse of her sexuality she still couldn't see it as anything other than normal, even though she knew that typical teenage girls don't think so poorly of themselves that they will have sex with anyone who wants it.

My first job was helping her see that what had occurred was damaging to her sexuality so that she could make sense of her current sexual behaviors. I suggested books to read, including novels, so that she could identify with the characters. She could see that a woman in a novel was being treated badly, and deserved better. A therapy group for women addressing sexual issues also helped. Monica described her father's behavior, and was surprised to see other women reacting with disgust and sadness. These influences didn't fully change her beliefs, but she was, at least on an intellectual level, able to relate her current sexuality with the influences from childhood. She is now ending a relationship that has been sexless for several years and plans to be single for a time. When she eventually creates a new relationship, she will be more conscious of the factors that attract her, and her belief that she has to give sex in order to be acceptable.

DAMAGE CAN BRING MOTIVATION TO CHANGE

Those whose sexuality was damaged in ways that created havoc in their adult sexual lives are often able to heal their sexuality to a greater extent than those dealing with less damage. Sexual healing is difficult and painful, and taking on the task requires great motivation. Fearing the inability to have relationships at all, or facing the desire to have sex with children, can be a significant motivation to face sexual healing, a motivation that those who suffered less damage might not feel.

Two men had been arrested and convicted of child sexual abuse (Hastings 1994). As I spoke with each man for many hours over several years, I learned that both had been the object of severe abuse, sexual and otherwise, in childhood. After completing court-mandated treatment, each elected to continue therapy to heal more fully. By the time I met them, both were experiencing the healthiest sex they had ever encountered.

Their wives joined them in sexual recovery, which helped them explore new sexuality. I interviewed one of the men over a period of three years, and during this time he told me about the status of his sex life. In the final interview, he glowingly described the kind of sex he and his wife had discovered after persistently attending twelve-step groups, and questioning everything about their sexuality. He still found it necessary to avoid young boys who had a certain vulnerable, sweet look, as he was afraid that he could still be triggered into arousal. But he had been able to relinquish other forms of cross-wired arousal so that he could fully be with his wife. Both in their late fifties, they no longer believed that sexual desire came from outside stimulation or an inherent need for sex. Instead, they could allow their intimacy to suggest sexual activity, and go from there.

Interviewing these men at length, and meeting with their wives, touched me deeply. They have a good deal more work to do—perhaps a lifelong process—but they know how to do it and they enjoy it. Both felt a great deal of shame in telling me—another new person—about their sexual activities with children. This shame is the motivation for them to stay on the path of recovery.

ABSTAINING FROM SEX ISN'T A WORKABLE SOLUTION

Logic suggests that if sex is too shameful, a person might elect to give up sexuality. It is conceivable that sex would disappear if we didn't need it for survival of the species!

Richard (see Chapter 1) came to me because he had no interest in having sex with his wife when they married. His sex life consisted of fantasy and masturbation. He knew he had to do whatever it took to change. But the change was slow and tedious in the beginning. I talked about him frequently in my consultation group to gather support to tolerate the pace. At the same time, I sensed that he had the motivation to see it through, in contrast to others who flee when they feel shame or who fear having to give up valued sexual activities.

Richard had the necessary ego strength to tolerate the memories of being sexually abused by his father when he was 8 and 9 years old. In the second year of our work, he had severe body memories, thrashing around on the floor of his living room, gagging. After we talked about the first event, he had a similar experience in my office. He became intensely depressed during this time, lost weight, and went on antidepressant medication for a year. As he worked through this period over the next two years, he began to be able to have sex with his wife. They conceived a wanted child. Richard was determined she would not be left alone with his father. After four years of therapy Richard tearfully said good-bye, appreciating how dramatically his life had changed.

MASTURBATION AS A SEX LIFE

Richard might have lived a life like many men who choose masturbation as their sexual outlet and never marry. We tend to assume that "confirmed bachelors" are closeted gay men, but this is not always the case. Some people (men and women) have been so physically and/or sexually violated that they cannot bring themselves to have sex. While this decision does not require contact sexual abuse, sexuality has been damaged by some other serious disrespect to the body. Partners may be chosen who confirm the belief that abuse is unavoidable. Or the fear will continue even with a partner who is not abusive.

People who live out their lives alone, masturbating or having casual sex, or giving up sex altogether, either don't know there is help, or are unable to face the long and painful therapy necessary to change their beliefs.

Luckily, Richard's wife wanted him to seek help, and he was able to use the help he found.

CONFRONTING WITHOUT SHAMING

Clients who use pornography or fantasy to get or stay aroused, and to reach orgasm, may feel shame. They may also believe that fantasy and pornography are acceptable (unless the nature of the pornography is culturally unacceptable, such as rape). While our culture—thanks in large part to sex therapy—overtly approves, at the same time most people don't routinely mention to their neighbors that they found a great new video. When I saw the movie *Spanking the Monkey*, about mother–son incest, I noticed a high level of shame in the audience. People crouched into themselves, and the air was as moist as in a room full of group therapy clients revealing shameful material. People avoided eye contact, and there was none of the light chatting common in theaters before a movie starts.

As with anything shameful, when a client talks about pornography, the therapist's first useful reaction is acceptance and interest in hearing more about it. I tell clients that the content of porn and fantasy that arouses them can be useful in learning how their sexuality was damaged, thus encouraging them to continue. Questions about when they first discovered pornography, and how they felt about it, can demonstrate interest, as well as informing the client that it is something to talk more about. Conversation can remove some of the shame.

During this initial discussion, I say that sexual activity that is intimate with oneself or with another doesn't happen when either or both parties are responding to an outside stimulus. I might ask if they have noticed this. The nonshaming tone will invite clients to feel less shameful about the use of pornography, while examining the negative effects. This prepares clients to examine what it might reveal about sexual symptoms.

What I have described sounds simple enough, but it rarely is. None of my clients is shame free about using pictures or videos. (Many people are able to *avoid* the feeling of shame; see Chapter 3.)

It is a lengthy process to remove shame from behaviors that have been heavily shamed by silence and disgust. When the culture makes that shift, we will likely find little interest in pornography because people without sexual shame don't need its stimulating boost to engage sexual arousal.

UNDERSTANDING SEXUAL ABUSE

The field of sex therapy began well before the advent of sexual abuse as a clinical issue. With a behavioral focus, the discipline attempts to change sexual symptoms without examining the historical cause. While this can sometimes be sufficient, it can also divert a client without specific image memories from exploring the underlying cause. In other cases, clients may not wish to engage in the deep process of addressing sexual abuse, and prefer a more rapid, symptom-focused therapy. The sex therapist who can offer both will best serve clients.

SEXUAL ADDICTION THERAPISTS

Research has demonstrated that more than 80 percent of sexual addicts remember childhood sexual abuse (Carnes 1991). The information presented earlier about how disso-ciation during abuse can prevent verbal and image memory suggests that an even greater percentage of sexual addicts have been sexually abused as children. While the *Journal of Sexual Addiction/Compulsivity* addresses the complex causes and treatment needs of sexual addiction, some twelve-step programs and some sexual addiction therapists focus on preventing sexual acting out. While it is helpful to stop the behaviors, true healing requires working through the causes of damaged sexuality.

HEALING OF SEXUAL EXPRESSION

Training in sexual healing is sadly lacking. While healing from the original abuses of sexuality is recognized to be a needed arena of recovery, most writers of books for survivors don't go far enough in discussing this issue.

People healing from sexual abuse find healthier uses of sexuality, but they don't have the language to express the difference, nor does our culture.

6

The Complexity of Sexual Addiction

SEXUAL ADDICTION/COMPULSIVITY

Sexual compulsivity didn't become an area of study among general therapists until it was named as a sexual addiction in the early 1980s. Even though a journal emerged from the similarities in the two fields in 1994 (*The Journal of Sexual Addiction/Compulsivity*, which is a good reference for these overlapping fields), the two factions still debate the appropriateness of the concept of addiction and the forms of treatment.

Psychologist Patrick Carnes wrote the first book on sexual addiction, *Out of the Shadows: Understanding Sexual Addiction*, in 1983. He reports on his research in *Don't Call It*

Love (1991). He also wrote a useful 44-page booklet, "Counseling the Sexual Addict: Systems, Strategies, and Skills" (1985). Other helpful sources that address sexual addiction are Hastings (1991), Kasl (1989), Rutter (1991), and Schaef (1989).

Carnes and other psychotherapists (such as Terry Kellogg) started two twelve-step programs for sexual addiction in 1979. As with alcoholism, they discovered that twelve-step programs were far more effective in curbing the compulsion (addiction) than was traditional psychotherapy. Three major groups (and many smaller ones) have formed nationwide: Sexaholics Anonymous (SA), Sex Addicts Anonymous (SAA), and Sex and Love Addicts Anonymous (SLAA). The National Council on Sexual Addiction/Compulsivity (P.O. Box 161064, Atlanta, GA, 30321-9998, telephone (770) 968-5002) provides information on these groups and names of therapists. Helpful books on sexual addiction are listed in the references at the end of this book.

Sexuality is considered addictive when sexual thought or activity greatly interferes with other aspects of life, such as work, love relationships, creativity, family life, parenting, recreation, and finances. A sexual addict might miss work in order to pursue a drug-like *sexual trance* (a useful term coined by Carnes to indicate the altered state sought in order to forget feelings of shame, failure, or loneliness). Work can seem less important than the "fix"—unless the addict is also addicted to work. A relationship can be disrupted by sexual acting out (engaging in the sexually addictive behaviors) and the lying that accompanies it. Examples include men who masturbate in their cars while looking at, or trying to pick up, sex objects; masturbating in an office or restroom at work; going to bars to pick up someone (or be picked up) for casual sex: buying prostitutes on a regular basis; frequenting strip clubs; requiring daily sex with the partner; frequent and necessary masturbation with pornography or fantasy.

Sexual fantasy is addictive when it is used to create a pleasant hum to make otherwise boring or distressing activities seem more appealing. One client imagined being saved from loneliness by a woman who desperately wanted him. When his lover broke up with him, he had difficulty stopping these thoughts, particularly when he awoke in the morning.

While these behaviors distract from healthy sexuality, they are only addictive if they are also *obsessive* or *compulsive*, in other words, if the person has difficulty interrupting thoughts about sex, searching for sex, or acting sexually. While sexual addiction recovery tends to focus on behaviors, the trance state can begin many hours or days before the actual sexual activity. This is the obsessive part of the addiction. The sexual act can be brief, and is very often unsatisfying. Or it can go on for hours, to the point of damaging tissues of the penis or vagina. This is the compulsion.

The addictive nature of sexuality can be determined by gently suggesting that a client give up the behavior for a week to see what happens. Most clients who do not already know they are sexually addicted will say they can do that easily. During the week between sessions they will discover how important the sexual thoughts or behaviors are in their lives. As with substance addiction, sexual addicts might deny, rationalize, and distort, but then they report how shocking it was to be unable to stop for even one week.

Then we begin the process of exploring when and why the compulsion takes over—what feelings are avoided. Among the most common are shame, failure, loneliness, and alienation. Frequent, regular sexual arousal, even if not acted out with orgasm, can provide an illusion of meaning to a life that doesn't otherwise seem to have any. We also repeatedly discuss the exact nature of the behaviors in order to challenge the denial that prevents the client from understanding what he or she is doing. This process is extended in couple therapy, group therapy, and/or twelve-step programs, making it increasingly more difficult to isolate the behaviors from normal life.

ONE SEXUAL ADDICTION

Kenneth (discussed in Chapter 3) came to me knowing he had a problem with sex and ready to work on it. He even used the term *sexual addiction*, although he had not read about it. His urges were so out of his control that he himself likened it to the alcoholic who cannot stop drinking. His wife of ten years had confronted him more strongly than usual, and he was terrified of losing her. He told me how he loved his wife, and didn't want to lose his marriage, but he wasn't able to stop searching for prostitutes, masturbating to pornography, and flirting everywhere.

Our first session lasted two hours as he poured out his history, crying intermittently, pleading for help. He desperately needed hope. We began meeting twice a week to define his symptoms, and map out a course of action. Kenneth, like many sex addicts, resisted the idea of going to twelve-step meetings. He believed he was different from other sex addicts, and wouldn't fit in. In truth, he didn't want to fit in, preferring to see himself as superior to most people, while, of course, feeling vastly inferior.

Kenneth joined my therapy group for men who were addicted to sex and, while specific sexual interests were different, the compulsive nature of the trance was the same. Kenneth, and most of the men who have been in the therapy group, had extreme behaviors that required a therapist specializing in sexual addiction and group therapy with other sex addicts, as well as a twelve-step program. Referral for group therapy can be made by therapists who don't specialize. Consulting with the group therapist, and hearing reports from the client about what goes on there, can be powerful and efficient sources of learning for the referring therapist.

SEXUAL ADDICTION MAY NOT BE IMMEDIATELY APPARENT

My client Jake provides a good example of how sexual issues can be confusing for a man who occasionally goes to prostitutes and masturbates to pornography. It is too simplistic to see such a person as only doing what our culture has programmed men to do. His wife is allowed to get angry, but she is to tolerate him. I will tell his story in detail.

When I met Jake in his mid-forties he had been to a therapist who specialized in the treatment of sex offenders. Jake's "offense" was minor compared to those who are mandated to attend this kind of treatment—he had been arrested for soliciting a prostitute. His wife, Janet, knew he had been to a massage parlor a year before because she found the charge on their Visa statement, but she didn't suspect that he was having sex with prostitutes.

The therapist worked with them for several months after the Visa charge, and again after the arrest, but terminated therapy when he couldn't do any more. Jake had found it helpful to write out a complete sexual history, and take a lie detector test to prove to Janet that he was telling the truth. Jake was glad to do this because he wanted to rebuild Janet's trust in him. This brought out the fact that he had had two affairs when away on business, and that he masturbated to pornography, and looked lustfully at women on a regular basis. He agreed to take lie detector tests every year, which is often a part of the treatment of sex offenders.

According to that therapist's framework, Jake wasn't a serious offender. He and his wife loved each other deeply, and Jake promised that he wouldn't continue his sexual behaviors. But he and Janet knew they needed more help without knowing how to get it. They arrived in my office six months later with a copy of my book.

After talking with Jake and Janet, and reading his sexual history, I understood why their first therapist thought there was little problem. His perception of healthy sex was supported by the culture and by sex therapy. Masturbation to adult, heterosexual pornography and lusting after attractive women are socially acceptable. The therapist suggested to Janet that she have breast enhancement surgery to be more sexually appealing to Jake to keep him at home. She did.

Jake had "only" two short affairs and one arrest for prostitution solicitation in his forties. When he saw prostitutes, he masturbated while looking at their breasts. He did not have sex with them. Yet as I asked questions, I discovered that Jake's issues were very serious.

Jake led an almost entirely sexualized life. He had to have regular orgasms with his wife in order to feel safe in her love. He couldn't touch her, or anyone else, without feeling sexual. Late in his recovery, he feared that he was falling out of love with Janet when he didn't lust for her body parts—actually a sign of his growing health. He couldn't hold his daughters as they were growing up because he didn't want to feel sexual toward them. He felt safer with his son, but even there he had to limit touch. He sexualized all the pets the family had over the years, unable to touch them without feeling sexual. He sexualized me (in my fifties, plump, and married), commenting that how I sat and moved was attractive to him. When I had a new haircut, he worried that I was going to wear glamorous makeup, project sexual energy, and want to be seen sexually, because he knew that if I did, he would quickly respond to it. He couldn't walk down the street or drive anywhere without looking for women to lust after. He was drawn toward the street in town where sexual services were most available, and when in the area was unable to drive across this street on his way to work without fighting a strong urge to stop.

The only distraction from sex was work. He held high-pressure employment in another state where he went for a few weeks at a time, alternating with a few weeks at home. He worked long hours with no days off, supervising a crew in sometimes dangerous, and always demanding, conditions. This commanded his attention, often providing an adrenaline rush, and always a challenge to do the best possible job. Masturbation put him to sleep at night.

Jake came from a family that rewarded him for being "good," and he tried his best to qualify. He never rebelled, and became excellent at everything he did. He made a lot of money from being good in his work, and established a high standard of living for himself and his family. He presented a model of a good person to the community, and reaped the benefits of creating a mirror in which he could see himself as good. It was very important to him to be moral and ethical.

The arrest for prostitution solicitation and diagnosis of sexual addiction were mortifying. Many people feel relieved when they are diagnosed as sexually addicted because it means they are not bad or hopeless, they just need help. But for those who see themselves as good, the diagnosis makes them aware of their belief in their all-pervasive badness that underlies the good facade. Jake was one of these.

How did Jake associate all touch with sex? We explored his childhood for an answer, and came up with a number of influences. One is the culture. The media train us to respond sexually to body posturing, flirting, and sexualized interactions. But we don't all have Jake's associations.

Jake's parents were highly sexualized people, who had parties in their home that Jake believes included sexual interaction. His mother wore sexy clothing into her sixties, and continued to flirt. When Jake confessed to his parents that he had been arrested for prostitution solicitation, they thought nothing of it, saying it was just the way men are. They laughed at the idea of sexual addiction, assaulting me for even suggesting he had a problem. They believed I convinced him he needed help so I could take his money while rendering no service.

Throughout Jake's childhood, he believed his mother wanted to have sex with him, and would have responded if he initiated. This was supported by several things. First, he remembers being breast-fed until he was 4. His exclusive interest in prostitutes' breasts while masturbating could be an outcome of his mother's arousal when feeding him, and her choice not to wean him at a more appropriate age. Second, his most vivid memory—and masturbation fantasy—is his mother coming into his room at night, drunk and naked, and falling on the bed next to him. He pretended he was asleep as his father came to retrieve her, but he felt her sexual interest in him. He believed his father's presence was the only reason she didn't pursue it. He has a collection of memories like this, including being in the bathroom as a teen when she pulled back the shower curtain, revealing her nude body.

Jake's belief that all love and physical contact are sexual comes from being raised by parents who felt sexual in ways that spilled out onto their children. It is possible that his mother created, by classical conditioning, the association between love and sex by looking at him lovingly while feeling sexual. He experienced his mother as lusting for him, in the same way he lusted for his wife and other women.

I explained to Jack that one of the reasons children become sexualized when they have been sexually abused is that it prevents them from feeling trauma when the adult wants to be sexual again. For example, one client, as an adult, became immediately aroused when he

thought about anal stimulation. He had been repeatedly anally penetrated as a child, which was extremely
painful. His body discovered that if he became aroused,
the pain could be converted into arousal, creating what
seemed to be a positive experience. After puberty he
started using fantasies and pornography of anal sex for
arousal and orgasms. In addition, even if he weren't
trying to be sexual, he would become aroused immediately if he heard anal sex mentioned. His healing
included feeling intense physical pain in his rectum and
abdomen, which decreased his sexual reactivity.

Jake was not aware of how he had become so
sexualized. We were left to guess that it came from
breast-feeding from a sexualized mother, and perhaps
other sexual intrusions, in addition to his memories of
his mother lusting for him.

Jake was able to prevent himself from passing this
on to his own children by refusing to touch them. This
is damaging to their sexuality, too, but he did prevent
passing on the particular kind of harm he received. In
addition, he monitored his wife for evidence of sexual
attraction to their son, and was relieved to find none.
Until these subjects came up in therapy, he had never
been able to discuss them, or even be entirely conscious
of his concerns.

Early in his recovery, it was extremely difficult for
Jake to give up his sexual behaviors. He used the "white
knuckle" approach, as it is called in twelve-step program
meetings; he made himself stop by sheer force, and had
little compassion for his slips. His therapy group spent
many months showing him how he was trying to control
his addiction, which wasn't allowing him to recover.

Jake came to feel tremendously dependent on his

wife, the one place where he allowed himself to have sex even when it wasn't healthy. Janet's recovery led her to understand her need to say no to addictive sex. She had a long history of providing sex in order to keep him, and so it was hard for her to say no when he expressed intense need. This is a common dynamic for couples when the man depends on his wife for the sex drug. He selects a woman who is willing to provide it. She quickly learns that this is the contract for the marriage— actually wanting this contract in order to assure that she won't lose him. When she decides she can no longer obey the contract, the addict may divorce her unless he is in sexual recovery. (I am using the example of a male sex addict and female partner. This dynamic is also present for female addicts with male partners, and for partners of the same gender.)

Jake's healing process has been multifaceted. In addition to sex, he has had to look at his need to be "good," and face the shame from giving up that image. As with all people addressing sexual issues, many other issues are relevant to the healing. "Goodness" doesn't include being angry, and Jake had to work on expressing it. An accepting therapy group supported him, even when group members were the object of his anger.

He also had to work through his idealization of me. His father had spoken lofty philosophy as if he had the solution to life, inviting Jake to look to others as the source of wisdom. After repeatedly turning to me in group, asking questions, engaging me in his attempt to find a new path, he could finally be angry with me for my inadequacy in giving him clear solutions. Because I did not become the new guru, he was able to risk anger.

He gradually stopped asking questions, and became increasingly wise about himself.

He appreciates his long relationship with his wife because she is the only person he can safely touch. If he feels sexual, he won't feel bad about himself. In this relationship he has become able to touch and caress without becoming sexual. This brings up fear because of his association of sex and love. Does he still love his wife if he doesn't feel sexual when they hold each other? At the same time, he occasionally has healthy, loving sex with Janet, too, which encourages his understanding of how giving up one kind of sexuality makes room for another.

He has had a new dog for a year, and has not sexualized his relating with her. She loves him, licks his face, and climbs on his lap—behaviors he had associated with arousal. He uses this relationship as a model for what might become possible with his adult daughters, his grandchild, and the men in the group.

Jake argued with me for more than two years about the need to reveal his sexual behaviors and his true thoughts and feelings to those he was in relationship with. During this time, he increasingly expressed what he was feeling to group members, family, and friends who were also in recovery. Therapy group members correspondingly felt closer to him.

Jake's experience of sex changed over several years. In the beginning it consisted of turning to his wife, seducing her until she said yes (as he hadn't been able to risk with his mother), and then rapid intercourse and orgasm. As with many sex addicts, the sex itself isn't highly pleasurable, and when orgasm (and the relaxation that follows) is the goal, the sex is not prolonged.

As both Jake and Janet increasingly freed themselves from addiction to each other and to sex, they were able to decrease sex for this purpose, and increase the opportunity to come together from a place of gentle love and a wish to bond. At these times, sex lasted longer, and included talking before, during, and after. This allowed them to stay present so they could see if the sex was serving them or serving the addiction.

Both Jake and Janet are now in therapy. Janet has evolved from a shy woman who could sit through a three-hour therapy group saying almost nothing, to an alive person who can take the floor and command attention. After a period of separation from her family of origin, she began confronting her mother with the truth of her childhood and their relationship. Through this process, she is learning how her mother is available to her and how she isn't. She is learning the truth.

After four years of group therapy, interspersed with periods of individual and couple sessions, Jake and Janet are on a path that they will stay on. They have too much invested in their new lives, even while they sometimes hate that they have to "recover." They are self-propelled now, so if they drop out of therapy for a while, or stop going to twelve-step meetings, they will eventually continue the work. Jake and Janet's emotional growth demonstrates how this process can be awkward, and difficult to start, but once the change process is understood, people who are committed to working on any obstacles will adopt a lifestyle of moving toward health.

Different theoretical frameworks term Jake's symptoms sexual compulsion, difficulty with intimacy, or hypersexuality. These labels could have been useful in helping him get better. The advantage of the sexual addiction label is that Jake had the opportunity to go to twelve-step meetings and discover that many men he came to respect were also cursed with the same uses of sexuality. In addition to weekly meetings, SA, SAA, and SLAA hold regular regional meetings, which allow members to interact with even more people engaged in similar healing. This experience can greatly support individual therapy, which is limited by the presence of only one person—the therapist—who has probably not experienced these same uses of sexuality.

A CASE IN WHICH CHANGE CAME QUICKLY

Various factors influence the speed of recovery, including the intensity of the addiction, and sources of self-esteem.

> Henry came to me because he was worried about his use of masturbation. He went to work for a large company after leaving a highly satisfying job in another state. Henry masturbated at least daily, and occasionally in his office or in the bathroom at work. He constantly feared that someone would walk in on him, or wonder why his door was locked. After an initial look at his symptoms, we focused on a crisis he had left behind in the other state. After fifteen years of monogamy, he had an affair with the wife of a couple he and his wife were close to. He became infatuated with her, and considered leaving his wife. Finally, he couldn't go through with it, even though the woman left her husband and children. Henry's wife discovered the affair, and his shame became intense. He ended the affair, but living in neighboring towns kept the memory alive. In addition, he

feared that others at his high-status professional company might know.

Thus, Henry and his wife moved to a new area. Henry took a new job and made a fresh start. But his self-respect was further damaged by buying a house at the top of a housing market that subsequently dropped, and by leaving his son in the town they moved from to finish high school. In addition, his wife had a difficult time finding work in her profession, furthering his guilt.

We discussed how these factors had pushed him to sexual acting out for two reasons. One was the avoidance of guilt and shame by "mood altering." The second was establishing a behavior pattern congruent with his shameful self-image. By talking about his behavior choices, he was able to reduce his shame and improve his self-image, thus removing the cause of the acting out. In addition, his wife began employment during his therapy, and he was able to bring his son to live with them.

The irony is that because Henry was able to stop acting out after four months of therapy, he actually accomplished less healing than Jake, who still looks at women lustfully after five years. Those with more severe symptoms (and corresponding damage to their sexuality) have to engage in the deepest healing in order to establish satisfactory lives. They can leave therapy able to have better lives than those who finish their changes in a few months.

Because some people can complete their changes relatively easily, therapists who don't specialize in sexual addiction can continue working with a client long enough to find out what will be required. We can't predict in the first few sessions whether a person will want to engage in deep sexual healing, or will be satisfied with a return to a previous level of self-esteem and sexual functioning. Once it becomes clear that the process is moving slowly, but well, and that it will require time to cover the breadth of issues, then a referral may be relevant—at least for a therapy group addressing these issues.

THE CASE OF A CLIENT WHO WAS NOT A SEX ADDICT

While Richard (discussed in Chapter 1) was clearly sexually addicted, Raymond would not qualify for such a diagnosis. His therapist, however, thought that he did, and referred him to me. If his therapist had had a little more information about the addictive use of sexual energy, she would have been able to continue her work with Raymond and his wife, Jean.

Raymond had phone sex when he was angry with his wife, and flirted with many women. His therapist agreed to see the couple because Raymond was willing to stop these activities. But when Raymond again began calling the phone sex lines six months later, she referred them.

Raymond's behaviors weren't compulsive because he was able to relinquish them in a few weeks—this time not because he had been told to, but because he understood how he used these behaviors to express anger and alter his mood. His use of sexual energy was equivalent to the social use of alcohol to mood alter, compared with the alcoholic's seriously disruptive use. (However, with sexuality, even a noncompulsive use interferes with relationships, and is best relinquished.)

Raymond quickly came to see that he had given his

wife the power to decide how he was to spend his free time. Then he was angry when she objected to an activity, perceiving her objection as not allowing him to do what he wanted. Through discussion, and practice expressing feelings and thoughts, he lost interest in calling women for sexual conversation. He no longer had a need to express anger indirectly. Raymond began learning how to tell his wife what he felt so he wouldn't resort to indirect anger. In addition, he could finally see how upsetting it was for Jean, and delighted in her growing trust of him—feeling hurt when she still thought he was staring at women.

In this case, Raymond's use of addictive sexuality was not compulsive, and he could *decide to relinquish it.* He attended several Sex Addicts Anonymous meetings, which helped reduce shame.

His first therapist could have pursued the reasons Raymond called the phone sex lines, and helped him see the need to express his feelings to his wife. The therapist had the skills but she felt incapable of addressing his addictive use of sexual energy.

When I met Raymond and Jean, I thought Jean might be sexually addicted. They had sex every day, even when Raymond worked nights, and came home exhausted. Jean associated sex with love, feeling secure if they had daily sex. But once she saw how she made that connection, she realized she really didn't want to have sex that often. They immediately stopped—again demonstrating the lack of compulsivity—and had sex only when they both felt like it. In the following weeks they told me with delight when each had been able to tell the other they didn't want sex. Raymond was tremendously relieved because he had had to fantasize about other women in order to perform every day. Now he could wait until he was ready. He was able to give up all sexual fantasy. This couple's therapy is a vivid example of how better sex isn't always more sex—in this case, less was better.

WOMEN'S SEXUAL ADDICTION

Our culture tends to see men as the ones who want too much sex, or the kinds of sex that are "perverted." As a result, sexual addiction appears to be a problem of mostly men. This is reflected in their greater representation in twelve-step groups. However, women engage in just as much addictive sex. The form may be different or the same, but it carries different cultural judgments.

The expressions "slut," "loose," and "easy" refer to women who are sexually addicted. While the culture lets men off with a wrist slap for "sowing his wild oats" because "men will be men," women are heavily judged for the same behaviors.

Therapists are culturally programmed to take the side of women who have a history of promiscuous sex, seeing it as a symptom of sexual abuse (which it is), and then focusing on the abuses that brought about the behaviors. We want to see it as "not their fault." While acceptance is necessary, this stand can divert women from acknowledging their symptoms and seeking help. Women are deprived by the therapeutic stance that they were victimized and thus have little or no responsibility for the outcome.

Susan came to therapy with her husband, Lewis, because she didn't want sex. She had been sexually abused by her father at around age 4, and perhaps younger, and just lying in bed with her husband brought on dissociative freezing. She was unable to tell him she was frightened. Lewis felt like a perpetrator when she acted like he was raping her when he suggested sex.

When Susan and Lewis recounted the history of their relationship, they told of a time when Susan went away on vacation, to be joined by Lewis a week later. She had an intense sexual experience with a man she met, bringing about a separation from Lewis when she told him. The first time I heard this story, I minimized the implication of Susan's addictive use of sexuality, knowing how asexual she had felt for years. It was only when Susan herself realized she was a sexual addict who was *acting in* (a term Carnes uses as the sexual equivalent of the symptom of anorexia in a compulsive overeater) that she was able to make use of her understanding of sexual addiction. Then we could begin looking at how she went into two-week trances in the throes of a sexual "binge," whether she had sex or merely exchanged sexual energy. Once she could identify it, she was able to see when she was about to enter another binge period, and prevent it. Their perception of Lewis as the bad one for wanting sex from an incest survivor changed to seeing both partners working on their sexuality.

ROMANCE—THE "FEMALE" FORM OF SEXUAL ADDICTION

Bringing flowers and gifts and sending cards can be loving gestures, but they can also be offerings of the sexual drug when used to create a romantic feeling. New relationships are intense because sexual energy is busily bonding two people into a couple, but the falling-in-love feeling can become addictive if used for more than the first few months of a relationship.

Women bring their partners to therapy because the partner isn't romantic any longer. Romance is quite different from expressing ongoing feelings of love and appreciation when they are felt, a natural outcome of a loving relationship.

Just as women can be addicted to sexual activity, men can also be addicted to romance.

Deborah ended a bad relationship with a promise to herself that she wouldn't enter another for at least a year. But then David showed up. He was the "man of her dreams," they were perfectly suited to each other, and the sex was wonderful. Deborah talked effusively about David, unable to think clearly about much else, boring her friends with stories about their catered brunches in bed (both had little money, and planned to go to graduate school the next year), flowers filling their bedroom, and poems written to each other. When I encountered Deborah two years later, after the birth of the baby conceived during one of their transcendent lovemaking sessions, she was writing poems about her misery and hatred for David. All the relationship issues that both had submerged by romance had now emerged, strangling their love. They were occasionally able to reengage the romance, wishing it could dominate their lives as it had in the beginning. Neither was willing to see the romance as an avoidance of real intimacy. Nor were they willing to seek help with their addictive use of sexual energy.

Part III

A New Look

Part III

A New Unit

7

Body Parts and Sexual Functioning

SEXUAL ANATOMY

Sexual body parts are referred to by countless slang expressions. Therapists need to know the anatomical name for body parts, and be willing to use this language for several reasons. One is that slang expressions, such as dick, cock, cunt, and pussy, carry sexual shame that required the use of slang instead of real names. Some writers suggest that the therapist should use slang expressions used by clients in order not to shame the client. But this tactic avoids shame, along with the other maneuvers to become congruent with sexual shame discussed in Chapter 3. Using the clinical expression might very well elicit shame, but this shame needs to be elicited so that it can be discharged. The therapist's task is how to introduce clinical terms without shaming the client, so the only shame comes from within the client.

Helping the client remove shame from anatomical words and slang expressions can begin changing attitudes toward sex.

A client asked me why his wife's cunt didn't get wet like other women's. He was embarrassed to ask and didn't know what to call her vagina. I nodded, accepting his question as complete even with this slang expression, and in my response, used the word *vagina.* I have long since removed my own feelings of shame over the word *cunt* when used to mean vagina or as name calling, and so I was able to absorb his question as if he had said vagina. This helped him feel less shame about both the question and the word. I said no more about the expression, feeling that I had communicated sufficiently by acceptance and using the correct word.

To show a client I am not shaming him or her for using slang expressions, I will sometimes discuss the term, using it in the conversation. For example, to make sure the man who used the word *cunt* didn't think he had offended me, I might have asked a question about the word, demonstrating that I can say it without discomfort. I could have said, with real curiosity, "Do the two of you call her vagina a cunt, or is that a word that only you use?"

When a client told me he was finally accessing his anger at women, and actually using the "C" word in his head, I immediately asked, "You mean *cunt?*" He laughed with pleasure and embarrassment, and then launched into using the word to express his long-withheld rage.

As a feminist I used to react to this word. At that time it would have been better to tell these clients that I had a negative reaction to the word, although I didn't want to shame them for using it. I would claim the reactions as my own conditioning. I might include the funny story from when I was 8, and asked my mother what "cont." meant, which I had read in the newspaper. It meant "continued," but she was so flustered and upset by my question, she told me it didn't mean anything. I would hope that by bringing the word into conversation, I could avoid causing my client additional shame while telling the truth about my reactions.

A male client consistently used the word *pussy* to mean vulva and vagina. He felt no shame for it. During a session, I curiously asked him what women thought when he said "pussy." He was caught up short, and then admitted that some women criticized him, which he didn't understand. As we talked, he decided that he would ask several women friends about it. He came back the next week to tell me that the primary reaction was distaste, as well as thinking they couldn't tell him they didn't like the word. He promptly stopped using it.

VULVA, LABIA, CLITORIS, AND VAGINA

Texts on human sexuality provide pictures and detailed descriptions of sexual anatomy and physiology. The vulva is the outer area of a woman's reproductive anatomy, and includes the clitoris; the clitoral hood, which partially covers the clitoris; and the labia majora and the labia minora, the outer and inner folds of tissue that surround the clitoris and the vagina. The vagina is the inside area where the penis can be inserted. It is also the birth canal. The cervix connects the vagina to the uterus—also known as the womb.

The clitoris has a large number of sexual nerve endings, and is usually the most sensitive to sexual stimulation. The vagina is also sexually sensitive, as are the folds of the labia and the anus (the opening of the rectum through which feces pass during bowel movements). It is generally believed by those who research human sexuality that only the outer third of the vagina has sensation because the inner two-thirds have no nerve endings. But energy flow between the penis and the vagina, or fingers and the vagina, can create an electric sensation that is not dependent on nerve reception, making vaginal stimulation more intense.

PENIS, SCROTUM, AND TESTICLES

The penis fills with blood in order to become erect. The average size is six inches when erect and three inches when nonerect (when cold or in states of fright the penis can pull up to only an inch or two), which is useful to know because most men think their penises are smaller than average. I don't ask male clients about the size of their penis because it crosses a personal boundary. With this information a man can assess for himself if his penis is indeed smaller than average. If not, then he can confront his fears that he isn't man enough or large enough to satisfy women—common beliefs associated with penis size.

> Mark talked about going to the gym four days a week, and before taking a shower, massaging his penis in order to obtain a partial erection to look bigger. The trick was making it look big enough, but preventing it from becoming fully erect. He wanted men to be

envious of his size, but didn't want them thinking he was aroused by being in the shower with other naked men.

I received a call from a 22-year-old man, Will, who had never had sex, or even a long-term girlfriend, because he was afraid to show a woman his penis. He said it was four inches when erect, and looked nonexistent when flaccid, and he was sure a woman would not feel it during intercourse, and would humiliate him. He hadn't been able to ask friends or family members about it because of our culture's shaming attitude. I suggested that he talk with a potential lover before taking off his clothes, and find out ahead of time how she might react. I told him that some women when engaged in casual sex might very well react negatively, and women who want to be in a relationship are more likely to be accepting.

Will was able to talk to me because I was a stranger, and because we were on the phone. Many clients might mention a fear that their penis is small, but won't pursue it unless asked. Overcoming their shame in order to mention it takes courage. Help from the therapist is usually needed in order to continue.

The testes or testicles (testicle is singular, testes plural, but common language is adopting testicles as a correct plural) are the sensitive balls hanging below the penis that manufacture semen. They are encompassed by the scrotum, the skin that is capable of shrinking to pull the testicles up to the body for warmth, or relaxing greatly to allow them to fall away for cooling. The scrotum and testicles are sexually sensitive, but less so than the penis.

SEXUAL ACTIVITIES

Sexual activity is usually divided into two categories—foreplay and having sex (meaning intercourse.) The term *foreplay* should be abandoned. It implies that sex is intercourse, and everything else leads up to it, supporting our cultural belief that if intercourse doesn't happen, sex hasn't happened. Young people believe they are virgins until they have had intercourse—an arbitrary distinction even though centuries old. By this definition, lesbians don't ever "have sex," and gay men don't either unless they have anal intercourse. As clients heal their sexuality, they will increasingly experience fully satisfying sex with just kissing, or bringing skin against skin with arousal, or just touching each other's genitals. Their descriptions of new and different sex will have more to do with feelings about partners, or newly experienced energy flows, than with different sexual positions and activities.

Therapists who are attached to old-fashioned definitions of having sex will slow down the client's realization. Therapists who reflect an understanding of the completeness of sexual contact with less than intercourse can speed up the client's appreciation of how sex can differ from the cultural definitions.

MASTURBATION

The great majority of men masturbate by stroking the penis with one hand, and stimulating other parts of the penis or testicles with the other. Some men will rub against sheets or objects without touching the genitals. This is probably the result of shame about touching oneself, which is circumvented by creating sufficient arousal for orgasm without touching the penis with the hand.

Women masturbate by rubbing the clitoris, or by penetrating the vagina or anus with fingers or objects. Women often use vibrators directly on the clitoris or in the vagina. The drawback of this practice is that the intense stimulation caused by the vibrator cannot be duplicated by sex with a partner, and may cause reliance on the vibrator. This is also true for men who stimulate themselves for long periods and/or with great intensity.

When men say they are not aroused by intercourse or oral sex, I ask how they masturbate. They may require more intense stimulation in order to produce arousal. When asking such a personal question, I include some education to trigger less shame. I might say, "When you tell me that you don't find intercourse stimulating enough, I wonder about how you masturbate. Did you know that when men stimulate themselves too vigorously they can lose sensitivity?" With this information I convey why I am asking so as not to prematurely confront the client's masturbation shame.

When people discover healthy sexuality, very little stimulation can produce great arousal. Reciprocal energy creates pleasurable feeling. There is no need for increasingly intense physical stimulation.

People who have discovered healthy masturbation find they are not interested in using pornography or fantasy. Instead, self-stimulation is experienced as enhancing a feeling of self, expanding outward to include the room, the house, and the world. It will not be followed by shame, or a need to compartmentalize that experience. Healthy masturbation, like healthy sex, has no goals of arousal or orgasm, freeing the individual to discover arousal and orgasms occurring on their own time schedule instead of forcing them to occur. Genital and body stimulation is self-caring, and adds to life instead of replacing or diverting from it (Hastings 1993). This is difficult to accomplish if shame interferes. The *feeling* of shame is reduced by intensely narrowing the focus to fantasy and pornography.

Asking clients about the content of fantasies and pornography that arouses them will provide helpful information about how sexuality was abused earlier in life, and about the nature of formative relationships. Sexual sadism can reflect actual enacted sexual abuse in childhood, or it can reflect a parent–child relationship dominated by these complementary dynamics. For example, Barry read and imagined scenes of controlling women during sex, even though he didn't act them out with partners. We discovered that this resulted from an emotionally incestuous relationship with his mother. She gave him little attention until he engaged her with sexual energy, flirtation, and charm. This was a form of control, which he honed to an art, and later used as his primary form of sexual addiction. His fantasy and pornography could reflect more overtly the control of women that appeared more subtly in real life.

Fantasies, pornography, or situations acted out in relationships may be a direct replay of childhood events. They can also be a situation that re-creates the *feeling* of the abuse, or plays out the nature of a relationship incorporated into a sexual context.

THE SEXUAL RESPONSE CYCLE

Based on the research of Masters and Johnson, researchers who invented the field of sex therapy, and that of Helen Singer Kaplan, the *DSM-IV* uses four phases of the sexual response cycle to define a number of "sexual dysfunctions." The phases are desire, arousal, orgasm, and resolution. They are described in the *DSM-IV*, along with the dysfunctions that belong to each phase.

This view of "having sex" may be more useful than having no scheme upon which to base research and understanding of sexual problems, but it holds an inherent danger. Seeing sex as necessarily including phases makes people think something is wrong if they don't include all the phases, and feel pressure to complete the process. The phases can be seen as an outcome of culture that is based on sex for procreation, which requires heterosexual intercourse and ejaculation into the vagina. But healthy sex, as it is unfolding among those in sexual recovery, is more complex.

PHASE-FREE SEX

Lewis and Susan (introduced in Chapter 6) were in therapy for more than six years addressing her sexual abuse history and dread of sexual activity, and Lewis's constant demand for what he saw as his rightful sexual satisfaction. Soon after they began therapy, they agreed to a sexual moratorium (Hastings 1993) in order to take this complicated issue out of the relationship for a time. In therapy Susan worked on her abuse history, and she appreciated not having to have sex. Lewis worked on his childhood deprivation of love resulting from premature emotional separation from an enmeshing mother before he was 2. He was one of those babies who wrench themselves backward off laps. He had apparently elected to forgo physical contact in exchange for maintaining some sense of self, but, of course, grew up deprived. He translated this into an intense desire for sexual interaction with Susan.

As Susan uncovered the abuses of her sexuality (years before entering therapy), she had strong reactions to Lewis's sexual interest. Even going to bed at night with her husband required routine dissociation.

Over ten years of marriage, Lewis came to feel like a sexual perpetrator. His self-esteem dropped accordingly. His father had flirted with, and sexualized, all women, including Susan, and Lewis had observed women's negative reactions to him his entire life. Now his wife's behavior made him feel like that despicable man who had been the object of so much repulsion. Lewis discovered (not consciously) that if he became small, whined, and demanded his rightful due, he could ask for sex without feeling like a perpetrator. Susan treated him like an annoying child, and pushed him away with disgust. Lewis preferred this reaction to being seen as her father, watching her freeze up in bed, terrified of his touch even when he wasn't thinking of sex.

After five years of no sex (the longest moratorium I have encountered), Susan and Lewis began again. Now they knew, from years of therapy, that they didn't have to finish what they started, or define sex by intercourse or orgasms. They also traded in the goal of having sex for the objective of talking about everything that came up, and following their intuition.

They began by taking off their clothes, and going to bed. As they held each other, now free from fear of abuse, both realized that they had been deprived of skin-to-skin contact for decades. Their first encounter consisted almost entirely of holding and touching each other in ways that maximized nonsexual skin contact.

Both of them had occasional feelings of sexual arousal, but even Lewis, who had felt sexually deprived for years, did not find himself focused on sexual feelings. When it was time to sleep, Susan put on from habit her soft, cuddly nightgown, only to find that it now felt like scratchy burlap compared to the feeling of Lewis's skin. She took it off. In the next therapy session they excitedly told me they had had sex in a wonderful new way. Yet they had not experienced the "desire" phase or orgasms. They went right from arousal to resolution.

Over weeks, they explored sexuality every few days. Susan, who had hated thinking that once she began she had to keep going, was gratified by knowing they had full sexual experiences with no intercourse or orgasms. When Lewis tensed up and "desired" intercourse, both of them knew he was back in the old kind of sex. As soon as it was named, he was able to let it go, and return to being present and intimate with Susan. While intercourse is a wonderful sexual expression, in this couple's tender, new sexual contact, it was not the right time for it.

If this couple felt they had to include all four phases in their sexual activity, Susan would still be too frightened to engage in a spontaneous sexual exchange. And Lewis would feel pressured to have an erection in order to have intercourse, which would take him away from intimacy with Susan.

Lewis and Susan's emotional work demonstrated how both parties had to make significant changes in order to drop the old attachments to sex, and free them to discover what sex can be. When they came to therapy, Susan hated sex with Lewis, even though she loved and respected him. Lewis resented being deprived of sex, and hounded her incessantly. Even when he stopped asking, his energy pleaded. To the superficial eye, it appeared that Lewis could have worked on changing his approach so that Susan would be more drawn to him. He might have experienced desire for sex, and then initiated contact in "acceptable" ways. But this would have avoided examination of his childhood, and learning about how sexual caretaking seemed to be the antidote to love deprivation.

Susan's sexual abuse was overt in contrast to the damage of Lewis's sexuality, which came from struggling out of the enmeshing relationship with his mother. Susan's father had gone to her bed when she was a preschool child, and she had learned to dissociate, moving to the ceiling to avoid the distress. But of course, she didn't avoid it, and told the story when in bed with Lewis. By taking control of her body and sexuality, she grew to believe she was safe in her own bed. Finally, as both reached a point of removing enough childhood trauma, they were able to begin again. Couples who must go through the deepest search, and relive major ongoing childhood trauma, are often the ones who best create the possibility of discovering their natural sexuality.

EDUCATION ABOUT SEXUAL FREQUENCY

Emma came to me because she didn't want as much sex now as she had in the beginning of her relationship with Terese, and not as much as Terese wanted. We talked about her sex life, both in the present and past, and her childhood family environment. During these sessions I counseled her about letting go of the idea of having to have sex, or having to engage in any particular sexual activities.

I mentioned to Emma the book *Sex in America* (Michael et al. 1994), which describes new research revealing that the typical range of sexual frequency was from every few days to several weeks (in contrast to studies based on nonrandom samples showing much higher rates that have been generally accepted as valid). Emma's interest in sex fell within this range. She went home to tell Terese, and discovered that Terese was fine with their frequency, reassured by research statistics that their frequency wasn't an indication of Emma's loss of interest in her. Four sessions later I noticed that Emma didn't seem to have anything to work on, and asked if we had completed what she came for. She was startled, saying she thought these things took years. While she has issues she might work on at a later time, the sexual problem was solved by removing the requirement for a certain sexual frequency. Her reaction to the pressure to "do it right" had created a distaste for sex.

THE RELEASE OF SEXUAL TENSION

The sex therapy model holds that orgasm releases sexual tension, and brings about the resolution phase of sexual activity. My clients experience two different kinds of arousal (as have I). The first is based on lust. The body becomes increasingly tense and hard as sexual arousal grows. This kind of feeling is commonly seen as good, passionate arousal.

However, people who have been in sexual recovery, and

relinquished goals of intercourse and orgasm, discover that greater and greater arousal can emerge as the body *relaxes*. Instead of feeling tense and hard, when energy can flow freely, it will flow more vigorously through a relaxed body. This relaxed state permits partners to be more present with each other. Instead of being *distracted* by sexual feelings, they can be increasingly *joined* by them. This discovery is consistent with the Chinese study of energy movement called Qigong (*gong* is the movement of Qi [also spelled Chi], or energy), where good posture, relaxation, and removal of tension in the body is established to enhance movement of the *Qi*. Students learning to move energy typically find themselves feeling sexual more easily and more often (Tse 1995).

Sexual tension creates a need for the relaxation of orgasm. Relaxed sex doesn't require orgasm. The sense of fulfillment after sex is complete. Orgasm can be highly pleasurable, but not necessary. When clients talk about *needing orgasm*, one hypothesis to consider is that they experience a strong need to relieve tension.

SEXUAL INTEREST IS STRONGER IN THE BEGINNING

Couples fall in love, enjoy passionate sexual energy, and then find that a year or so later their sexual interest decreases. There are two reasons for this. The first is a healthy one. The initial bonding has to be intense to create "falling in love" in order to quickly form two people into a new family. The bond that keeps people together requires sexuality to create it. (From an evolution perspective, the bond ensured that a child would have two parents to take care of it, increasing his or her chances for survival.) The need to create the bond diminishes once the bond is formed.

The second reason sexual interest drops is shame. (There are also idiosyncratic reasons, such as relationship conflicts.) The shame carried by all of us in varying degrees appears when the need for strong sexual interest subsides into the everyday. The need to bond no longer overrides the shame. This is even more pronounced for homosexual couples because of greater cultural shaming.

> Marge and Jane found themselves unable to perceive each other's sexually bonded love because of the shame that accompanied it. This situation created conflict over sex, and even over nonsexual affection. The women were able to run a home together, and work in the same business, using their compatibility and mutual respect to their advantage. But after their first year, they were unable to comfortably have sex. We addressed this by talking about sexual activities in order to bring up the shame feelings, and then worked on emotional discharge. I explained to them how the purpose wasn't to tell the whole story about how they have sex. The purpose was to tell bits of the story at a time in order to access the shame. They couldn't address the shame until they could introduce the triggers for it.
>
> Marge wanted to focus on how neighbors and co-workers discriminated against them, transferring her attention to external homophobia, which is important. But the internalized belief that there was something seriously wrong, or perverted, about their sexual loving was the obstacle to the two women loving each other.
>
> I could see their love for each other, even when they focused on conflicts. They both cried when I said I

supported their love, and their expression of affection and sexuality. I offered myself as a new reflection of their lifestyle as acceptable and wonderful, to counter the influence of the culture and family members.

WITHHOLDING SEX

Some therapists talk about clients who "withhold" sex to control and punish the partner. The word "withholding" implies that sex is given to meet the partner's needs.

A partner can *feel* withholding and punitive when saying no to sex, and can certainly take pleasure in the partner's frustration. In addition, women (or men) can feel as if they are punishing and controlling because the partner feels punished and controlled. If the partner who doesn't want sex believes this reflection, she will feel bad for something she isn't doing. But no one should have sex unless it feels entirely right.

If the woman learns how to express anger, it won't automatically mean she will then "provide" sex. Instead, it might free her to say no for healthier reasons. And to say yes for healthier reasons. Healthy, spiritually based sexual activity doesn't include "giving" and "receiving" sex. It isn't about "meeting each other's needs."

When the man (or woman) feels as if he is being punished by his partner's withholding of sex, the therapist can ask questions in order to obtain a broader picture. For example, the therapist could ask how it would feel if *he* had to give sex when he didn't want to. Explaining to both that it is a violation to have sex when it doesn't feel right can encourage her to set limits and help him to see why it doesn't serve him to insist. The man can be asked how he would feel if he used his wife for gratification regardless of what she felt; the therapist can explore his reasons for wanting sex with an uninterested partner. For example, "Robert, I can see that you feel deprived by the lack of sex in your marriage. That feeling is so strong its hard for you to see much more, isn't it? So I want to ask you some questions that might help broaden the picture a little." Pause to see if he has a response. "Have you been in a situation where someone wanted you to have sex when you didn't want to?" If yes, "What did that feel like?" The response can be related to his mate's feelings.

"If (mate's name) had sex because you feel the need for it, you would be using her for your gratification. Using people doesn't enhance the relationship, does it?

"When you pressure (mate's name) to be sexual, I wonder if it makes you feel something like a rapist— someone who wants sex regardless of what the other person is feeling." Pause for response. "Feeling like a rapist isn't good for you—it must make you feel bad about yourself.

"Do you think you could consider giving up for now the pressure for sex in order to see what that feels like?"

Questions along this line are usually met with resistance, defensiveness, and rationalization. Even if they seem to get nowhere, the ideas have been introduced. In addition, his partner has heard you talk with him in this vein, supporting her intuitive knowing that she must not "give in" to sex.

MEN CAN LIVE WITHOUT SEX

Many couples come to therapy because one person doesn't want to have sex. Frequently, the other partner, usually the man, is very upset by this, and expresses a belief that he cannot manage without it. The spouses tend to believe this because it is supported by our culture. Monks, nuns, and priests who do not have sex are seen as strange, outside the norm. It is true that these men believe they cannot manage without sex, in the same way most people believe that sexual tension is a normal part of sexual feelings. The therapist can have compassion for this fear, and offer reassurance that it is, indeed, possible. Cultural repression of sexuality has brought about the experience of a strong sex drive, and the feeling of apparent need. Sexual moratoriums can be introduced in this context, offering the chance to experience giving up sex for a period of time.

Lewis reacted strongly to the idea of a sexual moratorium, and occasionally argued with me over the five years. He appreciates the function of going without, now that he is on the other side and having a very different, relaxed, passionate sexual love with Susan.

8

Paraphilias and Other "Cross-Wired" Preferences

DSM-IV defines paraphilias as follows: "Recurrent, intense, sexually arousing fantasies, sexual urges, or behaviors generally involving 1) nonhuman objects, 2) the suffering or humiliation of oneself or one's partner, or 3) children or other nonconsenting persons, that occur over a period of at least 6 months. . . . The behavior, sexual urges, or fantasies cause clinically significant distress or impairment in social, occupational, or other important areas of functioning" (pp. 522–523). Eight paraphilias are described: exhibitionism (exposure of genitals), fetishism (use of nonliving objects), frotteurism (touching and rubbing against a nonconsenting person), pedophilia (focus on prepubescent children), sexual masochism (receiving humiliation or suffering), sexual sadism (inflicting humiliation or suffering), transvestic fetishism (cross-dressing), and voyeurism (observing sexual activity). A final category, "paraphilia not otherwise specified," is for paraphilias "that are less frequently encountered" (p. 532).

Defining eight kinds of arousal patterns that are clearly outside our culture's views of acceptable sex demonstrates the culture's influence. In my experience of working with sexually addicted clients I have found that these eight are not the most common forms of sexual arousal that "cause clinically significant distress or impairment in social, occupational, or other important areas of functioning." In fact, *men lusting for sexy women* is. But this isn't considered a paraphilia, even though it might be considered a problem when taken to the extreme of frequenting prostitutes or losing relationships over affairs. In truth, many sexual activities that are socially acceptable belong in this category. Consequently, I use the term *cross-wired sexuality* to indicate any associations with sex that are not inherently about sex. This is a useful term when discussing sexuality with clients.

> Rick was capable of having intimate sex with women, and was in his second marriage. But he found himself staring at women's body parts any time he was out in public. He didn't seduce women, and his interest didn't interfere with his life, and it happened only when he saw body parts of the shape he found attractive on women he didn't know. Rick's sexual behavior doesn't fit any of the categories listed in *DSM-IV*, except, at a stretch, paraphilia not otherwise specified.
>
> Rick's wives and girlfriends had been jealous. They didn't like being with him in public because his eyes wandered, and they felt like they were constantly competing with other women. He tried to convince them

that he didn't flirt, and never pursued these women. After all, it wasn't even the woman, just her parts. They had nothing to be jealous about.

Rick had gone to therapy with both wives. The first therapist focused entirely on the wife's jealousy until she stopped therapy and started divorce proceedings. The second therapist tried to shame him into stopping. She asked him to read feminist writings that showed how it harmed women to be with men who lusted. He read what she gave him, but wasn't able to stop. And didn't want to stop. This common behavior that is considered an outcome of "men being men" is a sexual symptom. If a therapist can discover how this behavior serves the man, just as with any other symptom, then it can become possible to develop empathy, and to help the client see how "lustful looking" (a sexual addiction recovery term) actually interferes with sexual, loving relationships.

While paraphilias can be useful to understand, they are only a short list of the possible distortions of sexual expression.

PARAPHILIACS DON'T GO TO THERAPY

The writers of *DSM-IV* say that most paraphilias aren't seen in therapists' offices unless required by the court. This is because of shame associated with culturally unacceptable sexual interests. If those with socially unacceptable cross-wiring knew that there were therapists who were able to understand their story, listen compassionately, and offer hope of change, they might seek therapy. There is nothing in the media that suggests this alternative. Women's magazines cite sex therapists who encourage the use of cross-wired arousal for the purpose of increasing sexual desire. Nothing suggests that it is desirable and possible to *heal from* the cross-wiring. As the effects of sexual healing become more generally understood, which is an outcome likely to follow the sexual abuse healing movement, more people will seek help.

Magazine articles about sex are designed to serve sex addiction by provoking a sexual hum by providing soft pornography. Because this increases sales, magazines publish fewer articles about how to heal sexual problems. Saying no to sex doesn't sell magazines, nor does abstract talk about flowing energy, and other types of sexual experiences that cannot be obtained by reading an article.

CULTURAL SHAMING BRINGS DISTRESS

Sexually sadistic and masochistic activities, cross-dressing, and fetishism do not inherently harm people (unless carried to an extreme) any more than chronic lusting for strangers does, except if feelings of being abnormal and deviant damage their sense of self. Sex therapy has increasingly encouraged people to reduce shame by joining groups who use the same forms of paraphilia. The effect is reducing shame, which can be the greatest cause for "clinically significant distress," resulting in "impairment in social, occupational, or other important areas of functioning."

Bob (described in Chapter 1) was greatly relieved when he revealed his history of dressing in women's underwear. While he was sexually addicted, and understood why cross-dressing inhibited intimate sex with his wife, reducing shame for this socially unacceptable behavior was a vital first step—a first step not required of men who lust after women or body parts.

PARAPHILIAS ARE RARE IN WOMEN

DSM-IV states that sexual masochism affects men twenty times more often than women, and the remaining paraphilias "are almost never diagnosed in females, although such cases have been reported." This implies that only a very few women have unhealthy attachments to sexuality. The *DSM-IV* is influenced by our culture's views. We can be more helpful to our clients if we adopt the view that culturally acceptable as well as unacceptable sexual practices can be disruptive to healthy sexuality and to relationships. For example, needing daily sex with one's reluctant partner damages the relationship, and is a failing attempt to solve problems.

Women engage in just as much cross-wired use of sexual energy as men. It is less obvious, again because of the culture. Sexual addiction isn't limited to sexual activity (as is obvious in Sex and Love Addicts twelve-step meetings). Women are acculturated to romanticize relationships. The selection of clothing attractive to men can be carried to an extreme. Some women spend money they cannot afford on makeup, hair, clothing, and surgery to make themselves attractive. Romantic fantasy can disrupt real life. I myself didn't look like a "sex addict" in college classes taking volumes of notes. I learned how to quickly transcribe the instructor's words as I continued to play out fantasies in my head. Yet there is no paraphilia called fantasizing the process of meeting a new man, falling in love, and eventually leaving him when he becomes unloving. While this is more common than other paraphilias, and disruptive to life, it is not generally seen as a symptom. It sounds like a normal activity for a teenager or a young woman just falling in love. But it is symptomatic of romance addiction.

Women violate the sexuality of children, too. Men are arrested and prosecuted for sexual activity with children, but the women who accompany them are often not. The assumption in our culture, acted on by child protective services departments and the police, is that women don't do these things, and if they do, it's because a man got them to. Noel Larson and Sally Maison (1987), psychologists who treat women convicted of sexual abuse of children, commented that all of the women were seriously disturbed. One might assume this is because only disturbed women are sexual with children. Instead, only disturbed women engage in behaviors extreme enough to warrant arrest.

There were news accounts of a woman who breast-fed her 3-year-old daughter, and called emergency services when she became sexually aroused by it. Child protective services took her child away from her for several months. News accounts took the view that the response was a violation of the mother's rights, and that sexual arousal when nursing a child is not sexual abuse. Sadly, this case demonstrates how right and wrong becomes the issue instead of helping the mother with a reaction to her child that isn't healthy for either of them. The ideal response would have been a referral to a therapist who understood cross-wiring. The mother would learn that her fears might be well grounded, and that she must establish limits necessary for her daughter's safety. The therapist would have compassion for the mother, and a genuine desire to help her interact with her daughter in healthier ways. The response is not condemning, and at the same time, it isn't a blanket acceptance of the behavior. Arrest and court-ordered treatment is usually a necessary step for many pedophiles because their shame is too intense to get help otherwise. But if this process is conducted in a shaming manner, little real healing can take place.

The therapist could learn if the mother experienced regular sexual arousal, and if she had used that arousal for her own pleasure. If it was the first time, the therapist could question if she was "in memory" about something that happened to her when she was that age. The therapist would explore why the mother was nursing her child at age 3. Therapy for the child might be in order, too. She could have breast-fed to take care of her mother's needs, or to obtain a feeling of security not otherwise available.

The best therapist stance is one of helping the mother and the child, as well as using the authority of the law to enforce necessary changes if the mother hesitates. Neither shaming the mother nor scolding the authorities for intervening will help the mother or the child.

EMOTIONAL INCEST

After working with many male sex addicts, and discovering how many of their mothers used them as surrogate spouses when the father was physically and/or emotionally absent, I have come to appreciate how mothers can damage the child's sexuality as much as a father who sexually fondles a child. Because mothers' love for children is socially approved and encouraged, the "abuse" is difficult to name. It is also hard for men and women in therapy to perceive their mother's "love" as intrusive, employing bonding appropriate to a partner.

Issues like these are assisted by group settings because it is easier to see that another person's relationship with his mother is not healthy. Then, by extension, it can be seen that the same kind of relating went on with his own mother. Most men feel guilty for not wanting their mothers to touch them when their mothers seem to love them so much. It takes time to discover that the mother's "love" was contaminated by feelings that should have been reserved for her adult mate.

Given the difficulties men and women have with coupling, it has become a cultural norm for the woman to emotionally move away from her husband and bond tightly with her children. Emotional incest is difficult to avoid if parents aren't able to maintain their bond as primary, supplemented by their bonds with the children. Examples are seen in the family where each child successively bonds with the mother, or where the first child is for the mother, and the second for the father. Two "couples" are made up of a parent and a child.

These dynamics are difficult for parents to hear about from the therapist. Shame makes it difficult to know that they have been harming their children. Therapeutic help requires a gentle, compassionate approach to avoid shaming— and, at the same time, firmness in confronting denial.

Changing these dynamics means changing a system that might be working for the parents. One couple who wanted help with their sex life left therapy when I focused on the fact that their 5-year-old child still slept in their room. The mother had an emotionally incestuous dependency on the child, and the father was defensive about any suggestion of changing it. I was not able to engage them in taking a broad look at their sexual bonding and sexual expression.

CULTURAL ACCEPTANCE DOES NOT DIMINISH DAMAGE

DSM-IV says that cultural norms make a difference in what is considered mentally unhealthy. "The diagnosis of paraphilias across cultures or religions is complicated by the fact that what is considered deviant in one cultural setting may be more acceptable in another setting." This may be true when deciding if a diagnosis is appropriate, but it is not relevant when considering if the sexual practice is harmful. For example, in Sudan it is unacceptable for girls to retain their vulva. They are required to have it surgically removed in a procedure called circumcision or infibulation (Lightfoot-Klein 1989). While this is culturally acceptable and required, it is highly damaging to women, and to the men who must cause painful sex to the women and to themselves.

As therapists, we have to look beyond the culture in order to discover how to really help our clients with their sexuality. It is easier to see how other cultures' norms are harmful than to understand the harm of our own.

NEW CRITERIA FOR "UNHEALTHY" SEX

The concept of cross-wiring removes the question of what is moral and acceptable, and, instead, suggests a different set of criteria to decide if something is "wrong." The following criteria might be more useful than diagnosable paraphilias when assessing a client's distress:

1. Does cross-wiring interfere with finding and maintaining a loving, intimate relationship?

2. Is sexual focus more on how to achieve arousal and orgasm than on intimacy, that is, seeing the partner more clearly, and being seen?

3. Does cross-wiring dictate sexual choices (i.e., partners, activities, feelings, sexual frequency, etc.)?

4. Does cross-wiring bring feelings of shame, either from within, or because others know?

5. Does cross-wiring prevent using sex as a loving expression (toward the self or others)?

6. Does cross-wiring inhibit the use of sexual energy to bond into a monogamous, committed relationship?

CATEGORIES OF CROSS-WIRED SEXUALITY

Within the categories of cross-wired behaviors (see below), particular behaviors can be high or low on the scale of social acceptability. For example, a man who is aroused by overtly sexual, "dirty" language is not acceptable if he does this with strangers on the street, but is tolerated and even encouraged when he does it with a partner who is sexually responsive to it. Men are culturally supported in being sexually turned off by a woman over a certain weight, which renders a proportion of the population sexually unattractive. One client told of liking a woman in high school whom he couldn't date because she was unacceptable to his peers—not unacceptable to him. Cultural cross-wiring severely limited his choice of a mate.

The following categories are not inclusive. They are intended to offer areas to consider with clients. There are many variations on each of these categories:

1. Visual stimuli

Partner's hair color
Need for "sexy" clothing
Partner of a certain body weight and shape and other physical qualities, such as nipple placement on breast
Body positioning and movement

2. Specific sexual activities needed for arousal

Any sexual activity that is *necessary* for arousal, rather than just an option—can include oral sex, anal sex, certain body positions, etc.

3. Nonsexual activities needed for arousal or orgasm

Spanking or being spanked
Being tickled
Bondage
Talking "dirty"
Genital pain—biting, pinching, scratching
Urinating or defecating
Fetish objects

4. Erotic stimuli in the environment

Watching a "sexy" person walk down the street
Watching someone undress
Hearing a zipper
Smelling perfume or cologne
Sex talk
Pictures or movies of sexual scenes

5. *Feelings that produce arousal*

> Feeling aroused by a lover walking away from you
> Wondering if the person will arouse you or not (during massage, for instance)
> Needing to be seduced, or to seduce
> Feeling special and important
> Feeling sexy to your partner
> Feeling admired, physically or otherwise

6. *Clothing worn*

> Tight clothing that shows off the body to others, bringing arousal
> Men wearing women's clothing
> Feeling well dressed

7. *Altering oneself to seem "sexy"*

> Body positioning
> Strutting
> Smiles
> Sounds
> Touching one's body suggestively

8. *Romance*

> Needing to be charmed, swept off one's feet, made to feel special
> Needing to feel like a real man, a stud, with larger than average genitals, and ability to perform
> Taking care of, and being taken care of (financially, emotionally, physically, etc.)

Quickly believing that this is *the* relationship, and
   is permanent
Reading romance novels frequently

9. *Discussing sex as wicked, forbidden, naughty, dirty*

Telling "dirty" jokes
Approaching potential partner with overtly sexual
   come-ons
Talking "dirty"

10. *Sexual roles*

The "other woman" or "other man" in triangles
The "bad girl"—having sex with almost anyone
Super stud—getting any girl
Prude
The "good girl"
The gentleman or good guy
Knight in shining armor

11. *Fear of sex*

Avoidance of sexual activity
Lack of arousal when it would be appropriate
Staying out of relationships
Having impersonal sex to avoid fear brought on
   by awareness of partner
Preferring masturbation to sex

12. *Fear of relationships*

13. *Preference for sex without a partner*

Fantasy of sex and sexual relationships is preferred for arousal
Pornography replaces sex with a real person

Voyeurism—looking at strangers, telling sexual jokes, mentioning the night to come at a wedding, double entendres in conversation, flirting with relatives' or friends' partners

14. *New partners necessary for arousal*

15. *Having sex because you can't say no*

You are in a relationship
You did it once before with that person
Men can't turn it down
There seems to be no relationship without it
You're not allowed to say no

16. *Sexual activity has meaning*

You are loved
You are a loving person
You are valued
You are wanted
You are beautiful/handsome
Life has meaning

17. *Sexual activity has a function*

Tranquilizer or sleeping pill or other mood-altering effect
Something to do
Creating closeness when it doesn't happen in other ways

18. *Responding with sexual energy when choosing not to*

Television and magazine ads designed to trigger sexual energy

Responding to flirtations of people who are not available, or you are not available

Responding to the walk, dress, and facial expression of those who exude sexual energy (often seen as charismatic)

GOING BEYOND THE CULTURE AND *DSM-IV*

This chapter discussed how our culture limits understanding of how to help people discover healthier sexual energy. If we help clients *adjust* to the cultural norm, we will be preventing healing that is now possible.

DSM-IV uses the language of paraphilias, which reflects the older, sexual compulsivity school, and mixes it in with the newer language of sexual dysfunction. For example, in the discussion of fetishism, it is said that when an object is strongly preferred or required for sexual excitement, "in its absence there may be erectile dysfunction in males" (p. 526). The clinical language regarding sexual symptoms must change in order to accurately reflect sexual difficulties. For example, when a certain object (such as women's clothing, shoes, or large breasts) is needed for arousal and orgasms, erections may not occur in its absence.

In discussing sexual desire disorders, *DSM-IV* states, "Both partners may have levels of desire within the normal range but at different ends of the continuum" (p. 497). This statement reflects a practical approach to sexuality, as if a bell-shaped curve can make sense of it. Sexuality is far too complex to view "desire" for sex as something that has a normal range. A person can fully express one's sexual self with sexual activity once a day, once a week, or once a year, depending on the circumstances and the relationship with a partner. Healthy, spiritual (in contrast to normal) sexuality is something that evolves out of the relationship, serves the needs of the relationship, and will vary accordingly. When the sexual bond is strong, and energetic communication moves back and forth along it, then both partners will want the same amount of sexual expression. *DSM-IV*, as a reflection of the culture, looks at what is normal for the purpose of diagnosis. But in the therapy office, normal isn't a useful concept because what is normal in any culture is based on shamed sexuality, and will not create a context within which the greatest growth is possible. As sexual abuse of children is now being confronted, our clients (and eventually our culture) have available the capacity for a previously rare experience of sexuality.

IS IT CROSS-WIRING OR COMPULSION?

When working with clients, it can be helpful to sort out the nature of a person's cross-wiring from the intensity of the drive to act on it. People have countless forms of cross-wiring, but if there is no accompanying obsession or compulsion, distress will be less likely. For example, people will find themselves sexually aroused by rape scenes in movies, but find the idea of actually raping or being raped, or even fantasizing about these acts, unpleasant. The cross-wiring exists, but doesn't bring with it obsessions or compulsions. These associations might be useful to the understanding of a person's sexuality, and the history that created it, but it won't take center stage.

In contrast is the person who is cross-wired to rape scenes, and who is also sexually compulsive. This person may act out rape scenes with lovers or prostitutes as either the rapist or the victim, or masturbate to fantasy or pornography with this theme. Others will act out the compulsion by forcing another person to have sex.

Compulsive sexuality can also exist in culturally approved sexual expression, such as intercourse with a spouse. This behavior is not considered cross-wired, but it is when a person must have it frequently to avoid emotional symptoms.

Helping a client differentiate between sexual associations and perceived need to be sexual can help make sense of symptoms that don't fall into the categories of paraphilia or dysfunction.

9

Understanding Flirting and Jealousy

Flirting is intended to communicate nonverbally that a person is available for a sexual relationship. Those who express this availability sort through the responding available people for a good match. In a hypothetical sexually healthy culture, those who were not available would not respond. Some people who are in mated relationships flirt with others who may or may not be available, which confuses the communication. This is the addictive use of sexual energy to obtain a sexual "hit"; people also flirt to feel powerful, to feel valuable, and to make their partner jealous. Most flirting is seen as "innocent." It isn't.

People who feel jealous may be confused about why, if they know their partner wouldn't have sex with someone else. In our culture, if someone has sex with someone else, then the partner is allowed to be jealous—extremely jealous. But if sex doesn't occur, it is seen as just flirting, and shouldn't be threatening.

JEALOUSY

Some clients seek therapy because of feelings of jealousy, or because they have partners who are jealous. While jealous feelings can be symptoms of childhood relationships or past adult relationships, jealousy is usually based on more than imagination. This is because humans are monogamously bonding creatures. If the partner directs sexual energy toward another, the emotional response of jealousy emerges to protect the union. At these times, jealousy is a natural outcome of a monogamous bond, even if there is no actual threat to the relationship. Because we live in a culture that permits flirting and other exchanges of sexual energy, jealousy is often elicited.

FLIRTING AS SEXUAL ADDICTION

Flirting is a common form of sexual addiction. It may be accompanied by having sex with others or used as fantasy material for masturbation. Women who don't want sex may act out their sex life in the form of flirting. This might be with men who are not available for a relationship, or with heterosexual women. The movie *Sex, Lies, and Videotape* portrays the character of Anne as very flirtatious; she hates having sex with her husband. The flirtatiousness disappears when she falls in love, and her sexual energy is directed toward her partner.

Women also direct flirtation toward their children. This form is not easily recognized as sexual energy because mothers are seen as pure. It is a common form of emotional incest, leaving children—both boys and girls—struggling with their sexuality in adult years.

Barry (introduced in Chapter 7) was addicted to flirting, as well as to fantasy and pornography. Barry's mother responded to his flirtation from the time he was a small boy, creating his flirtation addiction. He enjoyed sex with women, but he found it easier to control with flirting than when engaged in sexual activity. His story is not extraordinary. Flirting, when used addictively, emotionally eliminates the partner during the flirtation. Sexual energy is usually exclusive, and so when it is shared with someone else the partner is left out. The exception to this is when the couple together flirt with another person, creating an illusion of intimacy. This is common at parties, usually causing problems when one partner begins to feel excluded, or when one wants monogamy.

> Roberta, Barry's lover, had intense reactions, an example of the natural outcome of mating with a flirting addict—particularly when flirting was part of the initial attraction. Roberta's therapist worked with her on her history of past relationships with men who were sexual with others. In her childhood people came and went with no regard for her needs. The therapist helped Roberta see why she was drawn to people like Barry, who directed sexual energy toward others, even though he was physically constant. But she also affirmed that Roberta had good reason to be angry with Barry.

Barry and Roberta met alternate weeks for couples counseling with Roberta's therapist and me, and during this time Roberta relinquished her victim stance in relation to Barry, and was able to express loud and intense anger. I supported Barry as Roberta unleashed her rage from every time she watched him flirt with women at parties, or at work, or with her friends.

Barry had completed enough emotional work to understand that her reactions came from a desire for a monogamous bond. Since he shared that desire, he could often tolerate the pain of hearing her rage. But often his belief that he was bad, and had caused devastating harm, interfered. At these times he needed to set limits about how much he could hear. His therapy then focused on his right to set those limits, knowing that limit setting is a form of self-care, challenging his belief in his badness.

WHEN A PARTNER ISN'T JEALOUS

Some clients have figured out how to avoid jealousy. One way is to create enough emotional distance that knowing a partner is flirting or having sex with others doesn't hurt. If there is no sexual energy bond, when the partner engages sexually with others there is no bond to be violated. But this isn't much of a relationship.

A second maneuver is for both partners to have sex with others in the same environment so the partners can monitor and control each other—such as two couples exchanging partners, or a couple including a third person. The partner can use the jealousy to fuel sexual arousal, much as people learn how to use shame to do so (through sex in places where they might be caught, being dominated, and other sadomasochistic activities). Jealousy is an intense feeling, and if it can be channeled into arousal it can create a strong drug.

> Mike and Lisa went regularly to a club where people had sex with others. Mike decided who Lisa could be with, and when and where. This excited him until Lisa met with a man from the club away from that setting. He became so jealous he couldn't eat or sleep, obsessed with anger and hurt. I tried to explain that this reaction was healthier than the intensified arousal, but he could not hear this. He left after two sessions because his goal was to get things back to normal by getting Lisa to agree to return to his control. I couldn't join him in this objective. Lisa was too frightened of losing him to face her objections to their sexual activities.

SOME GAY MEN AGREE TO NONMONOGAMY

Almost all gay men who have not engaged in sexual recovery have a difficult time being monogamous (see Chapter 11). Research studies consistently show that gay relationships are not monogamous, and almost none remains so for more than five years. To cope with this tendency, and still be able to form committed relationships, it has become part of the gay subculture to accept sex outside of the marriage (I use "marriage" in its true meaning of sexual bonding and commitment).

The pain of infidelity is dealt with in a number of ways.

One is for both partners to have sex elsewhere, which reduces the awareness of pain, but does not remove it. One gay man found himself grieving deeply for his mate's extrarelationship sexual activities only after they separated. He kept these feelings at bay by sexual acting out whenever jealousy might have come up. But jealousy was only temporarily avoided.

As with Lisa and Mike, above, both men can together have sex with another man, creating sexual excitement and less fear of loss. Others agree to limit their sexual activities to strangers in bathhouses or parks, and avoid threatening the relationship with ongoing sexual relating. Fear and jealousy are also reduced by an agreement to tell each other about sexual encounters with others so secrecy doesn't add to the fear. While these methods can succeed in *coping* with jealousy, it is possible to offer gay clients the hope of sexual recovery so they can bond monogamously from the inside out, relinquishing the addictive use of sexual energy.

It is not inherent in being a gay man to have sex with many men. Working with a monogamous gay therapist can provide a model of alternative solutions to gay men. Gay therapist Randy Fitzgerald (1997) explains:

> I chose to be in a completely monogamous relationship and was willing to deal with the shame, anxiety and fear that came up from that decision. Now, because of moving through those feelings, while remaining monogamous, I have achieved an appropriate or present day perspective on monogamy—so it's easy in this relationship to maintain monogamy as I carry the preference in my cells. That makes it possible to help other men move in the same direction (although not all men that I work with choose to do so). [p. 1]

JEALOUSY PATTERNS

Growing up in a culture that doesn't respect monogamous bonding, everyone who has been in a relationship has felt jealous. (Some people control their partner to prevent feeling jealousy.)

If our culture understood the role of jealousy in alerting both partners that there is a problem with the bond, then each time a person felt jealous he or she would be able to express it through anger, crying, and demanding that the partner return to the safety of the bond. But such reactions are not appreciated by those who have not engaged in sufficient sexual healing, and feelings can be stored up for years. As with Roberta, described above, the feelings that have been elicited by one relationship will trigger expression of feelings held back from past relationships. Roberta went to three therapists who didn't understand her need to express these feelings, and, when she finally had the support of her new therapist and myself, she could unleash them.

Given this cultural situation, most clients with the symptom of jealousy have feelings created by past experiences. The mistake made by many therapists is believing that the symptom is *only* about the past experience. This can be disorienting to the client, who needs to have her present reality affirmed, as well as past influences acknowledged.

Bret and Linda sought therapy because he was ready to leave her if she didn't stop her "insane jealousy," as he called it. Bret was a confident, successful man who appeared comfortable with his life. He had found Linda very attractive, and courted her passionately two years earlier. He liked everything about her, including her work, the way she created her home, her love of animals, and the fact that she, too, didn't want children. She fit his definition of a perfect mate, and he proposed within three weeks. But as the relationship settled into the everyday, he stopped being attentive, returning to his usual interests. He wanted her to support his lifestyle, while he revered her and took care of her financially. None of this had been overtly communicated. Soon Linda began to complain about how he didn't pay attention to her, and treated other women the way he used to treat her.

As we discussed Linda's past, as well as the nature of her relationship with Bret, we could see both the healthy and unhealthy aspects of the jealousy. First, jealousy from the threat to the bond brought about by his flirtations was appropriate, indicative of the lack of a monogamous bond (not necessarily a threat of loss, or even of affairs). His dramatic courtship triggered her pattern of wanting to be saved from an ordinary life by an extraordinary man. The threat of losing a life made meaningful by a husband's love was not a healthy cause of jealousy. Instead, she needed to focus on making her life meaningful instead of depending on him. As we could separate out these different reasons for her jealousy, she could express the real one, and work on relinquishing the others.

Bret came to sessions to help fix Linda. He saw his life as perfect, if only his wife would play the part assigned her when they married. When he saw us uncovering the real and unreal forms of jealousy, he didn't like either one. Bret spent a good amount of time explaining why he was entitled to have her support for his life as he chose to lead it without questioning him or wanting him to be different. He pointed out that he had made clear to her that he worked long hours, attended many social functions, and was very successful as a result.

Bret and Linda's marriage didn't survive. She engaged in therapy, and forged a new life for herself free from the sanction of a powerful husband. She abandoned the jealousy she had felt when observing him charming women because her anger had had no effect on Bret. She could see that he wasn't going to have a monogamous bond with her. Instead, he would share his sexual energy with many women.

Once she grieved for the loss of the desired bond, and was no longer jealous, she realized that she was emotionally divorcing him. Even the threat of losing her was not sufficient motivation for him to look at his lifestyle, one that prevented him from having a real relationship with his wife.

They separated, and even before the divorce was final, he had found a new woman to replace Linda. Prior to their marriage, Linda hadn't seen his pattern of abandoning one imperfect woman for another, searching for the ideal complement to his life. Linda had been perfect until she grew dissatisfied with her role. Bret was unable to see that it is not possible for a mate to be genuinely happy with the contract. All will become dissatisfied. Some will grow and leave. Others will stay and punish passively, feeling victimized by the contract even while spending the money it provides.

This combination of patterns is common in marriages of politically and economically powerful men. Couples come for one or two sessions, and then realize that neither is willing to address their lifestyles in order to create a better marriage. The community I practice in has many people who work for a successful software company that pays well and inspires great commitment. The partners of many men who work there begin to feel left out, and the high income does not make up for the men's absence. Jealousy can focus on a man's work rather than on other women.

When I see that the couple isn't able to consider this dynamic, I try to engage the jealous partner in a more general therapy process with the hope of addressing her (or his) self-esteem. Occasionally this is possible, and is followed by a lengthy pulling apart, and often divorce. Other times, the partner comes to therapy for the affirmation that the situation is hopeless, gaining strength to leave.

UNHEALTHY FUNCTIONS OF JEALOUSY

Jealousy can be a symptom. For example, fear of abandonment can elicit a fear that if the partner relates with others, the partner will leave. Dependence on the partner manifests itself in jealousy and anger.

Jealousy can also be a reaction to one's own desire to have sex with others or to leave the relationship. Guilt or fear can result in projecting this desire onto the partner, and then suffering the resulting jealousy. For example, Jake (described in Chapter 6) responded sexually to almost all women he encountered. Because of this, he assumed Janet had the same interest in men. He struggled with jealousy throughout their relationship, controlling her activities in order to reduce his fear of losing her. As she took back control of her life, he was forced into intense fear and anger until he was able to see that she wasn't looking for a new man. In addition, his own recovery helped him understand how his belief that all people sexualize others was false. Resolving his dependence on his wife also freed him from his fear.

Some clients project disowned desires for others onto the partner, and make accusations that are untrue. This feels crazy to both the jealous person and the partner because the fears and facts don't match up.

DISCHARGING OLD JEALOUSY

My own experience of relinquishing old jealousy demonstrates how, if the present relationship doesn't trigger jealousy, it is possible to have the feelings while understanding that they don't belong in the present. In my second marriage, I knew my husband wasn't exchanging sexual energy with other people. He didn't lust or flirt. But feelings were stored up from a long first marriage and other relationships without inherent monogamous bonding, but I hadn't known I was jealous because I flirted too. The experience of having monogamous bonding provoked the experience of old jealousy, making possible its discharge. Because we understood how this worked, I was able to yell at my husband as if he were the cause, while both of us knew he wasn't. After a few weeks of being mad about every person he had ever had sex with, or even been attracted to, I freed myself of the feelings (Hastings 1993). Now when women flirt with him I hardly notice.

> Sara's discharge of jealousy took a different form. Her husband continued flirting, even though he is in sexual addiction recovery. Sara tried to be patient, and learn to tolerate his acting out, but after repeatedly watching

him respond to women who were attracted to him, she began to grieve. In a weekend-long therapy group, she sobbed bitterly for an hour. She wept loudly, despair radiating through the room, bringing the rest of us to tears. When I asked if she was emotionally divorcing her husband, she nodded and sobbed even louder.

As the tears ran their course, I explained that she was grieving for the illusion of a monogamous bond, created when they fell in love. Sara's father flirted with women, and bonded with her sister, so Sara didn't have a model of monogamy. In addition, she expressed her competition with her sister for their father's love by searching for men who would want only her. But when they eventually took that stand, she lost interest and left. She could see how this set her husband up to continue his flirtation with other women because he sensed that if he gave this up, and loved only Sara, she would lose interest.

By grieving, and letting go of the illusion of monogamy, Sara gave herself the opportunity to detach from her husband's sexual addiction. By living more congruently with the truth of their relationship, she had to give up some of her feeling of closeness to him. But she gained freedom from jealousy that was unavoidable as long as she saw the relationship as monogamous when it wasn't. Sara and her husband loved each other deeply, and knew they would stay together. Now free of the erroneous belief in a monogamous bond, they could become loving, committed friends, freer to openly engage in recovery, and to support each other's process. They did not love each other less. They were no less committed to the relationship. All that changed was the perception of the relationship as sexually monogamous.

This freed the couple to work toward such a bond because she gave up some of her jealousy. (Giving up all the jealousy is perhaps ideally possible, but it is unlikely that anyone has the grief tools to do it. This may be particularly true if they continue to have sex.) Her husband was freed from his shameful reactions to her jealousy, and the desire to hide his addiction, which, in turn, increased her trust in him.

10

Men Are Not the Bad Gender

Our culture sees men as carriers of badness and women as carriers of goodness. Beginning with sugar and spice and everything nice compared with snails and puppy dog tails, it goes on from there. The beliefs include the following: men only want sex; men don't want to be close; men are controlling, depriving, and unfair; only men rape; kind men are different from typical men. Women are seen as good, pure, loving, and nurturing.

Many women bring their men to therapy to get them fixed, complaining about their qualities in a shaming, demeaning, controlling manner. But because women are considered the good sex, it is more difficult to introduce the idea that the woman's attitude toward the man is harmful, and might be examined in therapy. Men can more easily believe they are bad and have done bad things because they have cultural support for this belief. When a woman faces the abuses she directs at her man (or children), she will experience even more pain than he does because her cultural definition requires her to be good. His requires that he apologize and promise not to do it again.

If a 30-year-old woman is sexual with a 15-year-old boy, he is considered lucky and she is seen as immature, or perhaps wanting a lover who can perform. When the roles are reversed, a 30-year-old man being sexual with a 15-year-old girl is considered a statutory rapist, pedophile, interested in "only one thing," and one of "those" men.

A client told about confronting his mother when, in his late twenties, she continued to enter the bathroom to urinate while he was in the shower, behind transparent glass doors. She had done this his entire life, and was shocked when he objected. He asked her how she would feel if his father urinated when his sister was in the shower. She agreed that this was not appropriate.

We are more shocked when a woman kills her children, or is sexual with children, because women are good. It is considered terrible when a man does these things, but it is more congruent with his social image. This attitude shames all men.

My work with male sex addicts and other men addressing sexuality has given me an education about men's inner workings related to their culturally condemned symptoms. The therapist role allows seeing from the inside what it is like to lead other kinds of lives.

This chapter discusses the criticism of men by women (and the culture), as strikingly demonstrated in the writing of feminists over the past two decades. With the help of compassionately understanding therapists, men are able to look at behavior shamed by the culture. Sex therapy promotes acceptance of lustful, impersonal sexual attitudes. Instead, cultural change can come from acceptance of men who have sexually objectifying attitudes, offering an opportunity to heal from these influences. This will contribute to a culturally supported healing of gender issues, and freedom for men and women to come together lovingly.

The man who just wants sex, who looks at body parts and not the woman, who wants a trophy on his arm, who wants a woman to focus on his needs with no needs of her own, who believes he has a right to control because he brings in more money is a cultural stereotype (based on truth). Feminist writing opened doors for women to at last see that things were unbalanced, and that these attitudes were harmful. The next step is to see how men are as much victims of the culture as the women who let themselves be controlled, while hating men for it.

It has been suggested that women are monogamous because they need to have a man help raise the family, and that men aren't inherently monogamous. This attitude strengthens the rift between women and men. Men are expected to feel no pain, go to war and sacrifice their lives, and support the family financially and provide a comfortable life for their wives and children. The "men's movement" is making some progress in assisting men to become more human, and to participate in family—and access a desire for monogamous bonding.

Therapists have the opportunity to understand men in ways the rest of the population doesn't. Helping men with sexual issues offers a way to understand how the culture has violated men, setting them up to violate themselves and the women they want to partner with. Sexual healing requires working toward equality between the sexes. It also requires discovering how to bond with another person with sexual energy instead of using it impersonally. Helping men work their way out of sexual addiction allows therapists to see men becoming intimate—with women, and with each other. It vividly shows how many men are locked into a position of seeing women sexually. It can create compassion where only confusion and anger were possible.

I receive an education by working with men as they struggle to let go of the need to win in order to feel worthy. I have watched them begin to care about each other, only to pull back into classic distancing stances. I listened for three years to a men's group talk about wanting physical contact with each other, and not be able to touch. And when they began to touch, how they had to cut off awareness. They made it easy to see why they needed women for nurturing, and why they needed to control their partners to assure some semblance of intimacy. I feel compassion for men who act out acculturated roles, the same compassion I feel for women who act out the counterpart roles.

THE MYTH OF MALE POWER

Warren Farrell presents overwhelming evidence that men are as victimized as women by the culture in *The Myth of Male Power* (1993). He points out that real, healthy power does not include the power over women—or over anything else. Farrell's work is useful for therapists (both male and female) who are working to understand how the perceived victims (women) and the perceived victimizers (men) are both scripted by the culture.

Farrell describes how large audiences of women came

to hear him speak about his support of their anger at men. He finally realized that he was contributing to the schism between women and men:

> I wondered if the reason so many more women than men listened to me was because I had been listening to women but not listening to men. I reviewed some of the tapes from among the hundreds of women's and men's groups I had started. I heard myself. When women criticized men, I called it "insight," "assertiveness," "women's liberation," "independence," or "high self-esteem." When men criticized women, I called it "sexism," "male chauvinism," "defensiveness," "rationalizing," and "backlash." I did it politely—but the men got the point. Soon the men were no longer expressing their feelings. Then I criticized the men for not expressing their feelings! [p. 12]

As Farrell began to listen to men, he discovered that it took far more internal security to speak on behalf of men than to speak on behalf of women.

John Stoltenberg's *Refusing To Be a Man* (1989) supports giving up male stereotypes in his desire to support the equality of women. His book was praised by famous feminists. Farrell, in contrast, realized that he was abandoning his gender by speaking out only for women.

> Lewis was married to Susan for fifteen years (introduced in Chapter 6 and further discussed in Chapter 7). After the initial period of sexual bonding, Susan's interest in sex decreased markedly, and Lewis's increased. Susan had been sexually abused as a child, and responded to sexual attention with fear often bordering on terror. Lewis could make no sense of this for the first decade of

marriage. He felt that he deserved to have sex, he was married to this woman, and she was not upholding her end of their partnership. From this initial presentation, he looked like the classic "all he wants is sex" male.

Prior to the possibility of sexual healing, this situation was unworkable. Feminists felt men's requirement for sex was harmful to women, but didn't know that there was hope for change. A woman entered a marriage hoping her interest in her husband would be strong enough to take care of his needs, but in time she became unable to provide sex for this purpose. The classic "headache" excuse, reflected in jokes, established the pattern that men wanted it and women didn't. Women could say no, but only with an excuse.

The couples I have seen with this dynamic who have been in previous therapy were approached in two ways. One is helping the woman want more sex. The man's "need" and "right" (which only two decades ago had the sanction of law in every state) was upheld, and the woman's issues were addressed. The second reaction was a negative attitude toward the man for pressuring his wife for sex. The therapists took sides, which does not serve the couple.

Lewis and Susan had previously worked with a therapist who helped Susan with some of her sexual abuse history. But Lewis had been complaining for years about not getting what he deserved. His tone was whining and monotonous, even while he said that he didn't want Susan to have sex if she didn't want to. This man, who was very successful in the financial world and who had spent time exploring his spiritual and energetic nature in his early twenties, became a pitiful, powerless child as he berated his wife.

My first reaction was annoyance. My experience as a psychotherapist didn't help me see through the presentation to his pain. He seemed like one of "those men," who want sex, think they deserve it, and don't understand how to be intimate. Apparently I wasn't the only therapist who had this reaction, because he had not felt understood by the two before me.

I asked him if the powerless child presentation was experienced in his childhood. I knew that if I understood his past, and saw how it was being replayed in the present, I would have more empathy and compassion. I had to see more than his complaining. I also pointed out how the way he asked for sex was guaranteed to get him none, as no woman could lovingly respond to whining.

We spent many sessions learning about his childhood. His mother had not been able to love him for himself, instead treating him as a cute object she could handle and show off to her friends. But Lewis refused to play his part. Before the end of his first year, he chose rebellion rather than playing the role his mother had wanted. His brother, born three years later, took on the role of Mommy's little prince, which in his forties he continues to play. Lewis's anger, and refusal to play his part, left him desperately deprived of love and affection. After learning how to be sexual in his teens and twenties, and confused about what girls wanted, he fell in love with Susan.

Susan's fear of sex provided Lewis the opportunity to reenact his relationship with his mother. He could ask for love, but she couldn't give it to him in the form he needed. Now when Lewis turned into the whiny, demanding person, I knew what was behind it, and had more tolerance of it. I could point out the way he was asking, and invite him to further explore the relationship with his mother.

But there was more. After Susan had been able to resolve much of the effects of her history of sexual abuse (incest), the focus turned to Lewis. He and I met for several weeks alone so he could focus on himself, and less on the deprivation. I encouraged him to talk about what it had been like being with a woman for fifteen years who refused to give him what he viewed as evidence of caring. He poured out a story of feeling as unloved by his wife as by his mother. He talked about what it was like to come home from work wondering if she would love him or hate him. I saw the innocence of a man facing a woman who is terrified by life and who cannot accept him. In the past Susan offered sex because she thought it was required, but she dissociated during it, which left him just as unconnected as in childhood. He focused on the feelings of closeness for a day or two after sex. He didn't know how to seek help.

As we explored more of what was behind Lewis's demands, we discovered that he believed that if he stopped wanting sex, the relationship was over. They had a good working partnership, taking care of a home and raising two children. But he said they had nothing that resembled a marriage. Giving up interest in sex felt like giving up marriage.

A second discovery was his fear that he was a sexual perpetrator, through identification with his father, who sexualized all relating with women. Lewis saw women (including Susan) move away from him with disgust. Lewis feared that if he came across as strong when introducing sex, instead of weak and whining, he would become his father. This was supported by Susan's reaction to him as if he were *her* father—a perpetrator who had caused her incredible pain, leaving her with scars affecting her sexuality and her entire life.

As Lewis and Susan explored sex, after years of healing, Lewis enjoyed feeling like a whole, strong man as he told Susan he was interested in opening up to new sexual possibilities. Susan responded well to these overtures, and the two spent more time in bed finding out how they might be together—sometimes sexual, sometimes not. But after a period in this strong, new place, Lewis would revert to whining. Susan reacted negatively. Lewis again believed he wasn't getting what he deserved. But now he could see his old pattern as a symptom.

EFFEMINATE GAY HOSTILITY

Some gay men express hostility through a caricature of femininity that can be quite offensive. (This type of character is seen frequently in movies; the red-headed gay man on the television show "Ellen" demonstrates it well.) Prior to understanding more about homosexuality, I thought this presentation was natural to being gay. It isn't.

Being effeminate isn't inherently part of being gay. It is also not inherently part of being a woman. What we call feminine is usually an *act* of being female. Since this act is culturally accepted for women, it isn't seen as offensive unless carried to an extreme. But for a man to do the same is labeled perverted. Dolly Parton said on "The Tonight Show" that if she hadn't been a woman, she would have been a drag queen.

Women and men have different energy, whether they are gay or straight. A man and a woman who are fully in their bodies and full of life energy will look more similar to each other than acculturated demonstrations of gender now portray. But they will be easily distinguishable even if they are wearing the same kind of clothing and hairstyle. It is interesting to note that Chinese teaching about life energy demonstrates energy flowing differently for men and women (Tse 1995). During exercises to increase the storage of energy, men and women place opposite hands over the storage area. When not distracted by acculturated representations of male and female, we can perceive these different energy patterns.

Thus, gay men's use of effeminate mannerisms is not inherent to being gay. Couching hostility within effeminate behaviors attempts to communicate that the behavior isn't really hostile. (Women use effeminate mannerisms in the same way.)

Being on the receiving end of effeminate hostility feels affronting, even though it can be hard to identify why. Back when I thought effeminism was natural to being gay, and believed that I had to accept the behavior (a case of reverse discrimination!), I was waited on in a restaurant by a gay man who exuded this kind of hostility. It wasn't personal; he did it with everyone. I happened to be with a bisexual man in the restaurant who told me that this was indeed hostile and had nothing to do with homosexuality.

I didn't get to learn about this man, but I have seen other gay men who use this style when they are angry, relinquishing it when not. By getting to intimately know gay men who were real with me, discovering what their lives are like, and having empathy, I could see that effeminate hostility was a stereotyped expression of anger. Now when I encounter gay men enacting these patterns, I understand.

Hostility is not the only reason gay men use effeminate mannerisms. Some do so in order to join a subculture, taking on body movements and gestures that are new to them. I have known men who are quite real whose speech and actions announce that they are gay. The same is true for lesbian women taking on masculine-appearing traits.

THE CASE OF A MAN WHO THOUGHT HE HAD TO HAVE SEX

Alex told me a sad story about his friendship with a girl he grew up with. His family and hers had been friends, and they were much like siblings or cousins, going from year to year until they graduated from high school. Then they decided to work as itinerant fruit pickers. They lived together in his van.

Alex and Diane weren't able to talk about sex and relationships, and how a girl and boy could be friends without sex. If either of them had been dating someone else, this would have taken care of the definition of their relationship, but they were limited by their travels.

Alex had grown up feeling inferior to "real" men, and believed that if he traveled with an attractive woman without having sex, he was less than a man. So he initiated sex, and Diane didn't say no. The definition of the relationship changed to boyfriend and girlfriend. When Alex settled down, Diane stayed in another state temporarily with a relative. They stayed in touch as lovers, while feeling like cousins. With the time apart, they both began new relationships, allowing theirs to resume at the cousin status.

Alex didn't talk about it until he was in his thirties, then grieving for how he had been influenced by the cultural view of men. In our discussion, we could see that his actions made him look like one of "those" men. He is required to initiate sex in order to fit in with men—but if he does so, he is condemned by women. I felt his conflict, and saw how he violated himself to achieve externally derived self-esteem, and to see himself as truly a man.

MEN'S FEAR OF BEING SEEN AS RAPISTS

Men identify with classic males represented in our culture—which includes the capacity to rape, demonstrated during war when the acceptable object of the rape is one of the enemy. Even though a small proportion act on the conditioning, many men identify with men who rape. This is disconcerting, and avoided with a number of mechanisms. One is being unmasculine.

Richard (presented in Chapter 1) was shy and withdrawn, and didn't appear very bright in spite of completing graduate education with very good grades. He didn't want to be like men who treated women badly. By not acting "male" he felt safe from this possibility. It also inhibited him during sex with Terrie. She described him as the most passive man she had ever had sex with.

Other men become unable to obtain erections, or to maintain them upon entering their partner's vagina, because of a fear that they will be seen as rapists—or find out they are. The inability to perform prevents this.

Tad complained bitterly about his wife's disinclination to have sex, but I never quite believed him. As we began exploring his feelings about masculinity, we discovered that he feared he was a rapist, as he viewed most men. He had never been able to maintain erections once intercourse began—if he couldn't have erections, he was safe from raping. In addition, Tad prided himself on enjoying sex that brought pleasure to his partner. He valued his qualities that resembled those ascribed to women, such as tenderness, compassion, and sympathy.

Many men have some fear of hurting a woman with intercourse even though it might not interfere, as it did for Richard and Tad. When women feel pain, men usually feel guilty, even though they haven't caused it.

Some men can relinquish this belief once they become conscious of it. Most, however, require a good deal of exploration before the belief changes—it is pervasive, passed down over many generations. Men who would never rape women they know will sometimes find themselves doing so in war, especially when the subculture allows it, and when other men act on this conditioning. While this behavior is frightening and shocking, men would not rape if their sexuality had not been damaged by the culture.

MEN ARE VICTIMIZED BY MALE SOCIALIZATION

Therapists can help men by developing empathy for their plight as they try to live up to the culture's definition of manhood, but are unable to be true to themselves. Women want men who are tender and intimate, but the culture doesn't support this. Men who refuse to live up to the culture's model don't fit in very well. Yet this is the only way a man *can* discover a life with sexual intimacy, monogamous sexual bonding, and fully faceted love for his children.

Women have had increasing support since the beginning of the most recent women's movement to take on more male characteristics and actions. Men are now taking on more of what had been limited to women.

A classic example of the impossible conflict is the expectation that a man will have an erection any time he wants to. This is complicated by the fact that a woman doesn't like it when a man is sexually interested when she doesn't want him to be. He is either a failure or a perpetrator. This conflict encourages sexual addiction, as men need to be out of touch with their real sexual energy in order to live up to expectations, and to avoid shame when they can't. It also encourages men to hate women, without understanding why.

Men must have control over when they will be sexual, given the freedom to not meet the expectations of society. Sexual abuse recovery is discovering how women have to say no to sex. Men must be able to say no, too, in order to be able to heal their sexuality. Healing sexuality is far more than healing sexual problems.

11

Accepting Homosexuality

People who have sex with another person of the same gender are just that—people who have sex with the same gender. To best serve homosexual clients, the therapist must accept this. Any therapist who carries our culture's value that something is wrong with homosexual people, or with homosexual sex, should not take them as clients.

The cause of homosexuality has long been debated. It has been ascribed to childhood programming, developmental influences, gender abnormalities, character defect, brain differences, and genetics. The focus on cause is used to "prove" homosexuals cannot help it and thus deserve acceptance—or to prove they are sick and need help, or are sinful and deserving of ostracism. The phrase *sexual preference* has been replaced with *sexual orientation* to reflect the absence of choice. However, if cultures were accepting of homosexuality, these arguments would be pointless. It shouldn't matter if sexual orientation is a choice. In an accepting culture, perhaps more people would choose to partner with one of the same sex. In our condemning culture, primarily those who do not have a choice come out as gay.

If a therapist carries cultural programming to not talk about sexual orientation, or to act as if clients are normal even when the culture says they aren't, it can still be possible to serve a client well—if the therapist accepts homosexuality. In this case, exposure to gay people, particularly in the role of therapist which allows intimate exposure to who they are as people, can provide the therapist with the opportunity to unlearn the conditioning passed on by the culture. If the therapist's patterned responses are intrusive in the therapy, one way to prevent negatively affecting the client is to raise the issue.

For example, if the thought of anal sex is repulsive to the therapist, this attitude will be perceived (at least unconsciously) by the client. The therapist could say, "I know that anal sex is part of your sexual expression, and I don't want to judge that. But I have to tell you that I have my own negative reaction to doing that, and I think you might see it. I want to be accepting, and intellectually I think there's nothing wrong with it. But I have my own emotional conditioning that there is. I want to tell you this because even though I have reactions, I want you to be free to talk about it. I'm working on my reactions, too, so I hope they'll change." With this kind of self-revelation, the therapist doesn't have to lapse into the untenable position of trying to look accepting.

THE RIGHT TO LOVE ONE
OF THE SAME GENDER

An article by Ken Lovering published in the *Seattle Gay News* (1997) portrayed the experience of being part of a minority of people who are not allowed to love each other—even while being told they don't love each other:

> Recently, my partner Paul and I were awaiting an airport boarding call that would whisk him away to Washington, D.C., for five days. It would be our longest separation since we met and we were faced, for the first time in our relationship, with how to say good-bye in public. . . .
>
> To confront a monumental, long-term parting kiss at the airport with such anxiety felt unfair. . . . I felt as if something precious and timeless was being taken from me.
>
> . . . Paul and I never take our relationship for granted. Our good health often feels like something short of a miracle. But no matter how much wood I knock, I sometimes sense a specter in the shadows. Not because . . . of any tangible threat to our togetherness. But because we know life's fragility, that it can be torn from either of us unexpectedly and disastrously. . . . It seems to say, "Imagine for a moment that this is the last time I will see you."
>
> Who would we have to blame, then, if we never kissed good-bye? . . . I'm talking about a simple kiss (yes—on the lips) and an intimate hug after which my only thought as I strolled through the concourse would be how much I adore him, and his only thought as he boarded the plane would be how much he couldn't wait to see me again in five days.
>
> The sweetness of the departing kiss is too often snatched away from us. . . . If we are bold enough to plant one on our honey, we might know paranoia or fear. . . . A straight couple, after all, can kiss good-bye at an airport and it is seen by all (including themselves) as an expression of their love.

But if a Gay couple does so, it is seen by all (including us, it is unavoidable) as an expression of our politics, or at the very least, our subversion. After all, we are visibly undermining the status quo; we are proclaiming that we're here. . . .

HOMOPHOBIA

The term *homophobia* has come to include all negative cultural judgments of homosexuality, as well as fear and hatred of gay people, and the fear of being gay. The culture's values have been taken on by gays, too, which vastly influences their lives. Much of the work in therapy (and in life) is extricating them from these harmful, shameful beliefs about homosexuality. Gays will always have to face discrimination coming from outside themselves, although they can also take steps to reduce their exposure to these influences. This can be done by living in "gay friendly" cities (such as San Francisco and Seattle) and by living in communities with higher proportions of gays. But perhaps the most damaging form of discrimination comes from the inside. One task of therapy is helping the client discriminate between real oppression in the culture and neighborhood, and the fear that anything that goes wrong is a result of sexual orientation.

Marge and Jane (introduced in Chapter 7) lived in a community outside Seattle, and complained about the vicious treatment they received from neighbors in two different houses they had lived in. They attributed it to the neighborhood, even though this area of Greater Seattle has a sizable family-oriented gay organization. Normal neighbor activities, such as building a fence between backyards, was seen as a reaction to their sexual orientation. Of course, this is entirely possible. We worked on the differences between the felt sense of internalized oppression and actual oppression to assist the women in deciding if they should move to a neighborhood with a large percentage of gays.

SAME-GENDER THERAPISTS

Heterosexual therapists who have not had close gay friends or clients of their gender might find themselves confronting their own sexual interest in people of the same gender, particularly when they develop a close therapeutic relationship. This subject, along with any sexual feelings of the therapist, is not likely to be discussed in supervision or consultation groups (Pope et al. 1993). We all have the potential of attraction to anyone we are close to, and can make sense of it by talking about it. As with any sexual issues, consultation with colleagues can help.

A gay friend was in psychoanalysis with a married heterosexual male analyst who encouraged him to act out his compulsive masturbation while lying on the analytic couch. He was not aware this was sexual abuse until years later. A year after the analysis was terminated, the analyst contacted my friend, inviting him to have a sexual affair, revealing that he had had sex with another man and liked it. My friend knew this was over the line, and refused. We can assume this analyst did not discuss his feelings or actions with a consultation group, knowing that what he did was not acceptable analytic practice. This analyst was not able to address his own sexual issues, perhaps because of the lack of cultural and professional appreciation for the pervasive nature of sexual addiction.

HEALTHY HOMOSEXUAL SEX

In this unaccepting culture, sexual expression between men and between women is seen as deviant. In addition, many heterosexual men find thinking about, or watching, sex between women arousing. But the fact that homosexual sexual expression is just sexual expression hasn't become part of significant cultural awareness.

The heterosexual model for appropriate sex is based on intercourse. Oral stimulation and all other kinds of kissing and rubbing of bodies is seen as foreplay. A "blow job" is not having sex, it's an extra. Anal intercourse is a diversion from real intercourse. Therefore, sexual activity between people of the same gender doesn't qualify.

Therapists can work on changing their perception of the definition of "having sex" by examining the culture-based views of foreplay, the main event, and the goal of orgasm. Healthy, non-addicted sex has no goals, and can be complete without intercourse and without orgasm. When the need for intimate sexual contact with a partner has been met, the bodies may elect to have orgasms—or elect not to. When arousal naturally drops, and orgasms naturally don't occur, the experience is as satisfying as from orgasms. In addition, a sexually healthy heterosexual couple may have only intercourse in a given sexual exchange, or they may have no intercourse. The decision comes from their bodies, or their spirits, or their electromagnetic energy or Chi—the words depend on the framework used to name such events. It is not based on lust, or any other cross-wiring. Each sexual act unfolds as is right for that time. This model of healthy sex applies to people of all gender combinations.

Sexual energy is used for a number of purposes. One is to feel alive. Sexual feelings, arousal, or awareness is integrated into the rest of the awareness of life (in contrast to addiction, where arousal replaces other feelings). This is experienced in sexual activity.

A second function is to bond two people into a couple, and to re-bond them over the course of their relationship. The intensity of sexual relating allows a couple (of any gender combination) to rapidly become a family. It also makes the marriage (of any gender combination) more intense and more vital than other relationships. When children are added, parent–child bonds are also intense, but will take second place to the adults' bond. Sexual energy focused into the parental bond creates a boundary between adult sexuality and the developing sexuality of the children. This prevents incestuous relating between parents and children. The monogamous bonding of parents creates a clear, sexually boundaried environment (sexual energy is not broadcast to those who are inappropriate for sexual relating).

Homosexuals do not differ from heterosexuals in the role of sexual bonding. The differences in the gay male subculture are a result of belonging to a group that is ostracized by the dominant culture, and whose sexual expression is considered perverted. (Until the early 1970s, the *DSM* diagnosed homosexuality as a paraphilia.) The gay culture has reacted to this pathologizing of gay sex with a demonstrated acceptance of erotic relating. This shows up in the form of sexualized conversation, the inclusion of sexual references in correspondence and newsletters, and presentation of homosexual stimuli in bars, shops, and gay communities, such as the Castro district in San Francisco, and Broadway in Seattle. Under the guise of sexual freedom or sexual liberation, sexual expression can become obsessive.

Healthy gay sex includes masturbation without fantasy

or pornography, searching for an available mate, falling in love, "marrying," and discovering a commitment of sexual energy to the relationship. When gays have children, their sexual energy, when healthy, remains with each other. It does not threaten the bond by being directed toward other people.

HEALTHY OR UNHEALTHY?

The healthy or unhealthy nature of most homosexual sex cannot be entirely determined by the activity itself (as is true of most heterosexual sex). Oral or manual stimulation, and rubbing against each other can be used for arousal, and for expressing sexual energy. Anal sex and rimming (oral-anal contact) can be loving, bonding sexual expressions. (Anal sex can tax the immune system, and so care must be taken to relax the sphincter muscle, and lubricate to avoid tearing.)

These same activities, and those listed in Chapter 8, can be used addictively, and in a manner that doesn't respect each person or the bond between them. Sex between strangers is common in the gay male community, and an almost universally accepted practice. Bathhouses are created for this purpose, as are adult bookstores with holes in the walls between booths for penises to be inserted for stimulation by someone on the other side. There are parks known for gay "cruising," and bathrooms with holes between stalls. Less impersonal are gay bars where men interact with each other before going someplace to engage in sexual activity.

Most impersonal or semipersonal sexual activity is addictive. Gay men are particularly susceptible to sexual addiction, and to cross-wired sexual expression because the shaming of homosexual sex requires an even more intense effort to override the shame (see Chapter 3). As with the heterosexual culture, sexual activities that avoid shame have become part of the subculture. Some people believe that because certain activities are almost universal, they are normal or natural. As in the heterosexual culture, what is common is not necessarily healthy.

ADDICTIVE-LOOKING SEX MAY NOT BE ADDICTIVE

While park and bathhouse sex is generally a symptom of unhealthy use of sexual energy, there is an exception—men who are just coming out. This may be particularly true for men who have been married, or otherwise tried to remain in the larger culture and override their desire to be with men. Once a man admits he is gay, and sets out to discover what this means, it is natural to explore the gay world. The heterosexual parallel might be college students getting away from home and exploring the world of alcohol and sex before settling into a lifestyle that suits them. When assessing the role of alcohol, it is commonly understood that if a person drank heavily in college, but has since drunk moderately, it is probably not an indicator of alcoholism. In the same way that prior use of alcohol was not healthy but was not a sign of a more serious problem, impersonal sex can be exploration.

Ralph was in the army, married four years, and had two children when he finally realized that he couldn't live a heterosexual life. He filed for divorce when he met Ken, and the two fell in love and moved in together. However, Ralph hadn't had a chance to discover the gay world prior to coupling again, and he proceeded to do this, to Ken's despair. Ken always knew he was gay, and had explored the world of gay bars and casual sex, now finding it unsatisfying. He was ready for a committed relationship.

Ralph sought therapy to find out if he was sexually addicted, encouraged by Ken. Ralph went to gay bars and bathhouses when he was out of town. While being conscientious about safe sex, he took pleasure in showing off his body, and enjoyed being wanted and admired. When he was home, he had no interest in these activities and appreciated his life with Ken. He talked about spending time with neighbors, and how much he enjoyed cooking together. Their sexual relating was satisfying to him. But the attraction to casual sex in a group setting continued.

Ralph also talked about his struggle to deny his homosexuality throughout his early years, and how his desire for a career in the army conflicted with his sexuality. He loved his wife as a good friend. He also loved his children, and integrated them into his life with Ken on weekend visitations. Ralph had suppressed his interest in men, and it was bursting to get loose. We spent five sessions together, one with Ken. Ken was jealous and hurt, but he also understood that Ralph's activities were not about him because he had gone through the same thing years before.

I gave Ralph information about sexual addiction, and the caution that if he wasn't able to satisfy his curiosity in a year or so, he might consider that this is more than the exploration of a denied lifestyle.

This dynamic also occurs with heterosexual people who have subscribed to sexual suppression, and upon leaving home launch into exploration of casual sex, alcohol-laced sex, or a series of short-term relationships. This can look very addictive, but serves the function of breaking free from the old restrictive views. Some people go on to lead sexually addicted lives, but most gather the information they need, and find a healthier use of sexuality. A friend explained to me how this process worked for her, in contrast to her friends. She lifted the cultural repression, and through the help of therapy went on to sexual healing. She doesn't believe she could have accomplished this by just talking about sexual freedom.

ADDICTIVE SEX AMONG LESBIANS

When Laura came to me, I referred her to a chemical dependency treatment program for alcoholism. As she pursued this, we took a look at her other addiction—attraction to women not available for relationships. She had casual sex with women in her large lesbian community with whom she was not establishing a relationship. During her second session she revealed that she was going to secretly meet a woman who was in a committed relationship.

This use of her sexuality allowed several things. First, sex with unavailable women assured she didn't have to get involved. She was afraid to become involved because of a past relationship with an older woman (36 to Laura's 20) who abused her physically and emotionally. She still loved this woman, and constantly questioned if she should go back to her after a two-year separation.

The second function was feeding Laura's need to feel sexy and attractive. The sex itself was usually awkward and not fulfilling (partly because of Laura's alcohol consumption, which inhibited arousal and orgasm), but the pursuit was gratifying. At the same time, Laura complained about how women only wanted her sexually, and didn't really care about her.

Laura was terrified to give up alcohol because it allowed her to open up and be friendly, instead of feeling inhibited and shy. Alcohol was necessary to act out her sexual addiction. Becoming sober meant losing both addictions. Her entire social life consisted of alcohol-laced and flirting-laced gatherings of women. Being in a relationship was too frightening, as was being alone.

COPING WITH TRIGGERS

Jane and Marge had been in a committed relationship for eight years when Jane came to me to work on sexual abuse during her childhood and teen years. As Jane launched into this difficult work, she became frightened of having sex, which triggered Marge's fears. Marge came to therapy sessions to learn how they could love and support each other during this painful period.

Marge explained how she depended on sex to feel loved, and even though she understood why Jane wasn't willing to be sexual (Marge had gone through a similar period when addressing her own incest history), her fears weren't explained away. I asked if she could tell Jane she wouldn't leave when Jane talked about being terrified of losing Marge by not being sexual. But Marge couldn't. She said she had always gone on to be sexual with someone else when her lover stopped wanting her, and had ended relationships. She didn't want to lose Jane, but she also knew that her addiction to feeling safe and loved through sexual activity was so strong that she might act this out against her own wishes.

Over several weeks, through couples work and working with her individual therapist, Marge was able to handle the intense feelings that emerged when Jane said no to sex. We worked out a system to help. If Jane was triggered into childhood memories when Marge asked for a hug or kiss, and she couldn't explain this to Marge, then she should pick up a scarf as a signal. The scarf was a way for Jane to communicate without having to find words. It was also a shorthand communication to Marge that this wasn't her own loved-deprived history.

The women created a way to stay connected while they processed. They sat on the floor back to back (which felt safer than any other kind of touch) with the scarf over both their shoulders, each holding one end. With the scarf as a reminder of their conversations in my office, and the physical contact reassuring Marge that she wasn't being abandoned, they were usually able to slowly work through the triggering events. Marge could relinquish her solution of seeking sex with another woman.

INTIMACY OR ADDICTION—
A FRIGHTENING CHOICE

Fear of intimacy, sexual and otherwise, is a major cause of sexual addiction. When the addict gives up addictive sex, and attempts to relate sexually without avoiding intimacy, the effect can be too frightening to allow sex for a time. Seattle gay therapist, Randy Fitzgerald (1997) offered a case example that reflects this difficulty so prominent in the gay culture.

Frank and Ron came to me for couple's counseling. Their primary concern was Frank's addiction to anonymous sex in parks. While both of them were in individual therapy this was one issue that was not changing, nor even being talked about.

Frank, raised Catholic, reports feeling great shame and guilt, particularly at age six or seven when he was already identifying as a gay boy, and believed Christ died because of HIS sins. He lied about sex play with other boys at his first confession at age seven, which seems to have begun a strong split in Frank that separated his family and church life from his secret, shameful sex life. Frank came out of the closet when he quit seminary in his twenties, his park sex addiction in full swing. After a few short relationships, in his late twenties he and Ron began their 14-year relationship.

After entering individual therapy in his 30s, Frank had significant breaks from acting out when he was able to express his creativity through his work, relieving some of his stress, shame, guilt, and depression that led to looking for sex in parks.

When I saw Frank and Ron, the primary focus was learning to be honest with their feelings, and face each other as they truly were. Frank was filled with guilt and shame about his sexual addiction, feelings that had clear threads to the shaming he received as a child (frequently being called a "sissy") coupled with the sincere belief that he was damned to hell for being gay. When Frank talked about park sex guilt, it invariably led to discussing his Catholic upbringing.

Ron found enough support in our therapy sessions to be able to express his hurt and anger over the effects of Frank's sexual acting out. He also saw his own contributions to

Frank's addiction, and his pattern of relationships with men with whom he could not create a solid bond. Frank and Ron had little sex during the two years I saw them.

The bond between them was so insecure, a perpetuation of both men's inadequately bonded childhoods, that they were unable to contain in their relationship the intimacy that started to emerge as they became more fully honest. They ended the relationship, and our work.

Frank came for one session to check in about 18 months later. He was dating a man, free of acting out, and again involved in his creative work. He sounded sincerely comfortable with himself and his life. He attributed this to integrating his family/church life and his gay/sex life. He feels that therapy and ending his relationship with Ron helped accomplish this. But I believe Frank will have another step in his healing when he faces sexual intimacy in a relationship without park sex.

SIMILARITIES OF HETEROSEXUAL AND HOMOSEXUAL ISSUES

These case examples are in most ways identical to heterosexual clients. Sexual and relationship issues are very much the same. (With variation, this is also true across cultures.) After working with lesbians and gay men for many years, I find that I am hardly aware of the orientation differences when I sit with a person, working to obtain empathy and understanding of the issues, the causes of the issues, and the route to change. Most of the time I lose my awareness that this person (or couple) belongs to this other category of people. The awareness returns when the issues addressed have to do with the one difference—belonging to a group of people who are shamed, not accepted as a group, and who have to realistically decide who they can trust with information about a vital part of themselves.

HOMOSEXUAL MARRIAGE

As I write, the state of Hawaii is working toward legalizing homosexual marriage. The inability to marry has caused homosexual relationships to seem unreal—pretend, made up. Because of this devastating effect, the legalization of marriage is necessary in order to equalize the bonds of opposite- and same-gender couples. (Gay people don't have to marry in order to feel like a couple, but they must have the opportunity to marry.)

But even before marriage becomes legal, we as therapists can hold up a reflection of gay relationships as marriages. By doing this, we can reduce the culture's impact on our clients.

> My friend separated from the man he had been with for six years, and when I suggested that it was right to split their mutually acquired assets when they divorced, he went into shock. He had difficulty believing they were divorcing, because, of course, they had never married.
>
> The house they lived in was legally owned by his partner, and my friend thought it would entirely belong to the other man. But after my persistent naming of the relationship as marriage, and the separation as divorce, he found an attorney who knew that the state law views this relationship as similar to marriage in terms of ownership of combined assets. He is now seeking a share of the equity of the house.

AIDS

Male gay clients have experienced the deaths from AIDS of many friends. The grief for living a life filled with loss, fear of death, and guilt for surviving is a component of any long-term therapy. Gay sex addicts are exposing themselves to the AIDS virus, and need to be confronted, even though they already know about the threat of death. The ability to deny the consequences when in a sexual trance cannot be underestimated.

> I spent five years working with Jack, a gay man who had not come out when I met him. He wasn't sure he was gay because he had no interest in dating men, only in addictive sex with men he never saw again. He engaged in the most dangerous kind of sex, anal penetration without a condom, every two or three months. Each time we discussed the danger and ways to interrupt the acting out, but to no avail. After several sessions like this, I found myself filled with despair for him, afraid he would die from his sexual addiction, and knowing I would feel terrible grief if I had not been able to help him in time. I let the feeling surface, and told him that I didn't want him to die, how sad I would be if he caught AIDS. His face opened, and he visibly softened. He knew that one person really cared if he lived or died— something new to him. He never again exposed himself to unsafe sex, even though he continued acting out for another year or so before the compulsion abated. As he became more available for intimate relating, he discovered that his relationship interest was men, and came out to his family and friends. As dating and looking for

a relationship became part of his life, his interest in impersonal sex waned.

THERAPIST IMPACT ON GAY SHAME

If therapists reflect the culture's view of homosexual relationships as less real and more worthy of shame, they are limited in how much they can help gay people live the healthiest lives. But if they can reflect the truth—that gays differ from heterosexuals only in the gender of the partner— they can have a powerful influence in the lives of clients.

While gay therapists may often be the best choice for gay clients, the effect of being with an accepting heterosexual therapist who represents the larger culture can reduce the effect of rigid lack of acceptance. I can look at a couple like Marge and Jane and fully see them as rightfully married, creating their family, living in their home, and having sex.

WHEN TO REFER

Referring homosexual clients to homosexual therapists is sometimes most helpful. Clients may seek a heterosexual therapist when suspecting they are gay, but haven't fully admitted it to themselves, perhaps still hoping to be straight. In this case, working with the person toward acceptance can best be done by a heterosexual therapist; choosing a gay therapist can feel like admission of homosexuality. But once the client grasps that he or she is homosexual, a referral can be helpful. The client is given an opportunity to meet with a professional who has dealt with the same issues now facing the client. In addition, the gay therapist will know resources, and provide a mirror for the experience in a way that a heterosexual therapist cannot.

Sometimes a referral isn't the best choice, however. Some clients will be more comfortable working with an accepting person in the broader culture as a bridge between the two worlds.

Jack worked with me for over a year before he could acknowledge that he was gay. At this time I suggested that he join a group of gay men who were also coming out, and to this end I gave him the name of three gay therapists. He went to one session with each, and discovered that he was afraid they would be sexual with him. As a result, he continued his work with me, attending my men's group of heterosexual men. For Jack this was the best choice because it gave him a chance to work on his fear that all gay men wanted sex, and on how to set limits with the ones who did, before he launched out into the gay world.

Jennifer, 20 years old, was sent to me by her mother, who wanted me to make her heterosexual in spite of my telling her that it was not a likely outcome. I wanted to refer Jennifer to a lesbian therapist I consulted, but Jennifer's mother wouldn't pay for that therapy, which was otherwise unaffordable. In addition, Jennifer herself was not ready to see herself as belonging to a lesbian community. She associated only with straight friends, and didn't have sex even though she knew she was lesbian. I appreciated the terror she experienced at the thought of being homosexual. It demonstrated how the job of heterosexual therapists is to help homosexual clients discover the truth, and support them through the steps of revealing it.

When a client has developed a good relationship with a straight therapist, it can be helpful to also see a gay or lesbian therapist when they come out in order to work specifically on resulting issues. This allows the client to admit they are gay without being forced to lose the heterosexual therapist with whom they are working well. Jack was able to fully come out to friends, co-workers, and family while working with me and my men's group. Once he was ready, he quickly gathered information about how to access the gay culture.

READING ABOUT HOMOSEXUALITY

Heterosexual therapists can broaden their understanding of what it is like to be gay by reading books, as well as hearing client stories and having gay friends. I have found that reading novels with gay and straight characters can be a useful way to spend many hours "living" with people who are not like me in order to normalize a different kind of life. The series of six books by Armistead Maupin called *The Tales of the City* are a wonderful way to live in San Francisco for a while. The first book takes place in the late 1970s, before the AIDS epidemic, and the remaining books take the reader through more than a decade in a community of gay male, lesbian, and straight characters. Maupin is a delightful writer, bringing us humor and intrigue while letting us visit a community of integrated sexual orientations.

Stephen McCauley, author of *The Easy Way Out* and *The Object of My Affections*, also invites the reader into the lives of gay men and their relationships with the heterosexual culture. His third book, *The Man of the House* (1996) portrays the life of a sexually addicted gay man (without calling it addiction) struggling with his fear of intimacy and his inability to create a life with meaning. In one scene Clyde, the main character, describes having casual sex occasionally with a man he sees in no other context. Clyde and the man both look like each other's lover. Both find it easier to have sex with a stranger than with a chosen partner, while at the same time wanting to have sex with the partner. The tragedy of this situation is reflected by the emptiness Clyde feels when he leaves the man's house. McCauley puts the reader in touch with the sex addict's desperate desire for intimacy, as the other man wishes for Clyde to leave immediately once they are finished with sex.

12

Affairs

When a married person has sex with another person, our culture's stated value is that he or she is violating the marriage. Affairs are far more complicated than this picture. This chapter discusses the reasons affairs happen and the issue of telling or not telling the partner.

SEXUAL ADDICTION

Sex outside the marriage is one form sexual addiction takes. Some people have sex with a new person only once, while others develop lasting affairs to meet addictive sexual needs.

Terrie sought therapy because her husband, Peter, had swept her off her feet ten years before, but was now, in

Affairs

When a married person has sex with another person, our culture's stated value is that he or she is violating the marriage. Affairs are far more complicated than this picture. This chapter discusses the reasons affairs happen and the issue of telling or not telling the partner.

SEXUAL ADDICTION

Sex outside the marriage is one form sexual addiction takes. Some people have sex with a new person only once, while others develop lasting affairs to meet addictive sexual needs.

> Terrie sought therapy because her husband, Peter, had swept her off her feet ten years before, but was now, in

his fifties, having sex with a number of women in their early twenties. He ignored Terrie once she lost her ability to serve as a drug, and turned instead to new women he could sweep off their feet by being interested in their lives, adoring them, and giving expensive gifts. Terrie described how Peter spent hours on the phone with them, asking how they were, and taking care of things for them. At one point he left Terrie for a 24-year-old, but returned when he feared really losing Terrie—and when the new "drug" began to lose its effect.

Rob was married three times, and had affairs throughout. He was as addicted to the process of seduction as to the actual sex. Once when single, he had seduced a woman into spending the night with him, left her in the morning to go to work, and seduced a woman at the office into going home with him at noon for sex. He pulled up to his house to see the car of the woman from the night before in front of the car of the woman from the office. He drove away, shocked at what he had created. He came to me years later when his third wife had reached her limit, and was ready to leave if he didn't change. He entered therapy, but she left anyway. She had experienced too much pain to tolerate supporting him in a healing process. Soon after, he left therapy.

Barry, discussed in Chapter 9, didn't have sex with other women once he started his relationship with Roberta, but he still had affairs. By flirting and creating "special" relationships, he set up triangles with Roberta, himself, and the other woman. Some of Roberta's rage came from the fact that it went on right in front of her. Barry believed that flirting was innocent. Roberta felt crazy for being jealous when he swore to her that he wasn't having sex with anyone. The final straw occurred when Barry received a letter from one of his "friends" that had a sexualized note on the envelope. Roberta broke off the relationship until he sought therapy and entered recovery for sexual addiction. As we explored, we discovered that flirting was only one form of addictive acting out. He also had a collection of secret pornography that he used to masturbate regularly, sometimes injuring his penis from extensive and frequent stimulation.

Because flirtation can be difficult to define, Barry spent months examining his relationships with women. He explained to the women his need to heal from flirting, but they didn't easily give up *their* drug. He had been an excellent source. Some continued to contact him, and occasionally he played their voice mail messages to me for my impression of their sexualized language and tone. This gave him an objective verification of the sexually addictive nature of his relationships with them.

TELLING THE CO-ADDICT

Sex addicts who wish to recover learn right away that they have to tell their partner everything. If they keep secrets, it will be difficult to stop acting out. And, to create an intimate and healing relationship, it is necessary for both partners to be clear with each other about themselves and their lives. This kind of disclosure is best done in the therapist's office so the therapist can help the couple stay with their feelings instead of launching into blame, defensiveness, and argument. In addition, if the addict has difficulty remembering what he or she needs to tell, the presence of the therapist can help him or her understand what is needed.

> Barry confirmed Roberta's observations, but had difficulty telling her details about the women involved, or about addictive masturbation. Her therapist and I did a delicate balancing act of encouraging him to reveal while at the same time supporting him in setting limits about being vulnerable in the face of her attack. We identified the difference between honesty and revealing information. Often Barry told Roberta that he wasn't willing to reveal any more information at this time because he had only begun to look at it himself, and felt too vulnerable sharing it. He also said that in time he would reveal everything. This angered Roberta, but allowed Barry to create safety to continue his explorations with me, while at the same time not having to keep secrets from Roberta.

PREPARING THE CO-ADDICT

There is no standard way that information about addiction should be shared with the partner. Each case has to be evaluated and approached individually. Ideally, both partners have a therapist, or, when workable, have the same therapist who can see them as a couple and individually.

The concept of sexual addiction can be introduced gradually so the co-addict has a chance to absorb the concepts. This can provide a context for understanding affairs that might allow the partner to tolerate the information while the addict is engaged in healing from the compulsion. I have many times finessed the honoring of the partner's jealousy and rage, while at the same time honoring the out of control, compulsive nature of the addict's behaviors. Sometimes I think I must look like a crazy person to couples when I support a wife being angry with her husband, while at the same time having compassion and understanding for his behaviors.

> JJ called to ask if her husband was sexually addicted to a sadistic prostitute he visited regularly. I told her it was very possible, and I would be glad to see them. I didn't hear from her for several months, until Jerome was finally willing to come. Since they had both been in therapy, they didn't think I was crazy when I told her I perfectly understood her rage at her husband for sharing his sexual energy with someone else—and at the same time I told him I would like to hear all about what happened with the dominatrix, knowing his choice of sexual activity had significance.

Many couples are not able to understand that two sets of seemingly incompatible feelings are legitimate focuses of therapy. Often one or both will find this unworkable and decide to leave therapy. Other couples may take weeks or months to understand how sexual addiction healing works. It is during this tumultuous time that working with two individual therapists can often best support the couple. A colleague and I have seen couples in this manner, bringing them together when their anger and fear is sufficiently diminished. One or both partners can feel hate toward the other therapist as well as the partner—a situation not workable if they share the same therapist.

CREATING A CONTEXT

Preparing a context to confront the symptom of having affairs can help the secrets be received in a supportive way. One part of the context is the couple's presence in the therapist's office. If a person reveals to the spouse at home that he or she has been having affairs, the only reactions the spouse can have to this information are culturally determined. These include hopelessness, rage from betrayal, leaving the relationship, forgiving, making the partner pay, or having an affair to even the score.

Without help, couples don't have recourse to understand the affair, and to take steps to heal themselves and the relationship. When the disclosure is made in front of a therapist, the context for a different way to approach this situation already exists. It is possible for a disclosure to be made at home, if the addict explains that the affair is the focus of therapy. This can also indicate the possibility of a different resolution.

Context can also be created by telling the partner ahead of time that a secret will be revealed in a therapy session, and that it will be done there in order for both partners to have help.

A third way to create context can come from asking the partner to read about sexual addiction to see that affairs are something that can be recovered from. This education could convey hope that the relationship can become better than before, rather than contaminated by infidelity followed by apology and the promise to never do it again.

CONFESSING IS NOT THE SAME
AS REVEALING

Telling should not be confused with *confessing*. Sometimes spouses will feel so much guilt they tell to relieve themselves of it. This function invites the partner to forgive—withholding his or her reactions while removing the addict's guilt. When a partner tells about an affair it should be for the purpose of bringing the relationship into some kind of integrity. By having everything on the table, they have a chance to discover where to go from there. It is impossible to make good decisions without all the information. The truth makes more sense than suspicions and denials, which make the partner feel crazy.

A classic pattern among sex addicts is having an affair, followed by shame and remorse, followed by confessing and pleading for forgiveness. When the partner forgives, the shame goes away. (Therapy often begins when the partner can no longer tolerate their pattern.) If the shame is taken away through confession, then a foundation for sexual healing cannot be created. Instead, the partner needs to have his or her feelings of jealousy and anger, contributing this information to the truth of their lives. When the addict can take responsibility for the behaviors and the need to change, and when the partner can take responsibility for expressing natural feelings, then the groundwork is laid for healing the relationship—and the addiction.

HAVING AFFAIRS TO STAY MARRIED

People who find their marriages dreadful—sexually and in other ways—but feel they cannot divorce may choose to have sex with someone else, often in a long-term affair, to make their home life seem tolerable. Among the reasons for not divorcing are staying with the children, fear that a better marriage isn't possible, family pressure, and potential financial or business losses. The loss of self-esteem that results from criticism and other negativity in the marriage can seem to be offset by an affair with a person who "cares." This arrangement can continue until one or both partners cannot take it any longer, and seek help.

> Paul (discussed in Chapters 1 and 3) wanted to stay married to Alecia. He was unable to have sex with her because the cross-wired stimulus of "badness" needed for arousal could not exist in the marriage bed. Yet he loved her, and didn't want to leave. His solution was a series of affairs in order to have a sex life, to feel like a man, and to maintain some sense of self-esteem that slipped from his inability to make love with Alecia, and from Alecia's complaints about it.

When this situation is brought to therapy, the therapist is challenged to help the couple address their relationship and heal it, if possible.

TELLING THE PARTNER ABOUT THE AFFAIR

If the affair is not known to the spouse, the partner having the affair should be counseled to reveal it. This information can cause a crisis that could bring about change. Secrecy allows an untenable marriage contract to continue. The exception is a legitimate fear that the partner is likely to inflict physical pain, steal the children, or commit other acts

that could be too detrimental. In this case, the other partner
might be counseled to leave the relationship for safety
reasons.

> Paul had been unable to tell Alecia about his affairs
> because he thought there was no alternative. If he gave
> up affairs (or prostitutes) he would have had no sex life.
> After they had been married for two years, Alecia
> discovered Paul's affair with her best friend. She con-
> fronted him and gave up her friendship. He swore he
> wouldn't do it again, and tried to make it up to her. But
> there was no recourse for Paul to heal so he would be
> able to have a sexual relationship with his wife. He
> continued to have sex with other women.

> If Paul had been able to find a therapist to help him
> with his sexual issues, he could have told Alecia what was
> going on, assuring her that he wanted to give up that course.
> He could tell her that he had to address the reduced
> self-esteem and the self-criticism he would face if he had no
> sex life.

THERAPISTS CANNOT CARRY THE SECRET

Occasionally when a couple is in therapy, one partner will
tell the therapist in confidence that he or she is having an
affair, creating a difficult situation for the therapist, who
cannot hold this secret and expect to function therapeuti-
cally with the other partner. It can be explained to the one
having the affair why the secret cannot be kept, followed by
discussion of what will happen next. (This situation is different from the usual practice of not disclosing to one spouse

what goes on in the other spouse's individual sessions—
which is a matter of therapy boundaries.)

> I worked briefly with a woman referred to me by her
> husband's therapist. The therapist told me the husband
> was having an affair, but the therapist did not believe in
> confronting him with the need to tell his mate. I spent
> several miserable sessions with the wife, unable to
> address his affair because of confidentiality require-
> ments, listening to her berate herself for thinking he
> was unfaithful when she knew he wasn't. I saw the effect
> on my client of intuitively knowing something was going
> on, while being told it wasn't.

The person revealing an affair creates a triangle with
the therapist and spouse, placing the spouse on the outside.
The possibility that this reflects a childhood family pattern
can be explored.

I usually find that when one spouse tells me a secret, he
or she is preparing to tell the spouse, but needs to tell it first
to an accepting person. In this case, the therapist can
support the person through the process of telling, and
support the one who is hearing.

A DELAYED FORM OF GROWING UP

When a person stays in his or her first relationship, perhaps
entered in the teens, a period of exploring partners and
sexual activity has not been experienced. After many years of
monogamy, such a person may want to explore sex with
other people to fill in this information gap. This may occur
in the context of a mid-life crisis, or other major shift in the

normal routine of life. If this is the only function of sex with others, it will pass, and life with the partner will adjust to a different routine. This dynamic is particularly true for homosexuals who have been "in the closet" and who first encounter sex with others of the same gender. A period of obsession with sex, and trying new partners can be a natural reaction to withholding that part of the self (see Chapter 11).

The question of telling arises. While magazine articles and some sex therapists (e.g., Dr. Ruth), and common sense suggest not telling, keeping such a secret will prevent a couple from developing deep intimacy and trust. If a couple is satisfied with a superficial relationship, keeping the secret won't differ from the rest of their lifestyle. But couples who want to use therapy to obtain a more satisfying, rich life will have to be willing to risk revealing their secrets. This kind of life means learning to respect the other's revealed secrets— while at the same time, having intense feelings about something as important as an affair.

BREAKING FREE OF ENMESHMENT

In differentiating between affairs that are addictive and affairs that are an attempt to solve a problem, it is possible that the spouse is trying to dilute a highly enmeshed relationship. When a couple's dynamics hold them deeply entrenched in ways that torture each other, or inhibit their lives outside the relationship, one partner's affair can pull them apart and create room to breathe. The one with the affair splits his or her attention between two relationships, which can decrease need, criticism, and other inhibiting dynamics. These kinds of affairs may quickly run their course if the new relationship also becomes enmeshed. However, this dynamic is also present in some situations where a man will have a wife at home and keep a mistress (socially acceptable in some countries).

BEGINNING THE END OF A RELATIONSHIP

A common reason for beginning a sexual relationship is taking a step toward ending the current one. People come to therapy to "give the relationship one more chance," and then realize that it is over. People who are too frightened to be out of a relationship will begin a new one before ending the old. Falling in love with someone new can also alert the person having the affair that he or she is no longer in love with the mate, and that it is time to leave. This isn't easy to see as long as there is no overt reason to split up—if there is no fighting or conflict. When a sexual energy bond dies, it is natural to want to express and receive sexual energy from others. Ideally this would begin long after ending the old relationship, but for those who are not sufficiently aware to realize what is happening, or too dependent to take the risk, new relationships can make it happen.

PASSIVE-AGGRESSIVE ANGER TOWARD THE PARTNER

Most affairs are not expressions of anger toward the partner, even though most partners believe it is because of the intense pain that is caused. But sometimes an affair, or flirting, is designed to make the partner jealous, to get him or her to be less abandoning, or merely to express anger not otherwise expressed in constructive ways.

LACK OF MONOGAMOUS BONDING

Leland, who was bisexual, married Frances in the early 1950s in order to lead a socially acceptable lifestyle. But he didn't bond with her in a sexual energy–bonded monogamy, and later realized that he would have preferred partnering with a man. The 1950s were a time when leading a homosexual lifestyle, or even not marrying, would have interfered with his developing career.

Frances liked this arrangement because she had been afraid of sex, and his indifference made her comfortable pursuing him. She was dependent on him as a husband, but neither of them felt a loving connection. When Leland had casual sex or ongoing affairs with other men, he didn't feel unfaithful because he "never looked at another woman." When she learned of his decades of affairs, she was shocked. He didn't understand why she had a problem with it since they had never really been "in love."

There is truth to his assumption that he wasn't violating their relationship because they didn't have a monogamous bond. But of course the nature of their relationship wasn't spelled out, and she was able to believe they had what other married people had—an assumption of love and monogamy.

They had been married forty years when Frances learned the truth. Almost 70, she couldn't see any reason to divorce Leland, even though she moved to her own bedroom and took off her wedding ring.

Another example was the relationship between Prince Charles and Princess Diana. Charles was in love with a woman he wasn't allowed to marry, and was required to marry an appropriate virgin and have children. He married a stranger with a hymen, not a woman with whom he could monogamously bond. This kind of arrangement would make it difficult to forgo an already established bond. This common situation among royalty and wealthy families in history didn't use to end in divorce.

COPING WITH JEALOUSY

When a person has sex with someone else, the partner understandably feels intense jealousy when learning about it. One way to cope with this jealousy is to "even the score" with an affair. The healthier response is to feel the jealousy, and the grief it engenders.

LOSING INTEREST WHEN A WOMAN AGES

A sad outcome of cultural cross-wiring to lust after women of certain ages, body shapes, and skin texture has made it difficult for many men to want to have sex with their mates when they age. If her looks are necessary to become aroused, he will find his wife less appealing as the years go on. Sex therapists propose ways to adapt to this cultural outcome. One is for the woman to exercise and wear provocative clothing. Kaplan (1974) suggests that her male client fantasize about his wife when she was younger—supposedly not violating her by imagining someone else. But if he is fantasizing he isn't really with her. He is not offered the hope of changing his perceptions of sex so he can look at his wife and feel sexual.

Some of these men will have affairs with younger women so they can believe they are still men, and still able to perform. Others will divorce their wives and marry a younger woman. (There are other reasons, of course, including marrying a younger second wife because our culture views men as successful if they can attract a younger woman.) A tragic reason is a growing repulsion for a woman who is developing wrinkles, gaining weight, and changing shape.

Such men can have a revulsion for women's bodies even during their teens, but the cross-wiring of lust for breasts and body shapes can override this repulsion. Once the woman doesn't look anything like the lust object, his problems begin.

If a man is willing to admit to this problem, he can be helped with it. Questions about what turns him off, and the nature of his negative feelings, can get him started. Once he has accessed the feelings, and has decreased his shame by telling an accepting listener, he can be asked about the memory of this feeling when growing up. This can open the door to discovering how he might have had contact with women's bodies where he felt constrained, or used for comfort, or used for sexual bonding or sexual arousal. This revulsion is a common result of sexual abuse and emotional incest during childhood. As he is able to feel the disgust with an accepting and encouraging listener, he can gradually shed this reaction. Optimally he will be increasingly able to love his wife in the body she is in rather than having to find the right stimulus. Healthy sexuality is based on the loving energy flowing between the partners, not on body shapes and sizes. When couples in good health have discovered this energy, they are able to love each other sexually throughout their lives.

Men clients have expressed concern about discussing their aversion to women's bodies, including fat and wrinkles, because they fear they will offend me. While I am not entirely comfortable with my fat and wrinkles, I am no longer offended when I am not found sexually attractive. I let my clients know that I welcome hearing about their reactions and that I won't take them personally.

All therapists must work through their own feelings about inadequate bodies in order not to be offended by this kind of dialogue, particularly when the expression of distaste is directed toward the therapist's body. When the therapist is comfortable with these reactions, it can be helpful to educate the client about this ability to hear negative feelings expressed directly toward her (or him). Even then I find that men have difficulty. They have been taught how important it is to women to be considered sexually attractive. Therapists who haven't yet reached a point of acceptance of their own bodies must not pretend they have. The client will perceive it at least unconsciously. It can be powerful to reveal that the therapist is uncomfortable with her body, but wants to hear the client's feelings anyway.

AFFAIRS WITH MARRIED PEOPLE

When Margaret began therapy she had chosen to have sexual relationships only with married men. She didn't want the complexity of a real relationship that might lead to marriage. She saw this as a simple way to have sex, be loved, and go about her own life. Margaret lived in Anchorage, and worked alternate weeks on the

North Slope in the oil field office making a lot of money and holding a good deal of responsibility. The problem she faced was that eventually the men either wanted to leave their wives for her, or they moved on to a new lover. She tired of constantly falling in love and breaking up. She brought her current married lover to a therapy session to discuss his desire to marry her. They broke up instead. She returned to see me a couple of years later, after marrying a single man, to begin the hard work of learning how to combine her life with someone else's, and deal with her criticism of him. She now had to face her tendency to enmesh and control, which she had avoided.

THE PAIN OF AFFAIRS

Learning that one's partner has had sex with someone else is extremely painful. If such a client doesn't express distress, this is a symptom to examine. Humans are monogamously bonding creatures, and threat to monogamy is excruciating even if not threatened by actual loss of the partner. Jealousy and rage need to be given expression as valid feelings— although possibly contaminated by many other angers from the present and past. A therapist's office is a place where jealousy can be honored, while at the same time the one who had the affair can be supported. It is perhaps the most volatile couples' issue.

13

Paths to Sexual Healing

If we look at sexual healing as more than recovery from sexual abuse, and more than relieving sexual dysfunctions, and more than healing from sexual addiction—as well as more than the sum of these three areas of practice—then we need an alternative model for overall sexual healing. Healing sexuality from cultural and personal influences is a lifelong task, not to be completed in a few therapy sessions. Therapy can help people embark on this path, and the principles learned can be used throughout a lifetime. The process itself is intimate, allowing couples great closeness while they heal their sexuality together.

Some clients want to take on this intensive process. Those who do are often in recovery from sexual abuse and can no longer tolerate anything abusive in adult sexual relationships. Their sensitivity about unhealthy sex is heightened by past experiences, and from the process of examining them. Some sexual addicts are also able to examine shameful practices in order to throw out old views of sex, making room for the new. (But even clients who cannot embark on this healing can be greatly helped by open discussion of cultural and other factors that inhibit their sexuality.)

EQUALITY BETWEEN THE SEXES

The lack of equality between men and women (addressed by the women's movement) has prevented our culture from discovering the true nature of healthy sexuality. As long as one gender is considered inferior, or the property of the other gender, and is controlled emotionally, economically, or physically, sexuality cannot emerge equally for both partners in a couple. Couples who have not established decision-making equality may be able to improve sex, but cannot entirely heal it. If a couple comes for help with sexual issues, the dominance of one person will also have to be addressed.

The cultural movement toward equality for women encouraged women to begin telling about sexual abuse, which has initiated sexual healing.

SAYING NO TO SEX

People are prevented from saying no to sex for culturally imposed reasons. If a person cannot say no to sex every single time it doesn't feel right to be sexual, then saying yes isn't really an affirmative. It is contaminated with beliefs, such as sex has to be part of a relationship, real men and women must be sexual, or one will suffer without sex. One of the therapist's jobs is to help explore and remove the obstacles to taking full control of one's own body. These obstacles include fear that the partner will find someone else, and saying yes to avoid arguments.

Sexual healing cannot get under way until one or both partners refuse to engage in sexual activity if it doesn't feel right, which can result in weeks, months, or years of no sex.

In the beginning it can be difficult for clients to ascertain when it is right to say no. Clients can explore and assess how it feels to say yes and to say no. For example, one client watched her husband suffer for a week when she said no to sex, and finally, out of compassion, she agreed. She felt in control of the decision, and her choice came from caring, not from the obligation that had previously dominated her assent. She felt empowered by this decision, and enjoyed feeling as if she were truly in control of her sexuality. Only in later examination did she discover that using sex to take care of someone else didn't feel right. She saw how she was in the caretaker role instead of joining equally with her husband. In addition, she saw that she supported the idea that he had a "need" that she met. From this additional understanding, she decided not to have sex like that. But the new understanding didn't negate the power of this experience. At that time it was a good choice, and it allowed her to learn more about sex—something she might not have learned without the experience.

Jake and Janet (from Chapter 6) found themselves having sex when engaged in their sexual addiction. Jake was afraid to go without sex for long, and Janet wanted reassurance that Jake still loved her. They examined how sex felt before, during, and after as they educated themselves about when they should be saying no. Over time their education grew, and the amount of healthy sex did, too.

Years ago when I first realized that being able to say no to sex was necessary to begin sexual healing, I immediately assumed that people who had been having sex out of obligation would be happy to hear an "expert" say they could stop. When I made this suggestion, I received a rapid education about just how strong the cultural influence is. The list of reasons why an individual cannot say no grew. After hours of arguing, I gave up, realizing that a better focus was exploring the consequences of having sex when not wanting to. This allows increasing consciousness of the price being paid.

Culturally we believe that people who want to say no to sex are pressured by partners, and/or they are "frigid." They are usually thought to be women with male partners who, just because they are male, want sex. Responding to this belief, I offered a workshop on saying no to sex. Luckily I conversed with the people who attended before launching into my presentation because not one of them came to learn how to say no to a partner. They came to learn how to say no to themselves! Workshop members talked about how they got into sexual situations. I heard about how men felt compelled to think about sex when working with construction crews, and when they wanted to avoid fear and disgust that came from being in dangerous and dirty places. Women talked about having sex to fit in with a promiscuous social circle, and how they hoped sexual attention would allow them to feel good about themselves. Gays talked about how being gay automatically means being sexual. The common expression that if you have to be an addict, its great to be a sex addict, frustrates and saddens sex addicts who want to be able to say no to sexual opportunity.

Any time a person says yes to sex when experiencing negatives about the decision, it is harmful. Defenses will be strengthened against opening to sex in the future. The body is violated. The partner is violated by being cast into the role of rapist or perpetrator, even if he or she isn't conscious of it. Nothing but unhealthy functions of sex are served by having sex when it isn't right.

DISOBEYING CULTURAL RULES ABOUT SEX

Many cultural views are unhealthy, and so they have to be relinquished. These rules include: sex is owed to a mate, sex affirms being a man or a woman, sex assures the mate's love, having sex is a valid tranquilizer, having sex is necessary in order to meet a sexual "need," the person's only value is sexual, sex starts with kissing, sex ends with the man's orgasm, good lovers focus on the partner's needs, sex is a skill that results in "good" lovers and "bad" lovers, the loss of erection is automatically a problem, when a woman loses her arousal her partner isn't a good lover, men are responsible for women's orgasms.

REPLACING HAVING SEX WITH LEARNING ABOUT SEX

The rules mentioned above interfere with discovering healthy sexual energy. The alternative is to see each "sexual" encounter as a learning environment, a starting again of healthy adolescent explorations (Hastings 1993). Each social rule and personal belief is named, then observed, and the feelings that come with relinquishing it are expressed. Gradually, with practice, the sense of obligation to obey the rule subsides, becoming only a thought with no feeling enforcing it, and, finally, no thought.

DEVELOPING COMPASSION FOR THE SEXUAL SELF

Shame inhibits sexual healing. Compassion is the antidote to shame. Sexual healing leads to compassion, and compassion yields further sexual healing. The therapist can model compassion, and in therapy groups addressing sexual issues each member feels compassion for the others.

LEARNING TO TALK OPENLY ABOUT SEX

Ironically, sex is a subject that is talked about at length, and at the same time, is only rarely openly and comfortably addressed. While the last three decades have seen a great change in the overt acceptance of sexuality, it remains difficult for almost all people to talk with a therapist or therapy group without shame arising. Talking about sex in jokes, or sexualized camaraderie, is socially acceptable, especially while drinking alcohol, but this conversation won't remove shame from sexuality. It will open the door to the shame compartment, where the experience of shame can be avoided, not removed.

Therapy can help people learn how to talk about sex.

The therapist can help the client identify whom to talk with, and where boundaries are needed for protection. Some clients criticize themselves for not being able to talk easily with anyone when in truth they may be experiencing a valid need for self-protection.

Leading therapy groups with a focus on sexuality has demonstrated just how difficult it is to talk about. Even groups meeting for over a year experience fresh, new shame when the subject of sexual activity comes up again. When I interviewed five women (from a women's group that had met for three years) who had had sexual feelings toward their children, but who had not been sexual with them, the amount of shame was startling. These women knew each other well, and had developed trust from working together on their sexuality. But even this supportive environment could not assuage much of the shame they felt. To do this in a group of people without such trust is not good for the client. He or she needs clear boundaries and time to test the waters with any person or group.

I have taught many workshops on healthy sexuality, and they range from open and revealing to closed off and with little conversation. People eagerly pour out thoughts and experiences with others who are experienced as safe, but when one or more members demonstrate hostility, intense fear, or boundary crossing, the group becomes silent or argumentative.

EXPLORING THE HISTORY OF CROSS-WIRING

When a client has been sexually abused the abuse can become the focus of therapy while present sexual functioning might be put on the back burner. The client can be told that it is normal to lose interest in sex, and be encouraged to set limits. Sometimes healing the sexual abuse comes before learning about the healing of sexuality. Other clients embark on both at the same time, or alternate between them. Therapy must address the addictive use of sexual energy, the healing of abuses of sexuality, and healthy sexual functioning.

PREPARING THE BODY

Growing up in unhealthy cultures and unhealthy families produces bodies that guard against assault, both physical and emotional. With posture thrown off, and compensations created to allow normal uses of the body, our natural energy—sexual and otherwise—cannot move easily through us. This creates tension and exhaustion. To allow sexual energy to flow easily, and produce intense arousal from gentle stimulation, most bodies will need help. This help can be found in a number of forms. Acupuncture directly works on the energy channels. Qigong allows each person to learn how to move the energy, thus opening the body to increased flow. Rolfing loosens the tightened fascia, which holds the negative changes in place, allowing the body to take the shape it was originally designed for. Energy work, such as Reiki, can be helpful, as can massage that stimulates the energy points, such as Shiatsu. Feldenkrais practitioners offer inexpensive classes called "Awareness Through Movement." I personally accessed heightened sexual energy flow after about twenty Rolfing sessions, and thirty acupuncture sessions over a period of three or four years during which I was involved in sexual healing.

Part IV

Addressing Sexuality in Therapy

14

Why Clients Don't Talk with Therapists about Sex

Many clients can't express difficulties with sex, or even recognize they are troubled by sexuality, unless their issues fit into one of the three categories—abuse, dysfunction, and addiction. Few people ask their friends about sexual problems. Cultural shame prevents people from knowing what to say even when they know there is a problem.

THE DEPTH OF SEXUAL SHAME

In this culture, where sex is constantly presented through television, movies, and magazines, we tend to believe we no longer have issues about sex. In my writing I frequently think

I'm addressing something that no longer exists. Yet I conduct therapy groups where intense shame is provoked by the subject of overt sexual activity. Even I can feel shame when talking about overt sexual activities after more than a decade in sexual recovery and a psychological practice specializing in this area. It is pervasive and deep, and not to be underestimated as an inhibitor to sexual recovery.

We are prohibited from talking about sex unless it is in the form of joking, with a lover, indirect, or bragging—or in a way that our shame becomes congruent with who we are. When talking openly about sexuality, shame comes up and is felt or defended against. The therapist's manner increases or decreases shame, allowing most clients their first opportunity to talk about this vital facet of humanness.

HELPING THE CLIENT EXPLORE SEXUALITY

Regardless of the reason a person goes to therapy, almost everyone has sexual issues. Because of this, anyone who has sought more than symptom-focused therapy needs to be asked how sex is for them. While this may not materialize into further discussion, it communicates that the therapist is interested and willing to listen.

> Jan, married over ten years to Alan, told people their sex life was good. He was a sensitive lover, made sure she had orgasms, and thought she was sexually attractive. He ejaculated soon after beginning intercourse, but prior to intercourse he brought her to orgasm orally. She knew he enjoyed doing this. So Jan couldn't understand why she found sex with Alan repulsive. During years of psychoanalysis she never revealed her

feelings about sex. Finally, when Jan divorced Alan and fell in love again, she was able to discover that their sex had not been loving, but was an addiction for Alan. He needed sex on a regular basis in order to feel safe, and Jan provided that without ever being able to say she was doing so. She grew to hate sex without understanding that she was angry about the "contract."

By the time Jan reached my office to work on surfacing memories of childhood sexual abuse, she had come to understand all of this on her own. If her therapist had been able to ask her questions, and educate her about typical dynamics in sexual relationships, she might have been able to understand before divorcing Alan. The conversation could have gone like this:

Therapist: What is your sexual relationship like?
Jan: Oh, it's good, Alan's a good lover.
T: No problem there?
J: No . . . well, not with the sex, anyway.
T: With something else?
J: I don't know why I don't like to have sex with Alan when he's so tender and loving, just what I always thought I wanted. . . . I think something's wrong with me.
T: Not wanting sex with a partner can be caused by a number of things. One is abused sexuality from childhood—we could take a look at that. But another is the meaning of sex to the partner.
J: Really?
T: Yes. When the partner is sexually addictive, or emotionally absent, or needs certain things for arousal, it can be a turnoff. And should be a turnoff.

This conversation educates the client about dynamics not visible in our culture, and opens the door for questions that could demonstrate what's going on so she can take some steps. Recovering incest survivors are learning that it is harmful to be with a partner who isn't emotionally present, discovering that it feels better to not have sex than reenact that component of the abuse. It is only gradually becoming understood that none of us is emotionally served by having sex only for the sake of pleasurable sexual feelings.

If the therapy had gone like this, Jan might have told Alan what she was learning, allowing him to take a look at what sex meant for him. She would have permission to say no to sex without having to explain, thus throwing chaos into the marriage. Alan may or may not have been able to join her in the exploration of their sexuality, but she would have been able to identify one of the unhealthy aspects of the marriage.

THERAPIST LACK OF KNOWLEDGE

Many clients have told me about therapy experiences in which they couldn't address sexual issues. I have repeatedly asked why, what about that therapist made it difficult. No one has been able to explain it, instead expressing general discomfort with the idea. I think this reflects an intuitive knowing that the therapist didn't understand sexuality and would have been unable to understand the client. I was one of those therapists prior to undertaking my own sexual healing. A number of men were able to reveal that they went to adult bookstores and put their penises through a hole in a video booth to be brought to orgasm. With no understanding of sexual addiction, I didn't know what to do with this information. These men left therapy without being able to address an issue that brought them shame and interfered with their life. They might have felt even more shame by telling it to a therapist who just nodded, expressionless.

SYMPTOMS OF SEXUAL SECRETS

I have observed that when a person seems distant and not very real, or confused, or shy, or the eyes appear opaque, he or she may be hiding sexual secrets that prevent intimacy. The secret can be sexual addiction, or it can be shame about the stimulus needed for arousal. (The secrets may be about areas other than sex, of course. Or these symptoms may not indicate secrets at all.) As long as shameful activities remain hidden, a person cannot afford to be fully seen by the therapist. When I have sat with a client for a few weeks without getting a sense of the person, I will begin asking questions about sexual activities. I couch these questions within a good deal of education about the fact that we live in a culture that shames sexuality, and everyone has secrets, and how telling secrets in a safe environment can reduce shame attached to the behaviors or thoughts. I also point out the distance between us, and describe how keeping secrets can create it, in order to educate him or her about how this works. It is possible, of course, that the distance has nothing to do with sexual secrets, and clients will reveal this. In other cases, it is secrets, but the client isn't able to reveal them yet.

> Bob (discussed in Chapters 1 and 8) came to me because he was depressed, and knew it had something to do with his sex life. We spent two sessions talking about the low frequency of sex with his wife. I wove

questions about his sexual history around this discussion, but was left with the impression that I didn't yet know what we were to work on. In fact, I was so unsure of the real issue, I knew there was more he hadn't revealed. I didn't confront Bob with this information in the manner I described above. I could see that shame and fear were holding him back, and the best role I could play was discussing sex in a way that let him see that I didn't feel shaming about sex, and that I wasn't going to shame him. The therapeutic effect came from sitting with a therapist who would listen and not judge. This can take many sessions. Sometimes the client himself doesn't understand why he is there until he intuitively knows that he won't be shamed for what he does or thinks.

At the beginning of the third session Bob told me that he was highly aroused by wearing women's underwear. He had lived with tremendous shame since it began just before puberty. From a book he had grasped the idea that childhood experiences can influence the form of what arouses us in adulthood, and had begun looking at his childhood in order to find the cause. Knowing there was a cause reduced shame because if there was a cause, then the preference didn't mean something bad about him. Yet even during this session, Bob intermittently wanted to see his sexual problems as stemming from his wife's lack of interest.

Bob came to our fourth session with a list of memories. He had spent a traumatic week between sessions writing down every time he had borrowed or stolen women's underwear, and masturbated into them. And how he finally began to wear them himself. He urgently wanted to tell every single item in search of relief from the secrecy, and even stayed a few minutes after I said the session was over in order to get it all out. He felt tremendous relief in the following weeks, even though removing the shame over his sexual practices took many months. From this time on, Bob became clear about his sexuality. The fuzzy, subject-changing nature of our early sessions disappeared and Bob engaged with me in a deeply therapeutic way.

Bob's lack of clarity had to be respected as the product of shame that prevented even Bob from understanding what he needed in therapy. A decade ago I might have been frustrated by his manner, wondering if he would spend a session or two doing nothing and then leave. Or I might have quizzed him, asking him to clarify what he wanted from therapy. Now I know he wasn't able to tell me, didn't consciously know, and had to check me out before he understood what he needed. Passing his inspection required that I demonstrate comfort talking about sex by asking him questions in an open, nonintrusive manner.

THERAPIST SHAME INHIBITS CLIENTS

Therapists are products of this culture, and naturally feel shameful about discussing sex. This shame needs to be reduced.

The sexual shame and secrecy I carried in the early years of my psychological practice would have prevented Bob from accessing understanding of what he needed. He may have sought out another therapist, but this is unlikely. Instead, we might have focused on the only problem he could articulate—his wife's lack of interest in sex—and brought her to sessions to help her want more.

THERAPIST AROUSAL MAY RESULT FROM "SEXUALIZED" CLIENTS

Barbara came to see me after reading a book of mine (Hastings 1994). She understood from reading about the work of Eliana Gil (Gil and Kavanaugh 1993) why she felt sexual most of the time, and had difficulty deciding not to react sexually to touch. She poured out how she knew she had become sexualized by sexual abuse from her father up to age 5, and how she had been afraid she would abuse her own children. She knew that when she touched people, she might be conveying sexual energy, and felt shame for it, even though she could not control it. At the end of our first session, in a state of relief and gladness to feel under-stood and accepted, she reached out to me for a hug, but immediately pulled back. Shaking her head, she said she was afraid she had been sexual. I told her I hadn't picked up any sexual energy. I followed this by saying that if she did put it out, we wouldn't shame it, but just look at it. Her face lit up, and she came forward to hug me again, a warm, appreciative hug. And I became aware of the sharp transmission of sexual energy from her breasts, as well as sexual feelings in my own.

I had spent sufficient time learning when sexual feelings are my own natural ones, or cross-wired stimu-lators, or picked up from someone else. Because of this, I could remain clear about what was going on, and communicate that information to Barbara without shaming her. When she was uncomfortable with discovering what she had done, I could tell her that I had not been violated. I am an adult, I can set boundaries, and I can release the sexual feelings. They became no more than information that might be useful to her therapy—as when I experience anger, sadness, or fear belonging to my client.

Barbara was able to reveal information to me—both in words and with her body—because she knew the chances of being shamed by me were small. Her own shame came up but was moderate because she had already completed a great deal of work with another therapist. She came to me because her therapist, who specializes in healing from sexual addiction, didn't understand how the work of sexual healing can take into account present-day sexual functioning. Barbara had been hesitant to discuss her cross-wiring because she didn't think her therapist would understand that it resulted from her sexual abuse, and could be healed by looking at the present-day manifestations as well as the sexual abuse from childhood.

Barbara needed a specialist for help that might have been available through a general therapist who had addressed his or her own sexuality. While it is possible for therapists to intuitively understand many symptoms that they themselves have not healed, sexuality is so universally shamed that it is unlikely that therapists can offer a shame-free, understanding, and accepting environment for clients unless they have addressed their own sexuality.

Many clients in therapy for nonsexual issues were sexualized from childhood abuse and convey that in their touch. Consequently, all therapists need to be aware of the possibility. Our culture invites us to feel violated and offended by people who convey sexual energy. But seeing that some people have associated touch and sex and so are not able to inhibit sexual energy, and that they are not deliberately trying to engage us in sexual exchanges, allows therapists to have compassion for the plight of the client. In addition, when the issue is *expressed* between therapist and client, it allows a more immediate understanding, and potential for help, than when merely *discussed* (Gartner 1997).

Therapists who don't understand that sexual energy can be conveyed through the body will have difficulty understanding why they are sexually aroused by a client's hug. There is the possibility, of course, that the therapist is cross-wired to qualities of the client, or is touch deprived, or has been feeling lustful. Then sexual response to a hug can be understood as the therapist's issue. But if these phenomena are not going on, sexual awareness or arousal might be elicited by the client in ways that may not be recognizable as flirting, or otherwise conveying sexuality.

ACTING SHAME FREE WILL FAIL

Therapists cannot *decide* to be nonshaming of a client's sexuality—or act as if we are. Sexuality is a deep, unconsciously determined human facet, and all of us are equipped with radar for evidence of shame. Most clients will perceive the therapist's shame on some level, and withhold information, perhaps without consciously knowing why. The subject is hard enough to address with a therapist who has little shame. Because of this, therapists must address their own acculturated shame, as well as idiosyncratic forms, in order to be fully available to clients.

Therapists who can see they are feeling shame are in a position to take some steps. One is knowing they have their own emotional work to do. A second is acknowledging the shame to the client. For example, a therapist could say, "I really want to be accepting of what you are telling me, but I have my own judgments about it. I'm working on those judgments, and I don't want you to stop talking about it just because I have this reaction. You deserve to have a listener who doesn't judge you."

THERAPIST PREPARATION FOR SEXUAL EXPLORATION

We can become better therapists by looking at our own sexual shame, and taking steps to reduce it. This can be done through conversations about sex designed to elicit acculturated shame so that it can be reduced.

Watching a comedian talk about sex won't reduce sexual shame. I watched one of Eddie Murphy's videos recently, and was amazed to see that I didn't find it funny, as I had in the past. By removing a great deal of sexual shame, I no longer need to see a man walking around on the stage touching his genitals and using forbidden words in order to acknowledge that sex is part of my life. I got to see how he said shame-laced words with an invitation to laugh. This is evidence of the healthy need to talk about the forbidden, and the unhealthy need to use humor or some other maneuver to prevent shame, in fact to use shame to make it more enjoyable. If this same audience talked openly to one another during a break, factually describing the sex acts Murphy alluded to, their shame would indeed be felt.

Groups of psychotherapy students, or practicing psychotherapists, can talk about sex to remove surface embarrassment, and reduce shame. I have designed exercises (see Chapter 20) for therapists who wish to have some structure for the process of removing sexual shame. Pope and colleagues (1993) use vignettes of therapy sessions and questions about therapists' feelings about the vignettes, which can help therapists who wish to explore their feelings about sexual issues emerging in sessions.

15

Asking Questions about Sexuality

History taking is an essential part of conducting an initial interview or early psychotherapy sessions. When a client comes in with sexual issues, or the focus of therapy becomes sexual functioning or feelings, questions are asked so the therapist can integrate information into a general understanding of who this person is, and how she or he might best be helped.

Sexual histories, however, are different from other subjects because of shame. In addition, the client may not himself know what he needs to reveal until he feels safe enough to reveal it. Bob's story (in Chapters 1 and 14) demonstrated how a person will define sexual issues in one way until comfortable enough to realize what really needs to be talked about.

Learning about clients' sexuality takes a long time, not just because they don't want to talk, but because they have used many defense mechanisms in order to obey our culture's edicts. Clients have isolated their sexual cross-wiring from the rest of life. Many won't know the answers to some questions without time to allow the answers to come to them. This may take weeks or months.

ALLOW TIME FOR SHAME

Assessment of the presence of alcoholism or depression, or appropriate placement within a mental health center, can be accomplished in one to two hours. But the subject of sexuality cannot be covered so quickly. Even when a person has been referred to me for an evaluation of sexual addiction, and he or she is open to learning what I have to say, I can usually gather only a limited understanding of that person's experience in one to two hours. While most clients can provide an overview, the tolerance for questions regarding sexuality is much lower than for other subjects, even subjects that elicit a great deal of shame and guilt, such as alcoholism or the loss of a job.

Therapists can consider what it would be like to have someone ask them about their sex life, including questions about masturbation, the use of pornography or fantasy to get and stay aroused, sexual abuse, and how many people they have had sex with. Perhaps if these questions were asked in a cursory manner, intellectual responses could be given. In the therapy setting, of course, the question is just the door opener to gather other information.

Some clients offer a good deal of information, or dutifully answer questions, and later feel so much shame they are unable to continue with the therapist. This may be difficult to monitor, but can be assisted by asking the client how he or she is feeling about the revelations, making room to postpone.

For example, a woman came to me because she wanted to give up her sexual attraction to children. (She had not acted on it, so I didn't have to make a report.) She had been to several therapists to whom she spilled out the details. She then felt so much shame, she was unable to go back, blaming the therapists for not knowing how to help her with this issue. I encouraged her to wait until she had checked me out to see if I was worthy of her trust. She was relieved, but even with this permission to delay, she was unable to engage in therapy and left after five sessions.

In long-term therapy, many questions might not be asked for weeks, months, or even years. The time allows the client to face and discharge shame on his or her own time schedule, the therapist to adjust to her own feelings about the disclosure, and for new material to emerge as safety is established.

HOW TO ASK

Questioning resembling an interview, oriented toward gathering a complete understanding, is not helpful to the healing of the client. Below are examples of questions that can be asked *when warranted*. For example, if a person is referred for sexual addiction the questions will be different from those for a referral for childhood sexual abuse, which will differ from those for a depressed client for whom sexual issues begin to emerge. These examples are intended to be woven around the needs of the client, as the needs become visible.

These questions can also be used to reduce therapist shame (see Chapter 20).

WHAT TO ASK

"What is sex like for you?" This can be asked in many ways depending on therapist and client, such as, "I haven't heard you talk about sex. I was wondering how that area is for you." Or, "Is sexuality going OK?" Or, "This culture we live in makes most people think that sex is something not to talk about. And just about everyone has some sort of sexual secret. Is there anything you think could be helpful to talk about?" Working it into a context that suggests sexuality can be an encouragement to the client to bring it up more fully than he or she has been able to. Some people ask what I want to know, and I tell them I am asking an open question, introducing the subject.

This most general question opens up the subject, and allows the client to respond as he or she wants. The way the person responds will demonstrate sexual shame. Some clients will be able to talk with some embarrassment, while others will dissociate or become intellectual. The embarrassed client will demonstrate the feeling with smiles, blushing, and perhaps some stammering and laughter—a "normal" response to growing up in this culture. It can be helpful to name the reaction, and put it into a social context. For example, "This isn't something you talk about just every day, is it?"

When the reaction is more severe, the client may look frozen, with diminished breathing. When I notice I am not breathing fully, I check my client, knowing I am likely to reflect his or her experience. Reducing air intake is a quick way to reduce feeling by reducing energy provided by oxygen. At these times I comment, "You aren't breathing much." Sometimes this is followed by a deep intake of air, but when the need to not feel is strong, the client may not be able to increase air intake. One deep breath will be followed by a return to shallow breathing.

When a client has a strong reaction, fear can be reduced by explaining that he or she can take all the time they need to answer the question. I will often explain how the feelings are more important than the facts, encouraging the client to pace talking in order to manage the amount of shame and fear that comes up. For example, "I can see that this is a hard subject to talk about." Pause for possible response. "If you push yourself to answer my question, it won't be helpful because if you have to freeze up to talk, then you have to cut off your feelings. How about pacing yourself so you only feel some of the discomfort? We have plenty of time."

"What has sex been like in the past?" This is a good question for anyone who is looking at sexuality. It is another open-ended invitation to reflect, and the therapist learns from how the person responds.

This question, and the first one, might be answered in ways that suggest the whole story hasn't been told. Sex addicts who aren't ready to face their addiction are likely to give an emotionless explanation, perhaps with a rehearsed, flat quality. I pay attention to my own sense of not knowing, and wanting more information without knowing how to ask for it, because this response suggests that there is more. Searching for it can provoke resistance. For example, I might say, "I have the feeling that there is more, I don't quite understand how this is for you. Is there something more that will help me see what sex has been like?" If the client doesn't respond with additional information that yields a more intuitive understanding, the subject can be left until another time.

I have repeatedly experienced a feeling of, Oh, yes, now I see what was missing! when a client is finally ready to face the sexual addiction or shame of cross-wiring, or other issues that he or she isn't ready to reveal in the beginning.

"How often do you have sex?" This question shouldn't have a quick answer unless it's "never," or, "every day." Few people know how often they have sex, and the answer should be different at different times of life, as well as from month to month. A quick answer might indicate discomfort, or wanting to appear normal, or keeping track of how often the "contract" is met.

"How do you feel about how sex is for you?" This begins the search for feelings, and can offer information about what may be wrong for the person. For example, if a woman doesn't want as much sex as her husband, she may feel frustrated and deprived of getting to have an interest in sex—or she may want to have even less sex. She will learn that the therapist can respect any feelings she has.

"Approximately how many partners have you had? Not just intercourse, but any sexual activity." This is a general question to broaden the picture, and will reveal periods of low frequency, high frequency, casual sex, and the possibility of sexual addiction or fear of sex. Asking about "any sexual activity" will yield a better picture than asking about partners because in our culture partners aren't counted if there is no intercourse. For example, one client had been going to bars and finding women to kiss and fondle to orgasm, but because he didn't have intercourse, he didn't believe he was "having sex." He knew his wife wouldn't like this behavior, but he expected that she would have a far worse reaction if he had intercourse. By broadening the definition, people can take more seriously those times when they "only" fondled.

"How has sex been with different partners?" This question encourages reflection over the sexual history, and reveals possible difficulties. Again, sex can be defined as interactions with any sexual contact, not limited to those with intercourse.

"What does having sex do for you?" This might elicit associations with sex such as the need for love, for control, for the tranquilizing effect of orgasm, feeling like a man/woman, meeting an obligation, expressing anger, assuring the partner won't leave, and so on. Resistance to answering this question, or not knowing, may indicate fear of revealing cross-wiring, addiction, or a history of sexual abuse in childhood and/or adult years.

"Do you masturbate? How often? What is it like?" These questions are usually time stoppers. The client may answer quickly, but the energy in the room freezes. You could also ask what it's like to be asked such a personal question, weaving in an education about how no one is comfortable the first time. Because masturbation is the most common form of male sexual addiction, also common among female sexual addicts, it is a good time to watch for the presence of more information than words reveal. A reasonable response for someone who masturbates in a nonaddictive manner is obvious embarrassment, but the ability to answer clearly and completely. If no discomfort is demonstrated, or if the client becomes dissociative, it can be assumed that there is more material.

"What would it be like if you stopped having sex? Have you ever gone for several months without sexual activity? Without masturbation?" This question asks if sexual activity is compulsive, which could become the focus of the session. It also asks if a person would be relieved to stop sex altogether, opening the door to discovering what has caused this lack of interest. This question can gather information that may not appear naturally. More about sexual addiction, or fear of sex, might be revealed than from direct questions. For example, Richard's sexual addiction (Chapter 1) only became apparent when I asked about masturbation, and then suggested that he go without it for a week. Asking about giving up sex can reveal basic feelings about sexual activity.

"How do you start sex? Who initiates?" These questions can introduce subjects such as attitudes toward sex, and the causes for interest in sex. In addition, it will reveal if one or both partners has little or compulsive interest in sex.

"Do you have erections when you are ready for intercourse? If not, can erection be stimulated? Do you or your partner stimulate your erection? Do you lose your erection during intercourse? How do you reach orgasm? What is required? Does it seem to take too long? Not long enough? What do you do if it takes too long or not long enough?" These questions address sexual functioning.

* * *

"How do you feel about your genitals? How do you feel about your body? Size, shape, smell, color, texture?" This question could preface many other questions about negative feelings about bodies, and about sexual activities, as well as how these feelings are avoided, such as leaving the light off and avoiding sex with a partner.

"Do you fantasize sexually? This includes sexual scenes with a person or people, with or without yourself in them, or imagining sexual stimulation. Do you use fantasy to arouse yourself? To stay aroused? What is the content of the fantasies? The themes? Are they stories? Pictures? What are some of the fantasies?" This information is very important, and can help reveal what has caused sexual damage. Fantasies are a reflection of the past, whether of contact sexual abuse, exposure to pornography at a young age, or the imagination of a good life when the client was too young to create one. Fantasy addicts imagine whole movies of sexual or romantic scenes to provoke arousal, and can actually live in the fantasy during routine daily activities. The drug is a gentle arousal associated with love (or hurt, betrayal, shame, etc.).

"Do you use pornography? What kind?" This question includes magazines, books, videos, and telephone and computer communications. "Do you purchase sexual services?" This includes prostitution, strip clubs, adult bookstores, video arcades, peep shows, and group sex. Pornography and sexual services can provide the same kind of information as fantasy, and if it is used with any regularity is an indicator of probable sexual addiction.

*   *   *

"Do you have (or have you had) casual sex? How often? What was it like? How did you feel afterwards, or the next day?" Casual sexual activity can be an early form of exploring sexual activity, or it can indicate sexual addiction. It might also indicate fear of intimacy.

"Do you have specific cross-wiring to something considered unusual, such as dominance-submission, sadomasochism, urinating, defecating, cross-dressing, inflicting pain on yourself?" This (as with all questions here) needs to be asked with far more words than the above. The question can begin with an explanation of how common these kinds of activities are, although they aren't talked about because people feel shame for engaging in them. Explaining that the quantity of pornography on each of these topics shows us how common they are can help normalize the subject before looking for an answer. This is usually a hard question, but vital to discuss in order to remove shame. In addition, it can also provide information about the nature of sexual damage.

"What was your first sexual experience like?" (This doesn't have to mean intercourse, but most people answer as if it does. Some people assume this means postpuberty, others talk about childhood experiences.) "What was your first menstruation like? What was your first orgasm (ejaculation for men) like? Did it frighten you? Did you know about orgasm prior to having one? How did your family feel about sex, sexuality, and sexual body parts? They may not have said how they felt, but what did you pick up? How did you learn about sex?" These questions are helpful to engage clients in conversation about their sexuality. These questions tend to be less shame provoking, and can be eye openers for people who have never thought of talking about these experiences. When searching for causes of damage to sexuality, these questions can begin the process of making memories available. This information is usually not too difficult to remember, and once brought up for thought and discussion, makes room for more to follow.

"Have you had same-gender sexual experiences?" If gay, "Have you had any cross-gender sexual experiences?" Most people have had some kind of sexual experience with someone of the same sex before or after puberty, but feel shame. Asking the question, and comfortably accepting the answer with some validating information, can help remove shame.

"Does sexual arousal and/or orgasm provide any of the following feelings: loved, safe, shame free, tranquilized, stress free, not alone or lonely, powerful, euphoric, distracted, in control, relieved, wanted, calmer, reassured, good about self?" This question gets at the cross-wiring associated with sexuality, and opens the conversation to reveal the addictive use of sexual energy. These responses are not the result of a healthy use of sexuality, even though they are typical in this culture. This question can also help the partner see that these feelings are not a valid reason for sex. For example, when a person says he or she must have sex to feel safe, it is often difficult for a partner to turn him or her down.

"Does romantic love provide any of the following feelings: loved, safe, shame free, tranquilized, stress free, not alone or lonely, powerful, euphoric, distracted, in control, relieved, wanted, calmer, reassured, good about self?" Romantic sex is even more difficult for a partner to see as an unhealthy use of sexual energy. Romance is idealized in our culture, and woman are supported in wanting their mate to be more "romantic." But romance is as distracting from healthy sexual expression as any other addictive use of sexual energy.

WHAT TO DO WITH THE INFORMATION

Responses to the questions can be used to map out a picture of the client's sexual life. Questions can be asked as associations from the material that has come before. For example, if the client is asked about the effect of arousal or orgasm, and he or she responds with indifference, one might wonder if a sexual hit is coming from romantic involvement rather than the sexual activity itself, and then that is asked about.

16

Indirect Presentation of a Sexual Problem

WHEN CLIENT'S CAN'T NAME THEIR SEXUAL PROBLEM

Our culture distorts sexuality to such an extreme that many clients have difficulties with sex, some without knowing it. As a result, they come to therapy with other complaints, and the therapist must help identify the real causes. Sexuality is sometimes an answer.

Alecia (discussed in earlier chapters) sought for years to understand why her husband didn't want to have sex with her. Therapists addressed the problem as stated, and were unable to help her see the breadth of the issues that kept them apart. Her husband, Paul, did not tell therapists the rest of the sexual behaviors that would have helped identify the real problems.

Alecia read a self-help book (Hastings 1991) and saw her husband in bold print. He was sexually addicted to affairs. She had known about some of his affairs, having caught him in several, but didn't understand the significance of his behaviors. One psychiatrist told her to leave him, but was unable to offer help to Paul.

When an individual or couple come in with the complaint that one person doesn't want sex, it is time to begin asking the questions listed in the previous chapter. This issue can mask many other sexual issues. As with Paul, sexual addiction (when it doesn't include addiction to sex with the partner) will often make sex with the partner difficult. Sex addicts are so intensely focused on their drug of choice that sex with a mate may not provide sufficient stimulation to make sex interesting, or even possible. Some men masturbate with such intensity and for long periods of time that they lose the ability to be stimulated by the lesser friction of intercourse. Masturbating in this manner can cause irritation and even open sores. As the person needs greater and greater stimulation—physical or emotional—"normal" sex cannot stimulate sexual energy.

A second reason for lack of sexual interest is emerging memory of sexual abuse. People who are engaged in healing from sexual abuse typically lose interest in sex as they protect their physical body from remembered assault.

A third reason is feeling violated by the sexuality of the partner. Violation might come from the partner's sexual addiction, or the partner's need for stimulation by things that are offensive to the person, or from sex being used as a direct or indirect expression of anger.

These three areas can form the basis for initial working hypotheses for exploration.

EXPRESSION OF SEXUAL INTEREST IN THE THERAPIST

Clients sometimes find the therapist sexually attractive, and need to express it. Women and men who are considered particularly attractive by our culture's standards will need to know how to address this response, and be open to asking about it if this reaction seems to be held back. Cultural models of beauty are not set aside in the therapy office.

I had a colleague who had to stop seeing teenage girls because they routinely fell in love with him based on his looks. The relatively normal "crush" on an adult male authority figure made it difficult for him to help them with learning disabilities. But most of us don't provoke crushes based on looks. Sexual responses come from other sources.

Through examples, I will address some of the issues a client can be trying to bring up by having sexual feelings toward the therapist. This list isn't exhaustive.

A sexually addicted client may want the therapist to become a sex object. He or she may bring up sex in a way that only makes sense when looked at in the context of addiction. For example, a colleague described a client who lay on the analytic couch in sexualized positions, making yearning, sexual sighs, turning to look back at the analyst. (Both client and analyst were female, but the example works with any gender combination.) The analyst was unnerved by this assault, but didn't bring it up, consistent with her training.

A therapist who addresses this from an addiction point

of view would point out that the client seems to be feeling sexual, and ask her to talk about how else this shows up in her life. The therapist's discomfort would be revealed gently and with concern for the possible shame for getting caught having this "unacceptable" feeling. The function of feeling loved by the therapist would be questioned, but the use of sexual feeling to avoid other feelings would also be focused on. If addictive sexual arousal isn't identified as such, then the therapist is treating the equivalent of an inebriated alcoholic—something impossible to do.

> During my early days of practice I had a client, George, who grew attached to me. After talking about taking sexy underwear to a nurse at his doctor's office, he mentioned in a casual, offhand way that he knew I would wear such underwear if he brought it. I was too naive to know that he was planning to think of me wearing it and masturbate, carrying out his addiction to an affair without ever having the affair. He combined isolated sex with the fantasy of a real person.

> My cultural training not to hurt people's feelings urged me to take the gift, not shame him by saying I wouldn't wear it, and throw it away later. Luckily, I had enough experience not to fall into this pattern. Instead, I told him I wouldn't wear it. I helped him avoid the shame from bringing it and having it refused.
> This kind of situation is considered repulsive to most women who have not encouraged a man's sexual interest. It crosses the boundaries of a nonsexual relationship, and implies sexual contact. Men like my client are accustomed to being shamed by women who are not receptive, so they learn how to ask indirectly.

While I was able to set a proper boundary with George, I wasn't able to address the communication in his request. Now I would proceed differently. First, I would ask him to tell me about all the times he has given women underwear, how they responded, and what kind of masturbation fantasies he had about them. These questions would be asked one at a time, allowing plenty of time for him to be startled by the question, and feel shame when responding. I would show him how he defined his sex life as sexualized contact with a woman, followed by isolated sexual activity, and help him question if this felt like a reasonable lifelong style. George was a loner, who, even though he was married, lived at his job or in the garage making beautiful boxes and other things out of wood.

Once we understood the form his sex life took, I would bring up the question of the level of compulsivity with which he engaged in these practices. I would ask, What would it be like to stop masturbating for one week, and not interact with women you have given or want to give underwear? Most men will know right away they wouldn't like to do that. Some will think it an easy exercise. And for some it will be easy. If George could talk about the difficulty, I would postpone asking him to try it until he had addressed some of the fears.

I am sorry that I was unable to help George with his sexual issues. We worked together for about a year, and had some impact on his loner status, but did nothing for his understanding of sexuality. I am glad he let me take a look, however, because knowing I wasn't able to help him added to my motivation to learn more about sexuality.

As with the addictive use of substances, the sex addict will use classic forms of denial, which can be confronted. For example, I recently spoke with a woman who told me of a sexualized relaıonship she had with a spiritual advisor.

When I suggested she and her husband and this man sit down together and name the sexualized relating to render it difficult to pursue, she gave me the following reasoning. Her husband would be hurt by the information; the relationship was over and there was no point in bringing it up again even though she had said she would get on the next plane if he needed her; she had obtained many spiritual lessons by examining the relationship with him; he had mentored her development and she owed it to him to not disrupt his life; she didn't want to upset his wife since their relationship was in difficulty anyway; I wasn't respecting her wisdom; and she would leave it in God's hands. Each point sounded reasonable, but the quality was clearly denial of the fact that she carried this man around in her pocket ready to bring out any time life seemed unsatisfying. While this kind of "addiction" is common, and probably not of major concern compared with her other issues, she was teaching classes on healthy sexuality and proclaimed herself as sexually healthy. In addition, we had just discussed these same defenses directed toward her by her students.

INTENSE NEGATIVE FEELINGS

When a therapist finds certain sexual acts repulsive or abhorrent, this reaction may reflect shaming of these acts by our culture and nothing more. But it may reflect two other causes: a reaction to having suffered from abuse in the form of sexual acts that are repellent (such as incest, or being forced to perform certain sexual acts); or a reaction to wanting to engage in this kind of abuse, and negative feelings are created to prohibit it. I will begin with the second. If a person has inclinations that are socially and/or personally unacceptable, feeling intense shaming toward people who engage in it can have the effect of preventing the person from acting on these desires. It may also be a form of shaming the self for having this cross-wiring.

I saw this dynamic played out in a dramatic way when I visited a therapy group for men who had been arrested and convicted of the sexual abuse of children. Several of the men talked about how they had felt intense hatred for any man who sexually abused children. After years of this kind of expression, their relatives were shocked to learn that they had been sexual with children. The intense negative feelings made the unsuspecting listener believe this was the last thing this person would do. One man told of sitting in the living room watching the news on TV with his family when such a story came on. The child he had been molesting was in front of him, listening as he raged about "those people."

We cannot assume that such anger means the person is guilty of the same behavior he condemns. An equally likely reason for the anger is having been the victim of such abuse. Or the client might have grown up unable to protect someone else from abuse—sexual, emotional, shaming, beatings. These possibilities can be explored by gently questioning the nature of the anger, making room for more expression of anger, and listening for associations to the feeling.

CLIENTS WHO HAVE BEEN, OR WANT TO BE, SEXUAL WITH CHILDREN

Listening for information about sexual attraction to children is difficult because it is the most shamed form of sexuality. It is unusual for a person to seek therapy for this

symptom, particularly since all the states require an immediate report. I have clients come to me long after they have
been through court-mandated treatment to work toward a
healthier use of sexuality.

Threat of exposure is a major reason people won't tell
therapists, but perhaps just as important is the shame that
accompanies this most condemned form of sexual interest.
Even those who have not acted on the cross-wiring have
difficulty talking about it. In addition, the press has popularized the idea that pedophiles cannot change. This secret
has the greatest cultural pressure to be kept. I have worked
with many recovering incest survivors, and I know that many
of them must be sexually attracted to children. But only a
small handful have talked about it.

Other people with sexual cross-wiring to children or
young teens aren't conscious of it. The job of the therapist is
even more difficult here.

Jen loved her daughter until she was 3. Then Jen felt
repulsed by her daughter's desire for affection, and
pushed her away. The daughter came to seem like a
perpetrator.

Jake (discussed in Chapters 6 and 16) was never
comfortable holding his children, leaving that to his
wife. He entered therapy for sexual addiction after being
arrested for prostitution solicitation, and eventually
revealed that he sexualized all physical contact. He
didn't know it was possible to touch a woman, a child, or
an animal without having sexual feelings. Even massage
from a male massage therapist brought fear of a sexual
response. Recently, when his daughter came home to
announce her engagement, he was unable to reach out

to her with a hug because he couldn't do it without a sexual reaction. The healing process to relinquish this connection between physical touch and sex is slow. After four years Jake is able to be physically affectionate with his dog with no sexual connection, which brings him joy. He feels dependent on his wife, where it is acceptable to respond sexually to touch.

Jake wasn't trying to become aroused by touch. To avoid damaging his children, he had to avoid them. This offers a different picture from that of writers who are angry with men "who do that." I saw from working with Jake and other sex addicts that they don't have a choice about the reaction. The only choice they have is to avoid touching children while working on recovery in the hope of relinquishing this reaction.

I have not been able to use my intuition to ascertain if a client has this arousal pattern. Perhaps the need to keep it hidden prevents making the information available to intuition. However, even if a client cannot reveal it, therapists can talk about it in a manner that won't add more shame to the clients' views of themselves.

For example, when a client speaks angrily about a sexual abuser in the news, if the therapist joins in angrily shaming the person, then the client knows that if he has such attractions, he will not be met with acceptance from the therapist. If, on the other hand, the therapist speaks with sorrow, wishing for him or her to obtain helpful treatment, then the client will receive indirect acceptance. The therapist could comment that we have to provide good, helpful therapy if we are to stop this epidemic of sexual abuse, making the point that many people are engaged in this same behavior. And many are in recovery from it.

Clients who have been cross-wired to abuse children will, at the same time, take in a compassionate look at themselves. They deserve compassion and acceptance, even while having to take responsibility for healing themselves. Therapists must be able to accept the person with sexual attraction to children while not accepting the behavior. If the therapist cannot, the client will not feel accepted, no matter how accepting the therapist is of other behaviors and feelings.

I have not come to accept people who are sexual with children, and who refuse to take action to heal themselves. I am particularly incensed by those who believe it is acceptable to be sexual with a "consenting" child. But I don't intend to change these feelings.

Early in my work with incest survivors I found it difficult to believe that a person who was abused, and for whom I had tremendous empathy and compassion, could also have a sexual attraction to children. I encountered this with Kenneth (Chapters 6 and 10) who had been severely abused as a very young child. He told me about holding a 2-year-old child on his lap for the purpose of arousal when he was a teenage baby-sitter. I minimized the impact on this child, who was by that time about 18. Because I still carried strong negative feelings about people who use children sexually, I couldn't believe this person I respected and cared for could have done that. Over a period of weeks I was able to ask myself what it had been like for the girl, and how it had affected her sexuality in the present. I imagined her as my client, talking about body memories that interfered with her comfortable use of sexuality. I thought about my other clients who had been molested by baby-sitters. I thought about children taking care of children, how sitters can be too young and naive to understand the impact of what they were doing, and how no adults had been there to intervene. Finally, I was able to bring my two experiences of Kenneth into one person, and know that this man I liked and respected had actually been sexual with a 2-year-old child. Until then, I supported his denial, and by doing so, added further shame to his sexuality.

WHEN A "FRIEND" IS HAVING A PROBLEM

This line, often used in jokes, is occasionally used in the therapist's office. Sometimes clients really are asking about a friend. The difference may be revealed by the demeanor of the person asking. When asking about a real friend, people are usually more comfortable than talking about themselves. If asking for themselves, indirect evidence of shame will accompany the asking. Hesitance, looking sideways at the therapist or not making eye contact, shifting in the chair, and slower speech can be signs. In addition, he or she may use methods to cover shame, such as anger or joking. However it is presented, if the therapist has any hint that the person is talking about him- or herself, the answer can be couched in language that would not shame the person.

For example, if a client has a "friend" who masturbates every day, and is sometimes late for work, what do I think the friend should do about this? I might think of blurting out that his friend should take a look at his sexual addiction. But this could bring up the client's shame. I could be more helpful by talking about how masturbation itself isn't wrong or harmful, but it can be used in ways that are, and used to avoid other feelings. It sounds like his friend is using masturbation in unhealthy ways since he is endangering his work life. I would also add how he obviously cares about his friend's well-being, which communicates that I care about the client's.

Even if this client were not talking about himself, I have still communicated a nonshaming attitude toward sexuality, toward masturbation, and toward sexual addiction. I may not ever find out if this was relevant to my client, but I can assume that any interaction about sexuality that isn't shaming will create the beginning of a new way to look at it.

WHEN CLIENTS DON'T KNOW THEY HAVE A SEXUAL PROBLEM

Marvin was able to tell me that he felt bad about masturbating, asking if it was acceptable. At that time I had not yet learned about sexual addiction, and I gave him the pat response. I told him that masturbation wouldn't hurt him, it was a normal expression of sexuality, and our culture tells us it's shameful, even when professionals say it is not. Marvin was tremendously relieved, his energy changing from tense and contained to open and relaxed.

Soon after this I read about sexual addiction, and realized that Marvin may have needed more information. When he returned to see me after a break of several years I tried to bring it up with him. Through my questions about sexuality, he talked about how when he was on drugs (he had been recovering from drug addiction for three years) he exposed himself to a woman in the apartment across from his, believing even in the drug-free telling that this is what she wanted. He also talked about sex with two people, and how he was ready to have sex any time anyone wanted to.

By this time I knew it was sexual addiction, not an outcome of drug-induced lack of boundaries. This was supported by the fact that he continued to engage in addictive relationships with women, taking care of them financially with borrowed money, and intensely focusing on sex. He was addicted to the relationships as well as to sexual activity. While Marvin was able to give up more than ten years of drug addiction with one week in the hospital and steady attendance at Narcotics Anonymous meetings, he wasn't able to look at his sexual addiction during the several years I knew him. He came to see me for a few sessions at a time when his relationships got out of control. I wasn't able to help him.

With my current knowledge, I wouldn't answer his question about masturbation without first asking many questions to discover how he masturbated, how often, and how compulsive it was. While this may not have helped, I carry with me the feeling that I gave him a prescription for a sex drug, which he carries with him even after I tried to take it back.

ATTRACTION TO SEX ADDICTS

Diane came to me because her teenage daughters had told her that their stepfather was being sexual with them. This was in 1979, when abuse wasn't prosecuted and no treatment was required. Diane divorced him, and then went on to fall in love with a number of men, most of whom pursued her incessantly with romantic dates and gifts until they had sex, and then dropped her. I worked with her on increasing her self-esteem, something I would also do today, but I was unable to refer her to self-help books or twelve-step programs. Many relationship addicts will be attracted to sex addicts because they are the best source of the "drug." Diane loved men who wanted her so badly they were willing to spend money and energy pursuing her. But they were also the kind who moved on once the drug lost its power—some to other women, her husband to her daughters.

When I worked with Diane there were no twelve-step programs for relationship addiction (except for Alanon, for those in relationship with alcoholics). The two programs for sex addicts began that very year, followed later by Sex and Love Addicts Anonymous, and even later by programs for codependency. These programs provide an education about relationship addiction, and offer a route to change that way of approaching relationships, as well as support of others going through the same process.

SEXUAL ISSUES MAY IMPLY CHILDHOOD SEXUAL ABUSE

People who are experiencing sexual difficulties in the present may be able to name them, while being unable to name abuse from the past. They come to therapy to focus on a sexual dysfunction, and then discover a need to look at sexual abuse.

Brian (Chapter 4) came to me because he couldn't maintain erections, but once we began looking at his life and his history, he stopped focusing on the symptom. He was also incapable of intimacy, and was terrified of becoming involved with women, limiting himself to short-term affairs with married women, who seemed safer. As we examined his childhood with two drinking alcoholic parents, and a mother who was sexually boundariless, his present symptoms began to make sense as defense mechanisms to keep abuse at bay. Brian learned to respect his body's decision to prevent intercourse, and used this information to uncover how the fears had been created.

SEXUAL ISSUES AS INFORMATION ABOUT RELATIONSHIPS

Clients come to therapy to tell about how they aren't interested in sex, believing that lack of interest reflects a magical diagnosis of inhibited sexual desire they have read about in women's magazines. While lack of interest may result from past abuses of sexuality, it can also reflect issues in the sexual relationship.

Sex is culturally required of both genders. This provides an excuse to control the less interested partner by requiring sex. Men and women who are accustomed to setting limits in other areas may not feel they have a right to say no when the partner complains of not enough sex.

Nedra and Ron struggled with her lack of interest in sex for ten years before seeking help. She had grown to hate his nightly request for "snuggling" (which meant he would settle for cuddling but really wanted sex), because she felt guilty for not meeting his "sexual needs."

In the first session I told Nedra that she had to be willing to say no to sex for as long as she didn't want to be sexual, even if it meant forever. The couple looked at me in shock, unable to speak. Then they both argued with me about her obligation. I asked him if he wanted sex out of obligation. He said no, he wanted her to want him. I asked her if she could feel loving toward a man she felt obligated to have sex with. She began to realize how she had come to hate him because of the black cloud of disappointment hovering over her.

I suggested a sexual moratorium so they could see what it would be like if they dropped this hot issue between them. When they asked how long the moratorium should last, I discouraged them from setting a specific time. When a time is set, the one who wants more sex can wait it out, still hovering, still believing he or she is being deprived. In addition, the rule that relationships must include sex remains in place. If there is no time limit, the couple is more likely to take a look at their relationship without this dominating factor and work toward becoming sexual in new ways. Many of the damaging practices in relationships follow from the belief that sex has to take place. These include "giving" sex every few days, demanding sex every few days, blaming a partner for not doing it often enough, faking orgasms, treating the desirous partner as a perpetrator and the less interested partner as the victim, and so on.

Almost every time I make this suggestion, couples say they already have a moratorium. But they don't. A real moratorium occurs when both people are willing to set aside sexual relating in order to see what their relationship is like without the sexual struggles (Hastings 1993). If Ron refused to try a moratorium, I would ask questions to identify the dynamics he is trying to express through sexual entitlement.

Another client and I discovered that he refused a moratorium because demanding sex was the only way he felt any power in his relationship, and letting that go would relegate him to the position of a weak person. He couldn't afford to give up his demand for sex until he was able to stand his ground on other issues. The irony was that he created the loss of sex by making it impossible for his wife to respond lovingly. Once he gave up the demand she became attracted to him, and they became sexual again.

Nedra and Ron did agree to a moratorium, and were able to relinquish their struggle. Over time, they discovered they loved each other. Ron received a great deal more from Nedra when he didn't demand his due. Nedra had to express a good deal of anger she had bottled up for years in order to regain her loving feelings for Ron, but she was able to do so.

If Ron had not agreed to a moratorium, Nedra would have had to take on the task of saying no. Our culture works against this kind of growth, particularly if it goes on for weeks or months, or even years. But once a person takes the right to decide what will happen with their body and sexuality, it is enormously freeing, allowing sexual healing in ways that aren't otherwise possible. Nedra didn't have to confront that path to sexual healing, which made her work easier—but possibly not as complete.

THE SEARCH FOR HELP

The examples I have used in this chapter are not comprehensive, they only suggest ways people bring issues of sexuality to therapy. Each therapist must obtain experience listening between the lines for issues clients may be afraid to express, don't know are issues, or have presented to other therapists who couldn't help.

> Barry searched for help with his sexual addiction. Barry's story (presented in earlier chapters) is a good example of how people want help but don't know how to ask for it, and go to therapists who don't understand what is needed. Early in his teen years, Barry discovered he could relieve feelings of despair by flirting. He had a lot of sex, and even without sex, relating with women was fraught with sexual energy. Initially this was satisfying, but over the years Barry knew something was wrong, but couldn't name it.
>
> First he decided not to have casual sex, instead being sexual only with women he wanted to date over a period of time. He felt somewhat better about himself. But no real male friends, and sexualized relating with most women left him feeling lonely and isolated. He tried to decrease these feelings as well. By the time he met Roberta, he still masturbated regularly to fantasies, and continued flirting-laced relating.
>
> Barry and Roberta sought therapy because they could not discover the source of their conflicts. The therapist had no understanding of the addictive use of sexual energy, and could not help Barry understand how to bring his life into integrity. He told Barry and Roberta that Roberta's jealousy and anger about Barry's flirting was the problem. Our culture agrees with this assessment, and without training, the therapist didn't know how to help.
>
> Traditional sex therapists also believe there is nothing wrong with Barry's actions. He wasn't having sex with other women, and didn't buy prostitutes. He didn't

lose time from work, and his behavior didn't seem to be a threat to his relationship. Fantasy is considered a natural part of sexuality, even recommended by sex therapists. Flirting is called harmless. But Barry and Roberta felt this wasn't true.

A self-help book gave him some answers to what he had suspected, and then he called for an appointment. Roberta had gone into a rage about his incessant flirtation, finally letting herself know it was harmful to her, and pulled away from him.

When Barry came to me for therapy, Roberta didn't trust me because three therapists and her friends had seen it as her problem. I referred her to a colleague, and she spent weeks cautiously making sure her new therapist saw the nature of the addiction. Both Barry and Roberta had been damaged by their past therapists' lack of knowledge.

Barry and I spent several weeks determining the extent of his addiction. While it didn't look like it should be disruptive to his life—by our culture's assessment—he showed me how it was. He had no really intimate contact with anyone, including Roberta, because he was a master at creating an illusion of intimacy. As he tried to give up masturbation and flirting, he found that he couldn't. Over months of twice weekly individual sessions and the weekly men's group, he could stop the flirting he was able to recognize. But Roberta, who now allowed herself to see, pointed it out. When they were in public, she experienced how he left her emotionally when a woman gave him attention. He saw that he had to educate himself about flirting before he could change his behavior. When Barry was in a sexualized trance, and flirting, he was not able to observe himself—one of the functions of addiction. With the support of the men in the group, myself, and Roberta, he was able to become increasingly better at recognizing when he was acting out.

Recently Barry reached a crisis state. He stopped acting out in any way, and all the emotions emerged that flirting had held at bay. Now out of control, he was devastated by despair and fear, thrown back into his childhood where his needs weren't responded to, and instead, he had to take care of his parents' needs. He expected me to abandon him at any moment since he stopped being the "good client" he thought I wanted. Watching him go through this showed how intense and gripping an addiction can be even when the behaviors aren't much different from those seen all around us—behaviors even suggested by traditional sex therapists. The function of the behaviors, and the degree of compulsivity, are as important as the behaviors themselves (with the exceptions of sex with children, or in other ways harming another or oneself). Sex with a mate is generally considered healthy, but it can be addictive, and it can have functions beyond the pleasurable bonding and loving that make up healthy sexuality.

If Barry and Roberta's earlier therapist had understood sexual addiction, he would have referred them to a sexual addiction specialist. Roberta would have been spared the feelings that came from knowing something was wrong but receiving no validation for her perceptions.

17

When the Client Takes the "Sex Drug" in the Therapist's Office

Given that sexual addiction is very common, it should not be surprising that people can come to therapy sessions "under the influence." Understanding sexual addiction, and recognizing a sexual trance, can help in approaching these clients in a helpful way.

Our culture doesn't allow us to know when someone is feeling sexual unless it is in an acceptable context—certainly not a therapist's office. We are not supposed to tell others that they seem to be sexually aroused. We are conditioned to react with disgust when someone seems sexual in our presence without our consent. Therapists are conditioned this way, too.

A therapist, Ms. Y., referred Gary to me for evaluation. She had been seeing him for several months, and was frustrated by his constant desire to talk about sex. She tried to stop it by telling him she wasn't going to talk with him when he did so. When he continued, she silently looked out the window.

Gary did not go into his trance in my office because we immediately began talking openly about his sexual issues. When he launched into stories about sexual activity, I asked questions, and responded with comments that kept him on the track of observing his sexuality.

We discussed sexual addiction, and the opportunity to recover from it. However, Gary did not elect to do so. Now in his late fifties, he was physically disabled from decades of physically demanding employment that produced great fear and exhilaration and a lot of money. Greatly overweight, talking about sex was the only remaining way to elicit his adrenaline drug. He didn't want to look at giving up a way of life. I wasn't able to show him the possibility of an alternative that might be better.

Gary returned to Ms. Y. and continued to act out his sexual addiction in her office. She planned to work with him on loneliness, and historical issues that led him to addictive adrenaline rushes. If his life seems hopeless enough to confront the causes, perhaps her work will have some effect. If sexual addiction is sufficient to mask feelings, then the sexual trance could prevent therapy.

THERAPIST REACTION TO THE SEXUAL TRANCE

When a client comes to sessions with alcohol on the breath, most therapists can remain neutral while addressing the fact that no therapy can take place while he or she is in this state. But most people, particularly women, are conditioned by the culture to react with repulsion to someone who exudes sexual arousal. This is particularly true when the therapist is being used as the lust object, or expected to join in.

Prior to understanding sexual trances, I had a client who, in his late thirties, had already been to many therapists before me. The most recent, who referred him to me, said his behavior was offensive. He was described in condemning tones as narcissistic, controlling, and manipulative. Each female therapist had finally tired of his "disgusting" leers and sounds.

In the first session with Frank, I was able to address one of his manipulative stances—his history of mild suicide attempts had garnered a great deal of therapist attention. I told him that in order to work with me he would have to forgo these attempts, and if he tried one time, I would drop him as a client. He respected this limit for the year we met. But I was not able to identify, let alone set limits about the oozing of lustful, invasive, sexual energy. Frank made sexualized sounds throughout therapy sessions, and looked at my body parts. I felt almost constantly violated, and had no idea how to proceed. As with Gary, described above, as long as the addiction went unaddressed, nothing therapeutic could happen.

Frank left therapy with me to return to a previous therapist. I suspect that I didn't hide my disgust as well as other therapists had. Ten years later I ran into Frank. Sexual energy still oozed out of him. Apparently no therapists to date had been able to see what was going on, or if they had, Frank had been unable to make use of confrontation.

Frank is an example of clients who are seen as abusive to therapists. I felt abused by him. At the end of sessions I felt the need to bathe and change my clothes. By understanding how he was "taking his drug" in my office I would have been able to address it. I would have named it every time he looked or made sounds that were sexual, and asked him what function it was serving. By educating him on the subject of sexual addiction, referring him to twelve-step groups with others who experience what he does, and talking with him every time the addiction showed up in the office, Frank would have been offered hope for an affliction that alienated most people in his life, including those he hired to help him.

Cindy Rushin-Gallagher (1997) describes a male client who wanted to masturbate in front of her. She offered the case as an example of a client for whom all three approaches to sexuality are needed—addiction, dysfunction, and sexual abuse—as well as an understanding of healthy sexuality.

I have seen William for only six months, but he was ripe for intensive work on his sexuality. He had done a lot of previous work with many modalities and many therapists. William had a way of alienating female therapists with inappropriate sexual comments and becoming disillusioned or feeling betrayed by male therapists. He knew only one way to connect with people—through some type of sexual contact. It was immediately obvious he was sexually addictive. He focused constantly on sex through fantasizing, masturbating, using pornography, and engaging in high-risk behaviors.

William said he wanted to masturbate in front of me in his first therapy session. Of course, I told him this would not be allowed, but that I was interested in understanding his desire to have me witness this sexual expression. I presumed he was attempting to resolve some unfinished trauma. He continued over the next several months to test my limits with sexualizing behavior as we explored his psychosexual history. When we approached material that was particularly emotionally charged, William dissociated into a sexual trance. In therapy, I became the object of his trance.

William had been sexually abused in his past, experiences he had pushed away with pot, alcohol, and rationalization. The earliest was with his grandmother. He remembered this abuse several years ago, suffered a psychotic breakdown, was hospitalized, diagnosed with bipolar disorder, and put on lithium and antipsychotic medication. His grandmother's sexual stimulation was pleasuring and comforting for William until she became upset with his inability to ejaculate, and stopped. He felt confused, inadequate, and rejected. William had a hard time understanding how receiving sexual pleasure was a violation of his developing sexuality, but finally saw how she robbed him of his naturally unfolding sexuality.

In grade school, William was anally raped by a stranger. The resulting experience of being held down, feeling suffocated and trapped is a feeling that has continued to trigger him as an adult. It also created some gender confusion which led to a long-term homosexual relationship in junior high, episodic homosexual experiences as an adult, competition with male peers, and resistance to male authority. William discounted the abuse because he blamed himself for willingly going along with the man. He has come to see that he responded out of loneliness and the need for attention and approval.

William was an only child and was left alone a lot. He

used masturbation to comfort and soothe himself from loneliness. When his mother walked in on him once, she shamed him severely. After this he continued to masturbate, but experienced greater conflict about it. He has slowly understood the connection between this experience (and his grandmother's rejection) and his desire to have me see him masturbate. He has been desperately searching for validation of his sexuality, particularly from a woman in a position of authority.

William also presented with several sexual dysfunctions. He was having difficulty getting and maintaining firm erections. He found that stopping the antipsychotic medication resolved this and allowed him to experience more of the anger, sadness, and grief about his sexual violations. William also complained of having no desire to ejaculate into his wife. He preferred she masturbate him. The two didn't have a satisfying sexual connection, and she was not interested in sex. (Not surprising!!)

William willingly eliminated alcohol (not pot yet), pornography, and has just recently experimented with giving up fantasy. He found it lonely, boring, and difficult to get and maintain erections at first. Without substances he realized he wanted to heal his sexual relationship with his wife, and they are just starting couples work. William has much work to do still, but his commitment is apparent.

Athough William has been a challenging client, the work has been satisfying as I see him learning to connect, and feel like a worthy person. I believe I have facilitated his healing by providing a container where he could express his sexualizing with acceptance, completing his interrupted developmental task. It has been difficult to not react negatively to being sexualized, but I hold several memories of how I failed clients by not being able to contain their feelings, staying close to my heart for strength!

COPING WITH SHAME

Sometimes when a client's shame is too intense, he or she will see the therapist as shaming. I saw William for one session months before he entered therapy with Rushin-Gallagher, but he felt so much shame addressing his sexualized behavior he was unable to continue. He wrote me a note saying he planned to come to therapy, but didn't follow up. He later told Rushin-Gallagher I had shamed him. Over several months, as his shame dropped, he was able to see that I hadn't shamed him, and he entered my therapy group for men.

QUESTIONS TO ASK

I have prepared some questions that could help therapists talk about sex. Consider what it would be like for a therapist to ask these questions of a client and how it would feel if the client responds with defensiveness, and perhaps refuses to remain in therapy.

Asking about sexual feelings going on in the session is likely to bring up the most shame and distress for both client and therapist. Therefore, the questions below should be included within a good deal of education about sexual addiction (and the therapist's own discomfort, if it exists) in order to create an environment that will provoke as little shame as possible. If a client leaves in the middle of the session, or cancels the next appointment without explanation, a call to express interest in how he or she is doing could reduce shame and help the client return to process it further.

With this in mind, here are some ideas for questions.

*   *   *

"You look like you're feeling sexual. Are you?" This kind of question begins the naming process that almost never happens in childhood when the words should get matched up with feelings. Most people think they can feel sexual and no one will know. If the client says no, he or she isn't feeling sexual, the answer may reflect shame for having been caught. The subject can be dropped, allowing time for integration of the idea that the feelings are sexual, and that someone has not only seen, but named it.

"Are you looking at me like I'm a sex object?" This might be prefaced with a brief explanation about how our culture trains men to sexually objectify women, and how sexual energy can be used to avoid other feelings. Then, in this context, the person might be asked if this is going on for him now. If the client cannot tolerate such a direct naming of his or her objectification of the therapist, another question could be, "Can we talk about the way you are looking at me right now?" This question allows the client a little more time before the shameful feeling is named, while drawing attention to what the therapist has seen.

"I'm not comfortable when you look at me like that." Whether the person says yes or no to the previous question, further information about how the therapist reacts might help bring the person out of the sexual trance. He or she could begin seeing that there are implications to this addictive maneuver. By continuing to discuss sexual feelings going on in the room, and without using cultural shame-savers of humor or sexualized attitude, the client is having perhaps his or her first exposure to open communication about this secret topic.

Sexual addiction flourishes in secrecy. Many addicts say they fantasize about people around them, even while having conversations about work, and fully believe the other person doesn't know they are feeling sexual. Other people may or may not consciously know, but may find themselves feeling flattered, or violated. Addiction does not flourish as easily when named, particularly when a negative reaction is revealed. A client may leave therapy because the discomfort of being seen is too strong, but therapy isn't possible if the behaviors aren't named.

"Are you flirting with me? I noticed that you seem to be flirting with me." Sexual energy can be directed at a therapist in a seemingly more innocent manner, with flirtation. As explained in Chapter 9, there are many functions to this use of sexuality. Once the subject is out in the open, it allows examination of its use. Clients feel shame when I first mention that they are flirting with me or a group member. The most common first reaction is emphatic denial. I let the subject go, knowing the person is having a reaction, and won't be able to discuss it until he or she has had time to get over the shock and ponder the question.

WHEN THE THERAPIST IS SEDUCED

Some sexually addicted clients focus on the act of seduction rather than on sexual activity. This skill might be directed at the therapist, too, and can look like it isn't sexual. A skilled seducer will have the seduced person thinking it was his or her idea, and the seducer is only going along with it. When therapists feel sexual toward a client, one question to ask oneself is, What might the client be doing to provoke this?

Asking about history of nonsexual relationships might reveal if sexual attraction to the client is common.

> Kenneth flirted with women in grocery stores in such a way that they didn't know he was in addiction. He commented on items in the cart, and on the fabric of their clothes, highly knowledgeable about both. Naming beautiful fabrics and designers of the clothing allowed him to touch the fabric and stand closer. Allowing him to charmingly cross the line placed him within sexual bounds, and most women responded by openly flirting with him, and often asking him for a date. He apologetically turned them down, saying he was married. But he got the hit of success. The women left the store feeling flattered by the interest of an attractive man.

> Barry's skills were even more refined. He could quickly figure out what pleased a particular woman, and provide it. As my client, he set out to learn what pleased me, because he didn't believe I could be truly interested in him. He sensed right away that sexual flirtation wouldn't work. But early on we discovered that he could bring me a pleasant feeling of cheering him on in his progress. By examination, I came to see that this cheering feeling was very different from being truly glad for him. The latter came from deep inside, and was very satisfying, while the addictive hit was superficial and intense. Barry's method of eliciting this feeling in me was so unconscious that it was impossible for either of us to see how he did it. I had to rely on the *nature of the feeling* to know that it wasn't mine, that it was created by him. When I felt it, I immediately told him, even if it

meant interrupting him in midsentence. We then examined his need to control my feelings, and to see whether it was addictive mood altering, or if it was a way to tell his story by getting me to act out his mother's part.

THERAPISTS WHO HAVE SEX WITH CLIENTS

Many dynamics can lead a therapist to engage sexually with clients. One can come from not talking about the client's attempt to seduce the therapist (Pope et al. 1993). If a therapist is seduced by a client into sexual arousal and doesn't know how to address it openly, then he or she could feel compelled to act on it. Neither Kenneth nor Barry wished to have sex with their therapists, but some clients set out to create that result in order to play out their history, or to fuel a powerful addiction, or to win a power struggle, among other reasons. When the therapist feels prohibited from directly naming what is going on, the chances of playing out the assigned part in the drama increase.

Therapists can prevent such reactions by asking the client to join in the process of understanding why he or she would want to create such a reaction in the therapist. During this process the therapist can tell the client directly, clearly, and more than once that he or she will not be sexual with him or her. This might be expressed in the following way: "I know that your sexuality has been violated by people who were important to you, and maybe you fear that I will do that too. (Pause to see if there is a response.) I think you already know that I don't want to violate you, but I want to say it anyway. (Speaking distinctly, with full attention in order to fully impart the information) Jenny, I am not going to be sexual with you." I usually stop here to make room for a reaction. While this information seems obvious, clients with a history of sexual violation will benefit from hearing it stated out loud—even if they know it intellectually. I find it helpful to say it in one sentence for impact. While it seems like the most obvious thing to say, I have repeatedly experienced clients expressing relief, often in tears. Some clients need to hear it over and over, particularly if they grew up believing that adults wanted them for sex.

Sexual addiction thrives in secrecy—even more than other addictions. A therapist has to gently and tactfully describe everything that is going on in order to bring it out in the open where it cannot thrive behind cultural secrecy. While this is true with any kind of therapist seduction, it is particularly true with sexuality because of the strong cultural edict of secrecy.

WOMEN WHO FLIRT

I have given examples of men in sexual trances, and men who seduce. Women are just as likely to arrive in the therapist's office in sexual trance, and attempt to seduce an erotic response. But we don't have labels like "dirty old woman," or "manizer." A woman is a "slut" only if she is dressed like the stereotyped prostitute or if she sleeps with many men. A woman may not be feeling sexually aroused when using body positioning and gestures to convey sexuality. It is difficult to describe a client who was in a full sexual trance; the woman didn't flirt with me, she wasn't wearing provocative clothing, and she didn't communicate with body positioning. But the thought "sex" came to my mind as soon as I saw her. As the session unfolded, she talked about sexualizing with her spiritual leader that formed the basis of her addiction. Since I specialize in sexuality, I observed, and worked my observations into my understanding of her issues. If I had been confronted with this kind of energy ten years ago, without an understanding of how sexuality manifests itself in the therapy office, I would have felt defensive and uncomfortable, unsure how to proceed. While the energy didn't seem directed toward seducing me, it brought the subject of sexuality into the room. Psychotherapists can address it verbally as part of our job definition.

AROUSAL WITHOUT ADDICTION

Not all sexual feelings of the client, and of the therapist, are symptoms. Clients can be telling a memory of sexual abuse in childhood or adulthood, and find themselves aroused as they had been at the time. This can be a healing experience as the client is not violated, instead respected by the therapist. In addition, as with sadness, anger and fear, the therapist might feel sexual feelings for the client, either because the client has disowned them or because the client is finally owning them. When this experience of sexuality doesn't lead to sexual activity, and doesn't bring up shame for either party, it can provide an experience of boundaried sexuality for the client.

> Matt struggled with sexual addiction, and worked on the effect of his mother's sexualized touch throughout his childhood and teen years. During one of our sessions he felt particularly free of the influences and very happy. He told me he was feeling sexual, and had an erection. He had no shame, and no need to do

anything about it. We could see that he was feeling celebratory of his new sexuality, as is natural to 3-year-olds. He got to have a sexual experience in the presence of another person without triggering that person's sexual response—both of us were sexually boundaried. We got to experience one person feeling sexual, the other knowing it, and that's that. If we lived in a sexually healthy culture, we would all be able to feel sexual without others feeling sexual in response.

18

Countertransference Is a Source
of Information

The term *countertransference* in psychotherapy is most often used to refer to the therapist's issues that interfere with therapy. (Transference refers to the client's projection of issues and relationships onto the therapist. Countertransference includes the therapist's projections onto the client.) The common usage is more limited than the psychoanalytic concept. The subject of sexuality is a likely source of feelings for the therapist—feelings that can result from the therapist's dynamics, or from the client's.

Therapists' sexual feelings during therapy sessions can be disturbing. A framework of understanding is needed in order to make sense of what is going on. Without it, the therapist has no recourse but to shut down feelings, abandoning the client and the therapy process. All therapists—

not just those specializing in sexuality—have to take into account their own sexual feelings in sessions, because clients will bring up sexual issues. Sexuality is part of being human—for both the client and the therapist. If sexuality cannot be observed and discussed, the therapy will be deprived of a vital function.

This chapter discusses some of the sources of therapists' feelings.

WHEN THE THERAPIST FEELS SEXUAL

Perhaps the most puzzling and frightening feeling a therapist can have in a therapy session is sexual arousal. Because this experience is not well understood and can engender shame, not many consultation groups discuss the therapist's sexual feelings in sessions (Pope et al. 1993). Arousal is usually seen as an issue of the therapist that must be addressed in his or her own therapy. Therapists are sometimes advised to refer the client to another therapist in order to avoid "inappropriate" feelings. While one cause of sexual feelings is the therapist's own cross-wiring or addiction, there are more possibilities that might be explored in safe peer consultation groups or supervision.

THE THERAPIST'S OWN SEXUALITY EXPRESSES ITSELF

It is possible that therapists' sexual feelings will emerge as a result of being a sexual human being. If these feelings have nothing to do with the client, and don't include a wish to be somewhere else having sex or thoughts about a sexual partner, then the therapist can consider that it is nothing more than evidence of sexuality. When I find myself with genital arousal, or body arousal, I can differentiate it from countertransference by the boundaried quality. It seems to be all mine, not something I would share with anyone, or even tell others. An additional check is noticing how it is identical to what I might feel going for a walk or sitting at the computer. It is a sensation reflecting that I am a sexual person, and my body and spirit are enjoying it, and it does not distract me from such things as a client's humanity, or a page I am writing. Sexual feelings from other sources in therapy sessions have different qualities.

CROSS-WIRING OR ADDICTION

Another source of sexual feelings comes from the therapist's issues. As therapists' sexual healing proceeds, it becomes easier to differentiate between their own issues that yield sexual feelings with a client, and the client's issues. As people who have grown up in our culture, therapists have cross-wiring, and many are addicted to sexuality. Examination of these issues in therapy and consultation groups can free the therapist to differentiate the causes of his or her reactions. While thinking about having sex with a client can be a symptom, there are many other reasons therapists have these thoughts—reasons that can be valuable information in the therapy.

WHEN THE THERAPIST'S ISSUES SURFACE

Learning to be a therapist requires sorting through a mix of feelings, learning how to recognize the difference between the client's feelings and the therapist's. In addition, many become therapists to face their own issues and resolve them. Confusion is necessary to the learning process.

We are all sexually cross-wired. We cannot avoid the association of sex with many other things, and this cross-wiring will emerge in therapy settings. Being a competent therapist doesn't mean never having cross-wired sexual feelings emerge in response to something the client is doing or feeling. If we take on the cultural attitude of badness, we will be less available to our clients. We must examine our feelings, and see how best to address them.

THERAPIST REACTION TO OBJECTIFICATION

Jill Seipel (1997) saw a client early in her practice who was sexually cross-wired to hands. In his perception, her hands were sexual objects. As a new therapist, Jill didn't know how to address her discomfort when he looked at them lustfully. She tells the story:

> I was surprised that he could always find women to help him act out his behavior. After several sessions, I realized that I was becoming increasingly uncomfortable as he stared at my hands in a trance-like state. Rather than say anything, I stopped wearing nail polish and put my hands down by my sides, and consciously didn't use my hands while talking (a difficult task, indeed). I felt somehow I ought to be able to feel neutral. Finally, after talking with my supervisor, I brought it up, giving us both an opportunity to successfully explore what had led to this behavior. We uncovered other fetishistic behavior, as well. I remain convinced that what surfaced in the ensuing work would not have if I had not faced my fears in bringing this up with him.

Jill didn't remember what she actually said to her client, but we came up with possible ways to address this situation. Jill could say, "I noticed that you are looking at my hands. Are you feeling sexual about them?" This would open discussion of his cross-wiring, and short-circuit the acting out of his addiction in her office. The conversation might go something like this:

"Well, yes, I noticed what beautiful hands you have, I couldn't help but look. I'm sorry, I didn't mean to make you feel uncomfortable."

"Well, Steve, let's talk about it. We know that hands are sexual objects to you, and so if you look at mine, you are being sexual with me."

"Oh, no, I wasn't! I was just admiring your hands."

"Can you talk about what happened right before you started looking at my hands? Maybe we can learn something about the function of looking." This statement begins the education about sexual addiction, and the reduction of shame by suggesting that there is a reason.

"I always look. Right from when I walk in the door. I look at all women's hands."

"What does it do for you?"

"I think of those hands touching me. Comforting me. . . . Is that wrong?"

"Well, it's not a question of right or wrong, but maybe we can learn about why you need to imagine being comforted. . . . It sounds like you might feel lonely a lot of the time."

"Yes. Yes, I do. There are a lot of people in my life, my family, people I work with, but I don't feel like I really matter to anyone. When I look at a woman's hands, and think about her touching me with them, I feel good. Kinda sexual, and warm inside."

At this point the session can go in a number of directions. The loneliness can be explored further. A question about when this started can take him into the history. Asking what it would be like if he stopped looking can bring up the fear he is avoiding. Or the therapist could begin educating him about sexual addiction, explaining how he is giving himself the sex drug whenever he looks at a woman's hands. Near the end of the session the therapist might ask how he now thought of her hands, particularly if she noticed that he had stopped looking at them sexually. People usually give up their sexual trance once they are talking about it. He might feel genuinely connected to his therapist from revealing his loneliness and naming what he tries to obtain through objectification. If he has stopped objectifying as a result of the intimacy of talking, it can offer hope that it is possible to find another way. At some point, probably not this early, the subject of the reactions of people whose hands are objectified can be introduced so he can see why he is getting disgusted reactions from people even while trying to feel loved and comforted.

One way to continue the session is, "You want to be touched lovingly?"

"Yes! When my wife touches me, I don't feel that. Even when we have sex, and her hands do me." He looks shyly at the therapist, as if asking if it's acceptable to talk like this.

"She brings you to orgasm with her hands?" The therapist demonstrates the acceptability of talking directly and with no shame about sexual activity.

"Not to orgasm. Just when she touches me when we get started. . . . I'd like it if she did that. But I can't ask." Encouraging him to ask will not help him examine the hand cross-wiring, or to find real ways to feel loved and comforted. Questioning the function, and clarifying how the function is not served, can launch the recovery from sexual cross-wiring and addiction.

Therapist reactions to a client's sexualizing might be placed into four categories, based on examples from my practice and consultation groups and those of my three colleagues.

When clients are sexual in sessions, one response to the countertransference discomfort is to set limits. This would take the form of telling the man that he must not look at her hands, that it isn't appropriate to their relationship, which isn't sexual. This solution limits therapy because the subject of the hand fetish can only be brought up in the context of hands outside of the therapy setting. In addition, the client is likely to feel shame for acting on his cross-wiring, and then having it ruled off limits—and even more shame when he "slips" and looks—which is unavoidable. Limit setting places the therapist in the position of enforcing that limit—also impossible.

A second approach is the one Jill first used. By lowering her hands out of view she removed the "sexual object" from his sight so he wouldn't have this reaction—and she wouldn't have discomfort. One therapist who works with sex offenders chooses to change her appearance in order to avoid triggering clients' sexual responses. This reaction communicates the therapist's fear, and inability to deal directly with the issue. The client might feel shame as he sees he has made her uncomfortable. Or he can feel powerful in getting her to feel small and in his control.

A third approach is asking what is going on for the client, as I described. By asking in a curious, nonshaming manner, the therapist can create a new environment in which the chance of healing from this symptom becomes possible. Therapists might object to taking this approach when the client comes for something other than sexuality, and is perhaps limited to short-term therapy. But if this symptom is not addressed, the therapist will be left with negative reactions, and other work with the client will be compromised. In addition, if a client has this kind of sexual symptom, it can be very helpful to name it in a nonshaming manner, even if it can't be addressed fully at that time. You can assume this person has never had the experience of being asked with acceptance and curiosity about his shameful behaviors.

A fourth approach (which includes the third) is telling the client about the therapist's discomfort. Chances are, if Jill had been able to talk with her client, she wouldn't have felt the discomfort, but if she did, it could help to say it. When this man is in his sexual trance, he probably doesn't know he is offending women, even while he receives their shaming. Jill might have said, "I notice that I want to hide my hands when I am with you. And I stopped wearing nail polish so my hands would be less attractive to you. . . . It doesn't feel good to know you are objectifying my hands." This might be followed by asking him all about it—how do people react, and how does he feel about their reactions.

TO TELL OR NOT TO TELL

The question of how much the therapist should reveal in therapy sessions is a controversial subject. One agreed upon limit is that the purpose of revealing is to be helpful to the client, and not for the therapist's personal gratification. But beyond this, some therapists reveal a great deal of their reactions while others reveal almost none.

The psychoanalytic community proposes restrictive limits, while at the same time offering an in-depth understanding of countertransference. In contrast to the typical views on self-revelation, Maroda (1991) proposes thoughtful revelation of therapist emotions, including anger and love, and sometimes sexual feelings. She addresses the question of when to reveal, and how.

My own preference is to develop a relationship based on the premise that the two of us will explore together to understand what the client is working on, how our relationship reflects that, and what is needed for the work to take place. I see my feelings elicited by the client as one source of information for us to take a look at. This is in contrast to the therapist taking a look at the meaning of his or her feelings, and providing information through interpretations or questions. When the relationship can handle it, I offer my feelings as raw data, from which I might make guesses. For example, when I feel sad I will say I'm feeling sad. My client might go on with what she was saying, or switch to her own feeling of sadness, or tell me how I'm like someone in her past. I will have educated her to these possibilities in early revelations of feeling. From this stance of working together, I don't have to have my feelings figured out before speaking them. I give the raw data—the facts—sometimes followed with my guesses about the source and the meaning of the experience. From there we can together figure out what is going on.

In deciding how much to reveal, the following are some points to consider:

1. Some therapists are comfortable revealing their feelings to clients, and can develop an understanding of

how to do this through practice. Other therapists are not, and to do so would feel forced and unnatural.

2. New therapists will have less skill in differentiating the nature of their feeling, and the most useful way to use it. New therapists might discuss their feelings in supervision, and perhaps in their own therapy, before revealing them to the client. It requires experience to differentiate among the various causes of feelings emerging in therapy sessions.

3. I typically reveal less to new clients than to clients I have been working with for a time, and whom I have educated about the nature of therapist feelings and how they can be used. We live in a culture that does not reveal feelings easily—particularly countertransference feelings—and so part of the development of a therapeutic relationship is learning together how emotions can be named.

4. The nature of the relationship with the client must be considered. Some clients are so afraid of intimacy that they will engage in therapy without ever addressing the relationship with the therapist. Such people can feel assaulted and perhaps frightened or critical when the therapist attempts to introduce more. I have had such people come for several months of successful therapy, and I have revealed no more than interest and compassion.

One client came to therapy to address his sexual addiction, and rapidly uncovered the causes. He expressed great appreciation of the fact that I was able to know all about what he was struggling with and to help him with it. But it was clear that he wanted nothing more. In addition, I had little feeling beyond interest and sympathy. He did not use the therapeutic relationship as a source of healing beyond the shame-reducing effect of being accepted and understood.

REVEALING THERAPIST ISSUES CAN BE HELPFUL

Therapy sessions are not for the purpose of resolving the therapist's issues, but occasionally a situation will occur where the therapist might need to reveal issues that are inhibiting the therapy. I have no clear guidelines about how to decide if it can be helpful to bring up issues in the client's therapy—or if they should be limited to personal therapy, or supervisor or case consultation.

I had a profound experience with a client and a therapy group that exemplifies how the appearance of the therapist's cross-wired arousal, and other feelings, can be helpful to the client, other group members, and the therapist.

> I found myself feeling sexual in a therapy session with Kenneth. We were looking at pornography that triggered him to learn about the causes so he could challenge his cross-wired reactions. It was powerful for him to look at it with me and experience no arousal. (This use of pornography in a therapy session is not common practice, and one I rarely engage in. It is too easy for the client to incorporate the therapist into the addiction. Kenneth had worked with me for five years, and I could be sure of his purpose.)
>
> We talked about the possibility that one of us might be aroused by the pictures, and agreed that it would be named. Kenneth had no sexual reaction, and valued having me see triggering sadistic acts. His shame lifted.

After half an hour of looking at cruel sexual acts and women's thin bodies with huge implanted breasts, I was surprised when I reacted sexually to a picture based on body positioning. I immediately told Kenneth what had happened, and stopped looking at the picture. The arousal vanished as another reaction took over. I was flooded with shame and fear because of my patterned belief that I had violated him by feeling sexual in his presence. Kenneth feels like a son to me, and I quickly recognized the feeling I struggled with when my own son was growing up—I was afraid I might sexually abuse him. Now this pattern that dominated many years of my life, with little consciousness, was right in front of my eyes for the first time.

I had a choice about what I might do with these feelings. I could have hidden them, and processed them later. If I had been a new therapist, or Kenneth had been a new client, or if I believed he wouldn't have understood, I might have made this choice. But because of the length of our relationship, and my belief that we would be able to work it through, I told him what I was feeling. Even in my reactive state, I was clear about my issue, and the potential impact of revealing it. This was not a time to focus on Kenneth's dynamics, because this countertransference did not come from his issues.

I pulled my chair away from Kenneth, explaining why. Kenneth was glad I told him because he didn't have to guess why I shut down and pulled away. The session soon ended, but the next day in a therapy group Kenneth sat next to me, and I again felt that I had abused him—even while I knew I hadn't. I became frozen, unable to perceive the state of any member of the group. It was untenable to play-act being a therapist.

I knew they would see that I was not myself, and if I stayed quiet their childhood experience of hidden feelings would be reenacted. So I started talking.

Pulling my chair away from Kenneth, I asked if I could tell what happened in our session so I could reveal my state. He immediately said yes, and together we recounted it, including the powerful experience he received from not being shamed for his use of pornography, or the arousing images. I explained how I was having feelings associated with an erroneous belief that I had abused Kenneth, and had pulled away from him in order to avoid abusing him further. As I saw six attentive faces, all knowing I hadn't violated him, and all appreciating my openness, I came back to myself. Over about ten minutes, the fear and need for physical distance dissolved. I pulled my chair closer and closer until I was back in the circle of the group.

My fear that presenting my own issue could be harmful was quickly erased by group members' reactions. They had previously seen me as a calm, collected, classic therapist, always in control. Now their perception included the fact that I am not without my own issues, and am willing to speak up when frightened.

This use of the group setting to work on my issue that was elicited in the group is different from using the group for my own therapy. I didn't become a group member, and I didn't bring issues there to work on. I confronted what had to be confronted in order to do my job.

If the therapist decides not to reveal feelings elicited by a client's material, the client will perceive the shame or fear, and will take it on, perhaps unconsciously. This will increase unwillingness to talk about things that could trigger the therapist's shame. A friend told me he talked about his shameful sexual behavior with his therapist, and left the session sorry he had brought it up. While this might have been caused by his own shame, he believes it was intensified by his therapist's unacknowledged shame. He has since shared these same experiences with me and with my husband, without adding shame. Perhaps it is ideal if therapists have no shame, but it is not possible. If we can acknowledge our reactions for the client's sake, we can prevent adding further negative associations to his or her cross-wiring and sexual behaviors.

My friend's therapist might have said something like, "I'm glad you're telling me this, M. I know you need to talk about it so you don't feel like a bad person for what you did. But I have to tell you, I'm having some discomfort hearing it. I haven't resolved my own shame about this." She might go on to say, "I will understand if you don't want to talk about it further, but I want you to know that I'm willing to feel my shame and fear, and I'll also get help with it. I know my feelings aren't about you." This would create a model for how the client might address his own discomforts with people close to him, as well as provide safety in the therapy room.

FEELING THE CLIENTS' FEELINGS

The English language is inadequate to express some vital aspects of human experience. One area of deficit is in describing the capacity of people to feel the feelings of another, particularly if the other person disowns them. Theaters demonstrate this phenomenon. Even when there is little laughter or other overt expression, sharing feelings with a group intensifies the experience for everyone. Energy is passed among members of the audience, as we access the human capacity to join, forming community. We are not meant to be solitary beings. This capacity to funnel feelings to another person and to receive them can provide useful information. Clients who are unable to feel their own feelings may take an intermediate step (unconsciously) between lack of awareness and awareness, and let the therapist feel the emotion for them. Sexual arousal is one of these feelings. This kind of countertransference has been called *concordant identification* (Kernberg 1995).

When I take on a client's feeling, I check to see if it is mine. The answer isn't always clear. Most often, the feeling that belongs to the client is of a lighter intensity than my own. It seems to land on me, perhaps settling in, while my own feelings emerge from deep inside. Another check is my attention. If I am having my own feelings, my attention goes to myself (as well as my client) as when I am angry about what happened to her. But if it is her feeling, then my attention is primarily outside. At times I will cry for many minutes, giving expression to his or her grief.

A context can be created so clients can understand why the therapist will share feelings. Early in therapy when a feeling first comes up, I use it to create a model. For example, if I find myself feeling sad, I might say, "I'd like to interrupt you, if that's okay. I started feeling sad, and I know it isn't my feeling, so I wondered if you were maybe feeling some sadness." I am communicating that I know I can feel clients' feelings for them. When the client acknowledges feeling sad, we nod together. The client might begin expressing the sadness herself. After the first or second time, the client knows from her own experience that this can happen.

Then if I begin to feel sexual feelings that aren't mine, she knows they are possibly her own. I have prepared her so she doesn't feel assaulted or offended by my statement of sexual feelings. She can feel supported by my naming something she has disowned.

My unresolved fear of harming clients by revealing that I feel sexual in therapy sessions often results in a different approach than I would use with other feelings. I am more likely to ask my client if she is feeling sexual instead of saying that I am. Once she says she is, then I might say I guessed that because I was too. This is a particularly good idea when therapy is new, when the therapist isn't sure the client will understand why the therapist is feeling aroused. Expressions of most countertransference require a developing relationship. (There are exceptions, such as a client who explained in our third session how she needed to hear the truth about my feelings toward her. When I became annoyed, and told her, she was greatly relieved, and more trusting.) Expression of sexual feelings requires the greatest therapeutic alignment.

BECOMING THE CLIENT'S PARENT (SIBLING, GRANDPARENT, ETC.)

As we are capable of experiencing the client's feelings, we are also capable of taking on the feelings of important members of their childhood families (this has been called *complementary identification* [Kernberg 1995]). Early in my practice I had difficulty believing this was true, but after years of seeing that I was right, when I start having feelings that don't make any sense in my life, and also don't seem related to the client's dynamics, I know I might be taking the role of someone else. I will describe what I am feeling to the client, and ask if this is familiar. She will usually tell me immediately who I am like. Then, after asking for permission, I might begin speaking from that place. Sometimes clients will become angry with me, able to express feelings they have been unable to express to the real person.

As a striking example, I once found myself so irritated that I wanted to look away from my client. The feeling was so strong, I followed it, sighed, telling him how I would like to have binoculars to study the birds outside the window. He laughed and laughed, finally stopping long enough to tell me he had bought his mother binoculars for Christmas for just that purpose—something I hadn't known.

When the subject is sexuality, I have more difficulty launching into the role, particularly when the person I am taking on is someone who abused the client.

> Susan's mother was controlling and domineering, finding fault with everything. I could play this part. But when I felt the sexualized wanting Susan's mother had often demonstrated, I changed to telling Susan what I was feeling instead of playing it out. My fear sometimes prevents me from being clear enough to discern when my actions are helpful and when I might go too far.
>
> Susan was in a therapy group that acted out this kind of dynamic. She took on the role of Kenneth's mother, and flirted with him. Kenneth understood what she was doing, saw the similarities with mother, and was able to fight back for the first time. After feeling the dread and disgust that dominated their sexualized relationship, he pulled out of historical immobility, stood up, and began yelling. When clients take on each

other's relatives, I can see more clearly than when I take them on.

This is not role playing. It is not a technique. It is not based on an intellectual assessment that playing a relative could help. It is responding to actual feelings that emerge within the therapist (or group member) in response to the need of the client to make his or her history overt.

ATTRACTION TO THE CLIENT

Given that we are all socialized to be attracted to certain kinds of people, and that we have idiosyncratic forms of cross-wired attraction, it is hardly surprising that therapists will find themselves attracted to clients. To make use of this attraction for the healing of the client, and for healing of the therapist, it should be discussed with colleagues or in therapy.

If this attraction elicits therapist shame, the therapist will be less able to see what is going on. (Lack of examination, followed by unconsciously programmed reactions, can lead to therapists having sex with clients.) If, instead, this attraction is seen as a symptom of the client's, or a symptom of the therapist's, or both, then it can be useful.

Here are some questions that might elicit useful information:

1. Is this the kind of person you are often attracted to?
2. What is it about this person that is attractive? (helpless, powerful, flirtatious, interested in you, depressed, needy, frightening, overtly sexual, sexy, overpowering, body shape, etc.)

3. How would you feel if you acted on this attraction?
4. If you were single and met this person socially, how would you feel if you acted on this attraction?
5. How would your attraction seem to serve the client? (client might feel in control, throw you off from pursuing painful information, invalidate you as all others have been invalidated, etc.)
6. Is the client playing out his or her sexual abuse history by offering you the role of the perpetrator?
7. What feelings of your own might you be avoiding by being sexually attracted?

Revealing the attraction can be couched in the language of how this is relevant to the therapy. For example, the therapist might say, "I've been noticing a feeling of mine that I think would be helpful to talk about (pause a few seconds to see if the client has a reaction). I had the thought that I'm attracted to you. I think there could be some relevance to our therapy. Do you have any thoughts about what that could be?" This introduction of the attraction as important to the therapy prevents the revelation from sounding like an invitation. The client might respond with, "All men (women) react like that," or, "Is that all you think about?" These reactions can become the focus of questions, such as, "All men (women) react like that?" or "No, it's not all I think about. Are you afraid it might be?" The subject has become part of the therapy instead of isolated from therapy. This kind of conversation can help the therapist differentiate his or her own cross-wiring that is independent of the client's issues, from issues of the client—as well as how the two are interwoven.

WHEN THE THERAPIST FEELS REVULSION

Revulsion is a feeling that has to be addressed early in the therapy because if it continues, no therapy can take place. Hiding the feeling will prevent therapy. The client will at least unconsciously know the therapist is disgusted.

Revulsion can come from a number of sources. First, the symptoms the client wants to address, such as wanting to be sexual with children, or cross-wiring to rape or other sadistic activities, can bring about strong negative feelings.

A second cause of revulsion is when the client is similar to someone the therapist found offensive in the past. For example, a colleague had a number of bad experiences with men from a certain country. These reactions become projected onto all men from that country. She handles this by not accepting such clients, knowing she cannot hide her reactions.

The client can bring about this feeling in any therapist if he or she is reenacting history in which he or she was found repulsive. For example, some children who have been used sexually in their first year or two become sexualized, and then approach the adult for sexual attention. But when the child is 2 or 3, the adult begins to see the child as perpetrating him or her. Then the child is treated with revulsion (other people respond with sexual attention). This dynamic can be demonstrated with people in adult life and with the therapist. Asking the client how others respond to him or her can begin the exploration. When the relationship can sustain the client's reactions to learning that the therapist feels revulsion too, this can be carefully introduced. Such a conversation might go like this:

"Do you find people responding negatively to you sometimes?"

"Why do you ask that?"

"I was curious. After hearing about how you look at people, objectifying them, I thought maybe they reacted badly."

"Well, yes, sometimes."

"What's that like, when they do?"

"I don't like it, if that's what you mean . . . but it seems natural, too. People don't seem to like me much."

"Maybe we can figure out what happened in your past that made you trigger negative feelings in people."

"Really? You think it can change?"

"Well, yes. *My* feelings are changing. I was feeling a little repulsed by you, but now that we are talking about your tender feelings, its gone away. I'm feeling closer to you."

Another cause of revulsion is when a sexually addicted client acts sexual toward the therapist in ways that feel intrusive and violating. Regardless of the cause, the therapist cannot afford to leave it unaddressed. We cannot act like we are accepting and caring without violating the client and limiting the therapy to superficial help (see Chapter 17).

WHEN THE THERAPIST FEELS THREATENED

When a client's dynamics create false power through intimidation, this can take the form of asking intrusive questions or sexualizing the therapist. Getting the therapist to squirm is an act of aggression. (Nonsexual forms include banging furniture, slapping a table, yelling loudly in a manner that doesn't reflect true anger, and other behaviors that are designed to frighten.)

Louisa Turner (1997) told of a client who asked her about the night before with her boyfriend, wanting to know who was on top when they had sex. Instead of addressing the content as a reflection of his sexual issues, she addressed the aggressive nature of his comment.

I received a call from a man who wanted help with sexual issues who berated me for not calling him back right away. It was clear that intimidation and control were more immediate issues than sex, and so I referred him to a specialist in anger.

SEXUAL AWARENESS

A client walks in the door and I think of sex, but without any indication of why. The person isn't *doing* anything—there is no flirting, no sexual energy exuded, and for the most part, she looks like her usual self. I wasn't feeling sexual before she arrived, and I don't have any cross-wiring that would elicit a sexual reaction.

While the exact mechanism for this transmission is not definable in Western culture, it is a reality that needs to be named in order to be able to perceive it. If a therapist does not know about this phenomenon, the sexual awareness will be perceived as coming from some other source, and this information will not be available to the therapy.

When one female client arrived for our second appointment, I had a strong sense of sexuality, but with no information about the source of this perception. I was puzzled and curious, but because our relationship was new, I didn't bring it up directly.

As our session unfolded, she talked about a man who had written books, who had given presentations, and who lived in another city—three similarities with me. She had had a sexualized bond with him, which had not been acted on because both were married. It had not even been discussed. This information allowed me to see that I was now in his role, revered and idealized for my work, and offered an invisible sexual connection to enhance our relationship. Although both of us are heterosexual, this kind of bond is just as functional as in an opposite-sex relationship, and perhaps even more useful because its sexual nature can be easily denied.

People we think are sexy but who aren't flirting may be communicating sexuality. We might want to attribute it to a person's looks or body shape, but often such qualities cannot account for the perception.

One client had a glamorous, sexual presentation when I met her, and over the course of several months of therapy, she gave it up, along with wearing makeup. Intermittently she wore makeup, and again the sexual presentation appeared. For months I assumed the makeup created the change in my perception until one day she came to therapy with the presentation and no makeup! Another time she wore makeup without the presentation. This freed us to look at the felt sense that accompanied the presentation compared with feeling like herself. Obviously, when she needed to present herself as glamorous and sexy, she had also chosen to wear makeup—a connection that threw me off.

THERAPIST REACTION TO FLIRTING AND SEDUCTION

Clients who flirt and seduce in order to feel safe and cared about will sooner or later try this long-standing habit with the therapist. Reactions typical in social situations are not useful in the therapy setting. One, flirting with the client, indicates that the relationship has a sexual component, which it must not. Two, a negative reaction will further shame the client's sexuality and self, and has no place in therapy (with the possible exception of anger if the client continues to pursue this course). Three, the absence of a reaction might communicate that the client might as well give up, and while this can be helpful, it avoids the chance to use the flirting as information about how the client leads his or her life.

Pointing out to the client that you notice her or him flirting, and wondering what this is about, can open discussion about sexuality. It is my experience that most clients will be shocked, and want to deny it at first. If they cannot talk about it at the time, the door is opened, and the observation is available for the therapist to refer back to when related issues come up.

For example, I had a male client who made himself feel big—and actually look bigger—by assuming a flirtatious, charismatic stance. He didn't mind the label of charismatic, but he didn't see himself as flirtatious. Over time I could relate this maneuver to its effectiveness in gathering attention, and how he liked the flirting it elicited in return. If I had not named it, he could have felt either rejected by my lack of response, or he might have believed it was what elicited my interest in him. The naming, even if it isn't pursued, cuts that short.

My colleague Louisa Turner (1997) wrote about the discomfort of other therapists when dealing with sexual invitations from clients that she observed over years of consultation groups she attended and supervised, and trainings and conferences.

It seems that there are a fair number of therapists out there (and it's mostly women therapists that I've heard about in this regard) who limit their clients' sexual acting out in the session in the name of setting limits and establishing clear boundaries. I mean to the extent that the offending behavior is not analyzed and the patient is warned to never repeat it or anything like it.

This reminds me of one of my clients, a middle-aged man with an erection problem, no sexual interest in his wife, and a long history of masturbation by hurting himself. In the third session he suggested that next week why don't we meet at the restaurant of a nearby hotel and then go upstairs to a room. I said no, that we would not do that, but that I wondered what it was about for him that that was what he wanted to do. In group supervision, several other female students (very bright and talented therapists) felt that I should just have said no and told him not to ever violate that boundary again, that asking him to continue into a discussion about it would only further stimulate his arousal and further encourage him to view me as a sexual object. Fortunately, I was supported by my supervisors to analyze his wish. Though the patient couldn't say much about it at the time, we went on to do much work over a several year period. Somewhere later in the treatment, as we were discussing his relationship with his critical and womanizing father, he noted that his father had always said that if you can't get a woman into bed by the fourth date, then you aren't much of a man. This clicked for me about that early proposition for our fourth session, and this led into a huge chunk of work about the connection between his sexual addiction and his relationship with his father.

Turner's gift to her client was naming, accepting, and questioning in order to help him heal. Her curiosity, instead of shaming, also established boundaries. She demonstrated that they would not engage in this manner, and she offered the healthy alternative. Acceptance of behavior through discussion of it does not mean the absence of boundaries.

The counsel Turner received regarding how discussion would stimulate and encourage him to view her as a sexual object is the opposite of what happens. It is our consistent experience that while talking openly and without shaming, virtually all men will be able to stop objectifying. Open questioning is the only way a man will be able to take an objective look at his behavior so that he can change it. As I discussed in Chapter 17, when Gary was referred to me by Ms. Y. for an evaluation of his sexual addiction, he talked about sex openly and with no sexualized "hit." While she tried to set a limit by refusing to engage with him when he talked about sex, he had continued to go into a sexual trance and act out his addiction in her office, with her as his sex object. When my male sexual addict clients come to sessions or groups in their sexual trance, they soon move out of it by open discussion of their desire to act out. Talking brings the person into the present, and away from the artificial world they have created using sexual arousal as the fuel. This is one of the functions of sexual twelve-step programs.

Barbara (presented in Chapter 14) wrote to me after

the session in which she pulled away from a brief hug because of her fear that she would harm me with her sexual energy. She was deeply touched by my acceptance of possible sexual cross-wiring occurring right in my office, in physical contact with me. If I set limits, saying she was not to hug me unless there was no sexual energy conveyed, she would continue to carry shame. But my willingness to experience it, and talk about it, freed her from being alone with this shameful issue that she desperately needed to address. Our clients need more than limit setting.

WHEN CLIENTS FANTASIZE
ABOUT THE THERAPIST

It is difficult enough to handle a client's direct statements of sexual fantasy about the therapist. It can be even more difficult when the client doesn't bring it up. Among the red flags that can alert the therapist are a feeling of revulsion for the client, feeling bored in sessions because little seems to be happening, a feeling that boundaries have been violated but with no evidence, or attraction to the client. Somewhat more obvious indicators might be indirect sexual references, such as asking if you saw the movie, *The People vs. Larry Flynt* with no obvious reason for the question. Or wondering what your bedroom looks like, or asking if your partner is a good lover. Early in my practice I ignored comments of this kind, but by doing so I created a rift by storing up my negative reactions. I felt violated. By seeing these questions as information about the client's issues, and addressing them openly, violation doesn't occur, and both the client and the therapist are alerted to important symptoms that would otherwise be overlooked.

I spoke with Al long after his three years of therapy in which he constantly fantasized about his therapist, but never thought it was something to bring up. He was a sex addict whose addiction wasn't recognized, and he played it out in therapy. Al was so familiar with this manner of responding to women, he didn't know it was a subject for therapy. His therapist didn't ask.

NOT ASKING ABOUT SEXUAL FEELINGS

Not asking about sexual feelings when it might be useful to do so can be a form of countertransference. Growing up in our culture has trained us that we must not talk about sex openly, particularly if the questions have to do with the client–therapist relationship. To demonstrate this, imagine yourself asking your client if he or she has sexual fantasies about you. If yes, what are they? Notice if your heart rate changes, or your breathing.

For Al, it would have been most helpful to begin with general questions about sexuality, then going on to masturbation, asking if he had gone to strip clubs, did he buy pornography, did he fantasize, and if so, what about? The answers to these questions would have led his therapist to asking if he fantasized about her, which would have greatly changed the nature of their therapy. It might have become real instead of providing material for his sexual addiction, and feeding his need for attention.

The therapist might have recognized that he wasn't really present, or she was bored because little was happening, even though he came back every week and expressed an appreciation for therapy. She might have felt uncomfortable without knowing why as she unconsciously perceived his sexual interest. He had told her about buying sexy underpants for a female massage therapist, and about the joke dildo he had given a woman he supervised at work. She didn't treat this information as worthy of further exploration. This therapist sought the consultation of a peer, who attended one of his sessions to help assess how to work with his anger. Neither therapist recognized the sexual issues that manifested in his life, and in the therapy relationship.

In these situations, discussion in case consultation can yield only guesses about what is going on, but can be useful in gathering support to ask difficult questions. When therapy seems stymied, and the reasons are not obvious, asking questions about sexual functioning might elicit valuable information.

Louisa Turner talked about what she can say to clients once she resolved her discomfort bringing up sexual subjects that are off-limits in our culture. When the subject of sexual fantasies comes up, she asks if the client includes her in the fantasies. If the response is no, she tells him or her that this might happen as a natural part of the therapy.

DRESSING FOR THE CLIENT

Any time therapists think about what they are going to wear to work based on a client they will see that day, it can be assumed that a countertransference reaction is taking place. This can be in the form of wanting to look nice, wanting to wear clothing the client finds acceptable, or wanting to avoid wearing clothing the client will react to sexually.

COUNTERTRANSFERENCE IS A SOURCE OF INFORMATION

While addressing some of the therapist's own feelings in therapy sessions can feel risky and uncomfortable, and may bring up feelings of shame and inadequacy, these feelings offer a wealth of information about the client's issues and avenues for addressing them. In addition, the therapist is offered the benefit of confrontation with her or his own issues. I personally feel some of the deepest work in therapy can be accomplished through using the countertransference.

19

How to Refer for Consultation

HOW TO REFER

If the subject of sexuality comes up, but doesn't unfold, it can serve the client to suggest one or two sessions with a specialist. I have seen that other therapists' clients can more easily talk with me, for two reasons. First, knowing that I specialize in sexuality, they know I have heard it all and am able to talk about it. Second, discussing sex can be easier with a trusted stranger than with a therapist with whom they have a relationship.

After meeting with the client, the specialist can help the therapist decide if referral for sexual addiction, or other sexual issues, is warranted, or if the therapist can handle it.

In the latter case, the specialist can provide information to assist the general therapist.

Gary (discussed in Chapter 17) had been meeting with Ms. Y. for almost a year, but had not told her that he wasn't having sex with his wife and was unable to sustain erections. When she referred him for evaluation of sexual addiction, he told me within twenty minutes. Before the session ended, he planned to tell Ms. Y., even though I had not brought up the need to do that. By talking he was able to see for himself that he had been keeping a secret unnecessarily.

Raymond and Jean (presented in Chapter 6) went to Dr. X. because of marital problems. Raymond's sexual acting out was just one of the issues they wanted to address, focusing more on his perception of her control of him, and her anger when he shut down and wouldn't relate to her. They hadn't told Dr. X. they had sex every day, and their feelings about it, because it didn't seem relevant. But in my office, where they came to address their sexuality, they filled me in on their sex life. I could question them further to learn that sexuality played a large part in their difficulties, and how they used sex to avoid other issues.

If Dr. X. had been willing to work with them on sexual issues, a referral for consultation instead of therapy could have served them well. We quickly defined the issues, and they rapidly made changes. They were capable of taking this information back to Dr. X., who could have continued the good work she had been doing. If, however, a couple were unable to quickly grasp their issues, then a transfer might have been advisable. Dr. X. and I would talk about how to best serve this couple.

REFERRAL FOR TREATMENT

A referral to a specialist is appropriate if the therapist doesn't feel qualified to work with the emerging sexual issues. In the area of sexual addiction, an available group is a vital part of healing. Therapists who feel capable of working with additional issues in individual therapy can refer clients only for group. This can be a good combination because it offers clients the complementary expertise of two professionals, and hearing the same thing from both therapists, perhaps in different language. This can more powerfully confront denial, a foremost challenge with sexual addiction.

It is my personal preference for the original therapist to continue working with a client on sexual addiction issues if that therapist is willing to learn about it and consult with specialists. The client can feel more supported by remaining with a trusted therapist than by being referred elsewhere. In addition, the addictive use of sexual energy is so pervasive in our culture that the treatment of it should not reside with a handful of specialists. It needs to become part of general practice. But if a therapist doesn't have the interest in learning more, or has negative feelings toward the client, then referral is preferable.

TWO THERAPISTS

Sometimes it is in the best interest of the client to have two therapists—the original therapist and a specialist. There are a number of reasons for this. One, when sexual shame is intense, clients may feel defensive toward the therapist who is helping with sexual issues. The support of the original therapist to work through these feelings, and to help with issues that are not sexual, can make therapy possible.

Second, shame decreases as additional safe people are told shameful secrets. Individual therapy is the best place to begin this shame reduction. Group therapy or twelve-step meetings will eventually broaden the numbers, but few people are able to talk in a group setting until a significant amount of therapy and education has occurred. In the meantime, talking with two therapists on an individual basis can assist with the need to tell more than one safe person. The client is less likely to believe that the original therapist is the only safe person—a belief common to clients in their first therapy experience.

> Ms. Z. referred Jerry, 35, after seeing him for about six months. Jerry was in his early thirties when his sister, then 18, told their mother he had been sexual with her from ages 8 to 17. His sister waited until she was 18 to reveal this so that Jerry would not be prosecuted. A report was never made. By the time Ms. Z. and I met him, he wasn't being sexual with other children. Consequently, we were not required to make a report. If we had, no action would have been taken. Therefore, sex offender treatment, which confronts the behavior and consequently the shame associated with it, had not been required. But Ms. Z. knew that Jerry needed to take a look at why he abused his sister, and felt attracted to girls, which interfered with developing relationships with women. She was not qualified to help him with this, and wanted to find someone who did.

Jerry hadn't been forced to confront his shame, and hadn't been able to associate with other men who had committed similar acts. Sexual shame is greatest for people who have been sexual with children. Suicide is not uncommon for those who have been reported. In addition to his own shame, he knows that our culture condemns him. Walking into my office meant remembering how he had treated his sister. Sessions were painful, and Jerry had great difficulty allowing me to become an ally. After three sessions he decided to come alternate weeks. He increased sessions with Ms. Z. to work through what was stimulated in our sessions.

Jerry worked with me for several months, but found the shame too overwhelming. He elected to continue examining his childhood with Ms. Z. and planned to address the incest at a later time. I believe he would not have been able to see me at all if he had not had Ms. Z. for support. He experienced me as shaming him because his own shame was so intense, and he couldn't imagine that I could know what he had done without condemning him. Ms. Z. maintained a position of support by not discussing the incest.

WHEN TO REFER

Clients will often bring up issues their therapist knows little about, and sometimes a referral is important. In the area of sexuality, I believe it is always appropriate to refer if the therapist doesn't feel capable of addressing the issue, or doesn't want to obtain supervision in order to be fully available to the client. It can be assumed that the client is revealing only part of the issue (see Chapters 14 and 16). I don't want to discount the secrecy surrounding other issues that bring shame to clients, but I believe the subject of sexuality will be more hidden, to both the client and the therapist.

TALK TO THE NEW THERAPIST FIRST

While all clients need a referral to be done in a compassionate way, sexuality requires even more empathy and compassion.

Here are some ideas to consider. First, call a potential therapist you want to make the referral to. Find out if this therapist has room in her or his practice to take on your client, and if the client's issues are within the scope of the therapist's practice. Discover if he or she is willing to have conversations with you to explore what is best in the long run. Make sure you can work with this therapist if the need arises in the future.

Ask the therapist for information about the kinds of symptoms he or she deals with. Most therapists who specialize in sexuality are limited to sex therapy, or sexual abuse, or sexual addiction, with only moderate overlap with the other two. In addition, therapists who treat sex offenders use either a behavior approach similar to sex therapists or a sexual addiction/compulsivity model. If this is the issue your client needs help with, notice if the therapist speaks with compassion or exasperation about sex offenders. Many sex offender programs advocate a punitive approach, actually increasing the offender's shame. This is different from confronting sex offenders with the truth about their behavior, and holding them responsible for change. Firmness, and even anger, can be delivered without shame—and must be in order for a sex offender to truly engage in sexual healing that can stop the harm of others.

Most people who advertise specialization in sexuality call themselves sex therapists. They may or not hold certification with ASSECT (American Association of Sex Education, Counselors, and Therapists), the organization that certifies sex therapists. Traditional sex therapy is behavior modification based, and focuses on the symptoms of sexual dysfunction. Sex therapists with additional training and experience may be able to address sexuality in a variety of ways. If your client needs to work on more than a specific symptom, it will help to interview the therapist about what he or she can offer in addition to sex therapy. There is a great deal of difference among sex therapists. Some are entirely mechanical, and others are able to become involved in real sexual healing.

When discussing with your client the possibility of referral to someone who specializes in sexual issues, the fact that this interaction with the potential new therapist has occurred can be included. By telling about your conversation with the potential new therapist, you begin the process of helping your client develop trust, and demonstrate that you are not abandoning your client by pushing him or her out the door.

John was referred to my therapy group for men who are sexually addicted. The referring therapist asked him for permission to ask me if there was room in my group, and if there was, to talk about him with me. She and I discussed his dynamics, and the current status of his sexual acting out. We discussed the other men in the group, and if John would be a good fit. I have learned from experience that there is no way to make sure that a person is a good fit because different dynamics show up in groups than in individual therapy. But it is possible to screen obvious mismatches. Sometimes a referral will be made even with serious reservations with the hope that a person will be able to connect with the group. We are often surprised. And often disappointed.

When John became established in the group, he appreciated the ongoing contact I had with his therapist, feeling supported by having two of us helping him in different contexts, in different ways, and on different issues.

Part V

Therapist Healing

20

Suggestions to Assist Therapists with Shame Removal

Therapists can read books about sexuality, but until their own shame and fear and secrecy are addressed, they will be inhibited in their ability to hear clients talk about sex. Therapeutic effectiveness will be reduced. Because of this, I recommend that all therapists take some steps to prepare themselves to be better therapists—as well as improve their own lives. This chapter includes questions to discuss.

The safest way to begin this exploration is probably in another therapist's office. Finding a therapist who has done some of his or her own sexual healing, you might begin by telling your story—memories about sex, yours and family members.

As with clients in sexual recovery, talking in groups is

necessary to challenge the culture's attitudes and beliefs. A subculture can support leaving the larger culture's views. It is radical to overthrow a society's closely held beliefs. Because of sexual shame, beliefs about sexuality are among the most closely held.

A MANUAL FOR ADDRESSING THERAPIST SEXUAL FEELINGS

The American Psychological Association (APA) published a book (Pope et al. 1993) that describes in detail how to go about talking about sexual feelings and issues that come up in therapy sessions. The book includes vignettes of sexual situations in sessions, followed by questions for therapists to discuss. There are no right or wrong answers. The questions are designed to bring up subjects that might naturally occur if we didn't live in a culture and belong to a profession that finds sex frightening to discuss. The authors do an excellent job of describing how to create safety in order to take on the task of discussing this fear-provoking subject. They address the lack of training regarding these vital experiences, as well as a disinclination to bring them up in consultation and supervision. Each therapist is left to address them alone. The authors wrote the book after discovering that 12 percent of male psychologists and 4 percent of female psychologists admitted on a confidential survey that they had had sexual contact with their clients. They rightfully believe that lack of understanding of sexuality and the fear of bringing up sexual issues, contribute to this high percentage of sexual abuse of clients. Instead of shaming therapists, the book takes a compassionate and helpful stance, offering solutions to the problem.

Pope and colleagues (1986) describe research regarding the frequency of therapist sexual feelings toward clients. They found that of the 575 psychotherapists surveyed, 87 percent (95 percent of men and 76 percent of women) have been sexually attracted to clients; 63 percent reported feeling "guilty, anxious and confused by the attraction" (p. 205). Sexual feelings are not something experienced by a few abnormal therapists. Most therapists have to confront sexual feelings, and few know how to do it.

SEX IS NOT DISCUSSED

I frequently hear from colleagues how hard it is to bring up sexual subjects—particularly if the therapist is feeling sexual—in supervision or case consultation. People are afraid of the reactions of others. An exception is gay therapist Randy Fitzgerald (1997), who had been in several consultation groups in which sex was discussed openly. We guessed this is because the gay community acknowledges sexuality more openly than does the heterosexual world.

Kernberg (1995) points out how infrequently sexual countertransference is brought up in consultation. He then models for readers how to acknowledge the possibility of sexual attraction by writing about a patient he had considered plain early in therapy, who became attractive to him as he developed an erotic countertransference.

Because of fear, some consultation groups will not be interested in pursuing the removal of shame with each other. Members who are interested in doing so can gather people together who share this interest.

THERAPIST GROUP WORK

Here is a list of suggestions for a discussion group of colleagues:

1. Discuss confidentiality until each person knows that others won't reveal what is said, or gossip about what goes on. Members can, however, talk outside the group about their own experience, which might include saying something like, "When one of the men in the group talked about his cross-wiring, I got aroused. It makes me wonder why, when I didn't have that reaction when other people talked about theirs."

2. Questions are designed to bring up feelings of shame that need to be relinquished. Eliciting the shame, breathing when it becomes strong, and letting the shame move through the body can release it, and, over time, allow sexual facts to become just facts. The feelings are not intended to be tolerated. The purpose is to bring up shame in order to release it. Focus should be on making room for the shame, not on completing the assignment. If too much shame comes up, stop, and attend to the shame.

3. In addition to shame, members may feel aroused, or angry, or frightened. We are conditioned to react with arousal, but this reaction will drop as more time is spent openly discussing sex. As sexual reactivity drops, the therapist will have an easier time hearing clients' stories without arousal. Arousal also serves the purpose of mood altering in order to avoid shame—a way of making shame congruent.

Don't shame yourself for becoming aroused. In this culture, dominated by sexual repression, and consequent reactivity, arousal is an almost automatic response to sexual discussion.

4. Don't use joking or other sexualized behaviors to become congruent with the shame. If anyone slips into this place, have an agreement to alert each other. If even one person does this without being confronted, group trust will diminish. (This does not include humor to discharge feelings. Laughter can be very helpful as a first step.)

5. Select questions that appeal to you. Do the easiest ones first. Make up your own. There is no right order or method. People must trust their own intuition about how to use these questions, who to discuss them with, and when.

6. Focus on the feelings that accompany telling and hearing others tell. Shame, fear, arousal, delight, and disgust are only some reactions. Observing and learning about these feelings are the reason for these conversations. Getting through all the questions is not the goal.

7. Breathe. Shallow breathing is an immediate mechanism for diminishing feeling. You will notice that a room of people will all diminish breath when an uncomfortable subject comes up. You can expect this to happen when discussing sex. Group members can remind each other to breathe. Or a timer can be set to go off every five minutes or so to alert people to check.

8. Movement can be helpful to reduce tension. If the air in the room feels humid and heavy, someone

can remind the group to move around, possibly taking a break to walk outside, to relieve tension.

9. Everyone should say at least a few sentences. When a person doesn't talk, the other members of the group are likely to project their fears onto this person, and expect judgment. At the same time, each person should not reveal anything he or she isn't ready to reveal. Talking can include talking about, rather than expressing, feelings of fear or shame.

10. Take your time responding to a question. The purpose is having feelings of shame, as well as fear, anger, and confusion, and bringing this subject into open conversation. If you force yourself to talk about sex and elicit too much shame, you will create harm, not healing.

11. As the group discovers that it is possible to have this kind of conversation, shame will drop in this setting. It may, however, come up again in other settings. Therefore, it can be helpful to create a second group, or find individuals who can have straightforward conversations about sex.

SUGGESTIONS AND QUESTIONS FOR CONSULTATION GROUPS

1. Bring textbooks on human sexuality, and take turns reading aloud about explicit sexual activities and sexual body parts. Next, other members can repeat what they heard.

2. Members describe in detail the sexual activities of their clients, or friends, or from books they have read.

3. Take turns taking sexual histories of each other.

Both the interviewer and the interviewee can interrupt the process to talk about any feelings that come up.

4. Give examples of times you have felt sexual in therapy sessions. See if you can differentiate among:

    a. sexual feelings that are all your own and have nothing to do with the client (which can be healthy or unhealthy sexuality);

    b. those that divert you from feelings (addictive use of sexual energy);

    c. those deliberately elicited by the client (through flirting, seductive poses, and/or clothing);

    d. those that are your client's, which you are giving expression (through projective identification);

    e. those for any other reason.

5. Have clients expressed sexual feelings in a therapy session? Talk about the variety of ways this can be done, including overt arousal for its own sake.

6. How do you feel when a client expresses sexual feelings that occurred outside the therapy office?

7. Have you been with clients you suspect were sexually aroused in your office? What did you do? How did you feel?

8. How do you feel about masturbation? How much cultural shame do you still carry?

9. How do you feel when you hear that a client or a client's partner is having an affair? Do you judge?

10. What are your own tendencies to use sex and/or romance addictively? What are your tendencies to use sex and/or romance in a cross-wired fashion? In other words, do you think it's normal for a client to lose sexual interest in a mate who has gained a few pounds? Or aged a couple of decades? Do you use

fantasy during sex to become or stay aroused? Do you wear sexy clothing to get aroused or arouse your partner? Do you have sex with people other than your mate? Have you used prostitutes for sex? Adult bookstores? Discuss how this influences your attitudes toward your clients' use of sex.

11. What kind of childhood training in sexuality did you receive? How did religion influence you? Did you feel guilt when masturbating? How did secrecy help you to engage in masturbating or sex?

12. Challenge the definition of what "having sex" means: orgasm, intercourse, foreplay? Can you hug and kiss while feeling sexual, then both lose arousal, and know you have just had sex? Or touch your genitals to bring arousal, stop, and know you have just masturbated?

13. Talk graphically about specific sexual activities used by women having sex with women. Then do the same for men having sex with men. As shame comes up, breathe. As the shame drops, if you are heterosexual, notice that these activities are part of normal heterosexual sex. If you are gay, notice how it feels to describe what you do, and what other gay people do. If you are in a group with heterosexuals, notice how you feel when they hear you talk about your sexual activities.

14. Talk about gay people you have met, how you felt about them, what you liked and didn't like. If you are gay, tell about discovering you were and what that meant in terms of fitting in, keeping secrets, wondering if others guess, if they have judgments.

15. Do you think you cannot live without sex? Share stories of times when sex wasn't available. Did mastur-

bation take its place? How long have you gone without sexual activity, including masturbation? If a long time, do you feel shame for this? What else?

16. Would you like to give up sex? Do you do it out of obligation—to be a partner, or because men and women are supposed to have sex in order to be men and women?

17. Describe first menstruation, first bras, first erections, ejaculation, orgasms, first sex. Take plenty of time for shame and fear.

18. Describe sexual body parts discussed in Chapter 7, using their clinical names. Also, name all the slang expressions, and note the feelings that come up. For example, women are socialized to have strong reactions to the word, *cunt*, both from mothers who abhorred it, and from feminists who view the word as the most repulsive expression that can be applied to a woman. We need to be able to say "cunt" without shame in order to help clients take the shame off. To do this, we have to take off our own shame. Practice saying "cunt" and "fuck" until they are just sounds. Caution: Don't use the words in the slang style that avoids the experience of shame.

19. Make up your own questions based on your clients' issues or listen to others in the group.

20. Repeat these questions as many times as necessary to remove shame.

Afterword

I have offered an overview of the three areas of treatment for sexual issues, elaborated on the role of shame, and discussed the healthier sexuality that becomes possible for people undertaking sexual healing. This understanding comes from my own healing, as well as observing people who are able to repair damage to their sexuality.

I hope this book helps therapists sit across from clients with an intuitive understanding and appreciation for the vast amount of inhibiting shame and cultural rulings. The therapist doesn't have to learn every intervention in order to offer what clients need. Instead, therapists can face their own cultural programming that prevents intuitive understanding. As more and more therapists undertake this task, more and

more clients will receive a mirror for their intuitively understood truth. As the ripples spread, the culture will be
impacted, and will continue to change. It will reflect the
rightness of sex that is relaxed, loving, respectful, gentle, and
passionate.

References

American Psychiatric Association (1994). *Diagnostic and Statistical Manual of Mental Disorders*, 4th ed. Washington DC: Author.

Bass, E., and Davis, L. (1988). *The Courage to Heal: A Guide for Women Survivors of Child Sexual Abuse.* New York: Harper & Row.

Brooks, G. R. (1995). *The Centerfold Syndrome.* San Francisco: Jossey-Bass.

Carnes, P. (1983). *Out of the Shadows: Understanding Sexual Addiction.* Minneapolis: Comp Care.

——— (1985). *Counseling the Sexual Addict: Systems, Strategies, and Skills.* Minneapolis: Hazelden.

——— (1991). *Don't Call It Love.* New York: Bantam.

Courtois, C. A. (1988). *Healing the Incest Wound: Adult Survivors in Therapy.* New York: Norton.

Davis, L. (1991). *Allies in Healing: When the Person You Love Was Sexually Abused as a Child.* New York: Harper Perennial.

Elliott, M., ed. (1993). *Female Sexual Abuse of Children.* New York: Guilford.

Farrell, W. (1993). *The Myth of Male Power: Why Men Are the Disposable Sex.* New York: Simon and Schuster.

Fitzgerald, R. (1997). Personal communication.

Fraser, S. (1987). *My Father's House: A Memoir of Incest and of Healing.* New York: Harper & Row.

Gartner, R. B., ed. (1997). *Memories of Sexual Betrayal: Truth, Fantasy, Repression, and Dissociation.* Northvale, NJ: Jason Aronson.

Gil, E. (1983). *Outgrowing the Pain: A Book for and about Adults Abused as Children.* New York: Dell.

Gil, E., and Kavanaugh, T. (1993). *Sexualized Children.* Rockville, MD: Launch Press.

Hartman, W., and Fithian, M. (1994). *The Treatment of Sexual Dysfunction: A Basic Approach.* Northvale, NJ: Jason Aronson.

Hastings, A. S. (1991). *Reclaiming Healthy Sexual Energy.* Deerfield Beach, FL: Health Communications.

——— (1993). *Discovering Sexuality That Will Satisfy You Both.* Tiburon, CA: The Printed Voice.

——— (1994). *From Generation to Generation: Understanding Sexual Attraction to Children.* Tiburon, CA: The Printed Voice.
(*The above three volumes are currently out of print but can be obtained by contacting the author at P.O. Box 40083, Bellevue, WA 98015.)

——— (1996). *Body and Soul: Sexuality on the Brink of Change.* New York: Insight Books.

Hawton, K. (1985). *Sex Therapy: A Practical Guide.* New York: Oxford University Press.

Heiman, J. R., and Lopiccolo, J. (1988). *Becoming Orgasmic: A Sexual and Personal Growth Program for Women.* New York: Prentice Hall.

Hunter, M. (1990). *Abused Boys: The Neglected Victims of Sexual Abuse.* Lexington, MA: Lexington Books.

Kaplan, H. S. (1974). *The New Sex Therapy*. New York: Brunner/ Mazel.

Kasl, C. D. (1989). *Women, Sex and Addiction: A Search for Love and Power*. New York: Tichnor and Fields.

Kernberg, O. F. (1995). *Love Relationships: Normality and Pathology*. New Haven: Yale University Press.

Larson, N., and Maison, S. (1987). *Psychosexual Treatment Program for Female Sex Offenders*. St. Paul: Meta Resources.

Leiblum, S. R., and Rosen, R. C., eds. (1988). *Sexual Desire Disorders*. New York: Guilford.

—— (1989). *Principles and Practice of Sex Therapy*. New York: Guilford.

Lew, M. (1990). *Victims No Longer: Men Recovering from Incest and Other Sexual Child Abuse*. New York: Harper & Row.

Lightfoot-Klein, H. (1989). *Prisoners of Ritual*. New York: Harrington Park Press.

Lisak, D., Hopper, J., and Song, P. (1996). Factors in the cycle of violence: gender rigidity and emotional constriction. *Journal of Traumatic Stress* 9:721–743.

Love, P. (1990). *The Emotional Incest Syndrome: What to Do When a Parent's Love Rules Your Life*. New York: Bantam.

Lovering, K. (1997). On Valentine's day, show off your PDOGAs! Must the personal be political? *Seattle Gay News*, February 7, p. 1.

Maltz, W., and Holman, B. (1987). *Incest and Sexuality: A Guide to Understanding and Healing*. Lexington, MA: Lexington Books.

Maroda, K. (1991). *The Power of Countertransference: Innovations in Analytic Technique*. Northvale, NJ: Jason Aronson.

Masters, W., and Johnson, V. (1966). *Human Sexual Response*. Boston: Little, Brown.

—— (1970). *Human Sexual Inadequacy*. Boston: Little, Brown.

McCauley, S. (1992). *The Easy Way Out*. New York: Washington Square Press.

—— (1994). *The Object of My Affection*. New York: Washington Square Press.

————— (1996). *Man of the House.* New York: Washington Square Press.

Maupin, A. (1978). *Tales of the City.* New York: HarperCollins.

————— (1980). *More Tales of the City.* New York: HarperCollins.

————— (1982). *Further Tales of the City.* New York: HarperCollins.

————— (1984). *Babycakes.* New York: HarperCollins.

————— (1987). *Significant Others.* New York: HarperCollins.

————— (1989). *Sure of You.* New York: HarperCollins.

Michael, R. T., Gagnon, J. H., Laumann, E. O., and Kolata, G. (1994). *Sex in America.* Boston: Little, Brown.

Milkman, H., and Sunderwirth, S. (1987). *Craving for Ecstasy: The Consciousness and Chemistry of Escape.* Lexington, MA: Lexington Books.

National Council on Sexual Addiction/Compulsivity Newsletter. Write NCSA/C, Box 161064, Atlanta, GA 30321-9998.

Plagenhoef, R. L., and Adler, C. (1992). *Why Am I Still Addicted?: A Holistic Approach to Recovery.* Blue Ridge Summit, PA: Tab Books.

Pope, K. S., Keith-Spiegel, P., and Tabachnick, B. G. (1986). Sexual attraction to clients: the human therapist and the (sometimes) inhuman training system. *The American Psychologist* 41:147–158.

Pope, K. S., Sonne, J. L., and Holroyd, J. (1993). *Sexual Feelings In Psychotherapy: Explorations for Therapists and Therapists-In-Training.* Washington, DC: American Psychological Association.

Rushin-Gallagher, C. (1997). Personal communication.

Russell, D. (1983). The incidence and prevalence of intrafamilial and extrafamilial sexual abuse of female children. *Child Abuse and Neglect* 7:133–146.

————— (1984). The prevalence and seriousness of incestuous abuse: stepfathers vs. biological fathers. *Child Abuse and Neglect* 8:15–22.

————— (1986). *The Secret Trauma: Incest in the Lives of Girls and Women.* New York: Basic Books.

Rutter, P. (1991). *Sex in the Forbidden Zone.* New York: Fawcett.

Schaef, A. W. (1989). *Escape From Intimacy: The Pseudo-Relationship Addictions. Untangling the "Love" Addictions: Sex, Romance, Relationships.* San Francisco: Harper & Row.

Schnarch, D. (1991). *Constructing the Sexual Crucible: An Integration of Sexual and Marital Therapy.* New York: Norton.

Seipel, J. (1997). Personal communication.

Stein, R. (1973). *Incest and Human Love.* Dallas: Spring Publications.

Stoltenberg, J. (1989). *Refusing To Be a Man: Essays on Sex and Justice.* New York: Meridian.

Szasz, T. (1990). *Sex by Prescription: The Startling Truth about Today's Sex Therapy.* Syracuse, NY: Syracuse University Press.

Thorsen, E. (1997). *Seattle Gay Couples Newsletter,* March, p. 2.

Tiefer, L. (1995). *Sex Is Not a Natural Act and Other Essays.* Boulder, CO: Westview Press.

Tse, M. (1995). *Qigong for Health and Vitality.* New York: Griffin.

Turner, L. (1997). Personal communication.

Vaughan, P. (1989). *The Monogamy Myth: A New Understanding of Affairs and How to Survive Them.* New York: New Market Press.

Westheimer, R. (1986). *Dr. Ruth's Guide to Good Sex.* New York: Warner Books.

Williams, L. M. (1994). Recall of childhood trauma: a prospective study of women's memories of child sexual abuse. *Journal of Consulting and Clinical Psychology* 62:1167–1176.

Index